D0325978

ALSO BY TONY HISS

The Giant Panda Book
(Children's book)

All Aboard with E. M. Frimbo
(with Rogers E. M. Whitaker)

Know-How: A Fix-It Book for the Clumsy but Pure of Heart
(with Guy Alland and Miron Waskiw)

Laughing Last

ILLUSTRATOR

The Bird Who Steals Everything Shining by Dieter Weslowski

EDITOR

Henry Chung's Hunan Style Chinese Cookbook

THE EXPERIENCE
OF PLACE

ALFRED A. KNOPF

TONY HISS

NEW YORK 1991

THE
EXPERIENCE
OF
PLACE

LONGWOOD COLLEGE LIBRARY
FARMVILLE, VIRGINIA 23901

BF
353
.H57
1990

THIS IS A BORZOI BOOK
PUBLISHED BY ALFRED A. KNOPF, INC.

Copyright © 1990 by Tony Hiss

All rights reserved under International and Pan-American Copyright Conventions.
Published in the United States by Alfred A. Knopf, Inc., New York,
and simultaneously in Canada by Random House of Canada Limited, Toronto.
Distributed by Random House, Inc., New York.

Portions of this work were originally published in *The New Yorker.*

Grateful acknowledgment is made to the following for permission to reprint
previously published material:
THE JOHNS HOPKINS UNIVERSITY PRESS: Excerpts from *F.L.O.: A Biography of
Frederick Law Olmsted* by Laura Wood Roper. The Johns Hopkins University Press,
Baltimore/London, 1974. Reprinted by permission.
THE NEW YORKER MAGAZINE, INC.: Illustrations by Kevin Wilson based on plans
by Dodson Associates, Ashfield, MA. Copyright © 1989 by The New Yorker
Magazine, Inc. Reprinted by special permission. All rights reserved.
THE UNIVERSITY OF ILLINOIS PRESS: Excerpts from *The New Exploration:
A Philosophy of Regional Planning* by Benton MacKaye. The University of Illinois
Press, 1962. Reprinted by permission.

Library of Congress Cataloging-in-Publication Data
Hiss, Tony.
The experience of place / Tony Hiss.—1st ed.
p. cm.
Includes bibliographical references.
ISBN 0-394-56849-4
1. Environmental psychology. 2. Regional planning.
I. Title. BF353.H57 1990
155.9'1—dc20 89-43357 CIP

Manufactured in the United States of America
Published August 20, 1990
Reprinted Five Times
Seventh Printing, November 1991

LONGWOOD COLLEGE LIBRARY
FARMVILLE, VIRGINIA 23901

FOR LOIS

Contents

Acknowledgments

This book was supported by a grant from the Graham Foundation for Advanced Studies in the Fine Arts; and by grants from the National Endowment for the Arts and the Municipal Art Society.

Four gifted editors have contributed their skills to this book: Ann Close at Knopf, and Robert Gottlieb, William Shawn, and Charles Patrick Crow at *The New Yorker*.

Many people have been extraordinarily helpful to me during the years I've worked on this project. Some are mentioned in the book. Some others are: Dorothy Alexander, Dorothy Schmiderer Baker, Martin Baron, Marie Behan, Lisa J. Betty, Kim Blakeley, Marisha Chamberlain, Adele Chatfield-Taylor, Amy Clyde, Barbara Cohen, Kevin Coyle, Mary Cregg, Dan Cullen, Linda Davidoff, Joseph DePlasco, Seymour Durst, Suzy Edelstein, Frank English, Mark S. Finnen, Mark Francis, Rosalie Genevro, Linda Gillies, Kevin Gilson, Don Guttenplan, Amanda Hirsch, Martha Kaplan, Vickie Karp, Cecily Corcoran Kihn, Larry Korner, Ann Kraybill, Alan Lapidus, Jeffrey Lewis, Agnese N. Lindley, Charles E. Little, Judith A. Livingston, Darlene McCloud, Bill McKibben, Kathleen A. Madden, Marc Matsil, Mary Means, Dorothy Marie Miner, Joseph Mitchell, Thomas A. Moore, Anne Mortimer-Maddox, Sonny Mehta, George Negroponte, Elena Pascarella, Allen Payne, Howard

Permut, Robert Pike, Michelle Preston, Patricia Raley, Thomas J. Reimers, Alison Rose, Melvin Rosenthal, Mark Rozzo, Suzanne Rubinstein, Klara Sauer, Herman Schaefer, Vincent F. Seyfried, Diane Souder, Gregory Spencer, Scott W. Standish, Tama Starr, Erna Stern, Paul Stoutenburgh, John Tauranac, Tupper Thomas, Amanda Urban, Elliot Willensky, Kevin Wilson, and Ervin H. Zube.

Introduction

This book is about improving our cities and countryside by perceiving our everyday surroundings in a new way, at a time when the places around us need it most.

We all react, consciously and unconsciously, to the places where we live and work, in ways we scarcely notice or that are only now becoming known to us. Ever-accelerating changes in most people's day-to-day circumstances are helping us and prodding us, sometimes forcing us, to learn that our ordinary surroundings, built and natural alike, have an immediate and a continuing effect on the way we feel and act, and on our health and intelligence. These places have an impact on our sense of self, our sense of safety, the kind of work we get done, the ways we interact with other people, even our ability to function as citizens in a democracy. In short, the places where we spend our time affect the people we are and can become.

As places around us change—both the communities that shelter us and the larger regions that support them—we all undergo changes inside. This means that whatever we experience in a place is both a serious environmental issue and a deeply personal one. Our relationship with the places we know and meet up with—where you are right now; and where you've been earlier today; and wherever you'll be in another few hours—is a close bond, intricate in nature, and not abstract, not remote at all: It's enveloping, almost a continuum with all we are and think. And the danger, as we are now beginning to see, is that whenever we make changes in our surroundings, we can all too easily shortchange ourselves, by cutting ourselves off from some of the sights or sounds, the shapes or textures, or other information from a place that have helped mold our understanding and are now necessary for us to thrive. Overdevelopment and urban sprawl can damage our own lives as much as they damage our cities and countryside.

The way to avoid the danger is to start doing three things at once: Make sure that when we change a place, the change agreed upon nurtures our growth as capable and responsible people while also protecting the natural environment and developing jobs and homes enough for all. But how do we go about doing three things at once when we're still having trouble finding ways to do two things at once—helping the economy prosper while at the same time preventing damage to the environment?

Luckily, we have a hidden ally—or, if not hidden, at least a long-neglected, overlooked, undervalued one. This ally is our built-in ability to experience places directly, an ability that makes it possible for people to know personally, through their own senses, about many of the ways our surroundings work within us. Paying careful attention to our experiences of places, we can use our own responses, thoughts, and feelings to help us replenish the places we love.

We can experience any place because we've all received, as part of the structure of our attention, a mechanism that drinks in whatever it can from our surroundings. This underlying awareness—I call it simultaneous perception—seems to operate continuously, at least during waking hours, even when our concentration seems altogether engrossed in something else entirely. While normal waking consciousness works to simplify perception, allowing us to act quickly and flexibly by helping us remain seemingly oblivious to almost everything except the task in front of us, simultaneous perception is more like an extra, or a sixth, sense: It broadens and diffuses the beam of attention evenhandedly across all the senses so we can take in whatever is around us—which means sensations of touch and balance, for instance, in addition to all sights, sounds, and smells.

Anytime we make conscious use of simultaneous perception, we can add on to our thinking. "One sees both close up and for miles, with the focus equal everywhere," as the art critic Robert Hughes has said of landscape drawings by nineteenth-century German Romantic painters. With the help of this extra sense, the familiar hard-and-fast boundary between ourselves and our surroundings seems softened, expanding our sense of the space occupied by "here" and the time taken up by "now," and uncovering normally ignored patterns of relationships that make us part of larger groups and events. It's simultaneous perception that allows any of us a direct sense of continuing membership in our communities, and our regions, and the fellowship of all living creatures.

Until recently, when people spoke about a vivid experience of a place, it would usually be a wonderful memory, a magic moment at one of the sweet spots of the world—an orange sunset over a white sand beach; or hearing the soft hooting of an owl while standing in a moonlit meadow; or standing up for one minute during the seventh-inning stretch of a sold-out playoff game at Fenway Park in Boston; or walking up Fifth Avenue in New York at Christmastime, dodging past roast-chestnut and hot-pretzel vendors, and catching a glimpse of the two stone lions in front of the Public Library, with fresh snow on their gray manes and big green wreaths around their necks.

These days people often tell me that some of their most unforgettable experiences of places are disturbingly painful and have to do with unanticipated loss. Sometimes there's less to see or hear or do in a place: A curving road in front of an old suburban house, for instance, gets straightened and widened, and suddenly a favorite grove of oaks or pines that the winds whistled through is chopped down and paved over. In the center of a big city, people who have been used to window-shopping from the bus on the way home from work find that they can't look out the bus windows at night anymore because these now have a dark-green or bronze tint—and then, squinting tight, they realize there are no longer any store windows to see, because they have all been covered over by steel grates.

Or a place may inadvertently give off two contradictory messages. A quiet downtown Manhattan courtroom may have been planned to convey the majesty of the law. There's a black-robed judge sitting, partially concealed, on a platform several feet high, so that only he or she can see the faces of everyone else present. The furniture is heavy and durable, made perhaps of oak, a tree that can live for hundreds of years; there's an American flag in one corner; and the words "In God We Trust" may have been emblazoned in bronze letters on one of the walls. But on a second wall there's a large clock whose hands have stopped moving—how long ago? And the paint is peeling away from a third wall, and maybe a chunk of plaster is missing too. "It takes away from the seriousness of the situation," someone coming off jury duty in New York said last year, "when the room itself tells you, 'Who cares?' The unspoken message takes a real toll— you see more jurors yawning and falling asleep."

An outdoor urban public plaza may have low ledges along adjoining walls that would make inviting sitting areas, except that, as William H. Whyte puts it, "another force has been diligently at work to deny these spaces," so that now the plaza's main message is "Move on!" In his most recent book, Whyte, a leading sociologist and city analyst, who has spent sixteen years thinking about the design and management of urban spaces, includes his own list of the most widely used ways of making ledges unsittable: "Horizontal metal strip with sawtooth points. Jagged rocks set in concrete (Southbridge Houses, New York

City). Spikes imbedded in ledges (Peachtree Plaza Hotel). Railing placed to hit you in small of back (GM Plaza, New York City)."

A damaged experience is not only numbing; over time we can begin to mistake it for the original. When art conservators in Italy, for instance, began a few years ago to restore the murals that Raphael and Michelangelo painted for the Vatican, they were shocked to find that a black curtain in the background of Raphael's *Coronation of Charlemagne* had originally been vividly patterned. Unnoticed, the curtain had slowly darkened, until at last it was obscured by hundreds of years of dirt and varnish. And in the case of Michelangelo, for generations art historians have revered him for his vision and grandeur—never once realizing he was also a brilliant colorist.

The fading and discoloration of places has been going on around us for generations. The American novelist Wallace Stegner in the 1960s uncovered a letter about this process written to a friend by an earlier American novelist, Sherwood Anderson, in the 1920s. "Is it not likely," Anderson asked, looking back across the generations before his own time, "that when this country was new and men were often alone in the fields and the forest they got a sense of bigness outside themselves that has now been lost? . . . Mystery whispered in the grass, played in the branches of the trees overhead, was caught up and blown across the American line in clouds of dust at evening in the prairies." Anderson himself had met people who had been changed by an earlier America: "I can remember old fellows in my home town speaking feelingly of an evening spent on the big empty plains. It had taken the shrillness out of them. They had learned the trick of quiet."

A brand-new science of place, growing up out of a body of formal research, like William H. Whyte's studies of plazas, is examining housing projects, train stations, hospitals, and sealed and sometimes "sick" office buildings; parks, lawns, and traffic-clogged streets; entrances, steps, and views from windows; meadows, fields, and forests; light, colors, noises, and scents; the horizon, small-air ions, and wind speed; and privacy. The investigators in this field include public health physicians, management consultants, architects, planners, clinical psychologists, ecologists, environmental psychologists, nature writers, political scientists, preservationists, and filmmakers. Although most of these students of place are still working separately, they have a common interest—safeguarding, repairing, and enriching our experience of place.

Human beings have always been an unfinished species, a story in the middle, a succession of families, tribes, and societies in transition to new awarenesses. Although we have always prided ourselves on our willingness to adapt to all habitats, and on our skill at prospering and making ourselves comfortable wherever we are—in a meadow, in a desert, on the tundra, or out on the ocean—we don't just adapt to places, or modify them in order to ease our burdens. We're the only species that over and over again has deliberately transformed our surroundings in order to stretch our capacity for understanding and provoke new accomplishments. And our growing and enhanced understanding is our most valuable, and our most vulnerable, inheritance.

The first time our surroundings stretched us, it was a gift— although it took us until the late 1980s to recognize either the gift or the gift-givers. Sometime between eight and thirteen million years ago, as primatologists and anthropologists have gradually learned, our remote ancestors came down from the East African treetops and moved out into the warmth and openness of the savanna. There, on the grasslands, over the course of many thousands of generations, they acquired larger brains and learned to stand and walk upright, to fashion tools and containers, and to live and work together cooperatively.

But this long era of human incubation was brought about by the work of other species, as conservation biologists have only recently discovered. "The savanna," says one of these biologists, Dr. David Western, who holds the Carter Chair for Conservation Biology at Wildlife Conservation International and is also chairman of the African Elephant Conservation Working Group, "has traditionally been thought of as the epitome of African landscape. But in fact it turns out to be the exception—something much more like what we would now call a managed landscape, like the meadows of a farm or the pastures on a ranch. Today the elephant is the keystone species of African savanna maintenance; it clears the brush, and keeps the forest from spreading back onto the grassland by uprooting any small trees. And this landscape management by the elephants allows huge herds of grass-eating animals to flourish—zebras, wildebeests, gazelles. When our human ancestors first emerged onto this same savanna, there were altogether fourteen species of megamammals, near-elephant-sized or bigger, engaged in grassland conservation, including now extinct species of sheep and goats as big as buffalo. These megamammals, including their still living kin, the elephants, were the first nursemaids of mankind."

An invented human habitat of much more recent origin, the city, has often had a similar experiential function, as Lewis Mumford a generation ago reminded people in *The City in History* when he described the benefits conferred by citizenship in the Greek polis, or city-state. Even though citizenship in the polis was denied to women, slaves, and merchants, and only grudgingly given to craftsmen—so that in Athens, for example, only one person in seven was a citizen—for those included in this company, citizenship was more like a school than either a rank or a reward. And the city itself constituted a framework of nurturing surroundings. As each Athenian went about his business, both public and private—going to the gymnasium, the theater, and the marketplace; climbing up the Acropolis and walking down to the harbor; attending annual citywide concerts and festivals of singing and dancing; and serving on juries, and in the assembly, and also in the military—the citizen was exposed to experiences that together and cumulatively produced, as Mumford said, "not a new type of city, but a new type of man. . . . For a while, city and citizen were one."

Now, late in the second half of the twentieth century, America's experiences are under siege. Sometimes the attack is subtle. Brown trout, according to Ted Williams, a naturalist who writes for *Audubon* magazine, "are (or were) prized gamefish, not because they fight well—although they do—but because they are moody and selective, a real challenge to outwit. Even skilled, patient fishermen who have taken the time to learn their ways don't fill up the cooler every time out." But the brown trout in many wild-looking streams flowing through still-unspoiled stretches of countryside have in recent years been replaced by "tiger trout," a man-made fish bred by fish managers at state hatcheries. The tiger trout, according to Williams, is an "idiot fish that gobbles everything in sight," a fish that "will streak to your side in the hope of getting fed." First-time fishermen used to have to extend themselves and learn to be patient as they worked on improving their ability to cast a line. Now they get the thrill of victory without also being able to take home a slightly different self.

Other attacks on America's experiences are far more blatant. In the northeastern United States, tens of millions of acres of near-wilderness woodlands in New York, Vermont, New Hampshire, and Maine may be thrown open for development in the next dozen years or so. In North America's most famous savanna landscape, the bluegrass country of Kentucky, half of Fayette County around Lexington, the region's hub county, has already been given over to "urban services." On many winter days, white haze from a coal-fired electric power plant eighty miles northeast of the Grand Canyon settles into the canyon and, according to a recent *New York Times* report, "washes out the famous vista of striking reds, purples, browns, and grays." In the more cautious words of the air-quality officials of the National Park Service: "You start to lose color; you start to lose contrast; you start to lose the detail of the different rock layers." Smog generated four hundred miles to the west in Los Angeles also drifts into the Grand Canyon. This kind of far-flung pollution now has a name—regional haze—and it's already a national problem: Long-term measurements taken at eastern airports, says the *Times,* show that "in the past 40 years the average distance that people can see has dropped from a range of 18 to 30 miles to exactly half that."

In the Northeast, according to Hooper Brooks, vice president of the Regional Plan Association in New York City and director of its Regional Open Space Program, development activities are for the first time becoming a uniform presence throughout the thirty-one counties in New York, New Jersey, and Connecticut that make up the New York metropolitan region. This means that shops on Fifth Avenue, theaters in Times Square, row houses west of Central Park, and unspoiled farmland in northern New Jersey and northwestern Connecticut, up along the Hudson River Valley, and out on the North Fork of Long Island—neighborhoods and landscapes often well over a hundred miles apart—are now almost equally at risk.

And all around the planet, the "typical" surroundings of vast numbers of people are radically changing character: Until recently, a large majority of the world's population lived in villages. Less than a decade from now, a small majority of the world's population (52 percent) will live in cities. And a hundred years from now, as many as 90 percent of all people may live in cities, and even today many city residents have little or no access to either wilderness areas or farming regions. And few cities nowadays are producing public experiences like those of ancient Athens.

In our planetary environmental crisis, we face an epidemic of extinctions—so many plant and animal species could be lost by continued destruction of the tropical rain forests that it might take twenty million years before basic evolutionary processes could regenerate as much abundance as exists today. Humanity, in its slow rise, has been nurtured both by abundant places and by its fruitful experiences of those places—and in some cases the experiences themselves are now millions of years old. By keeping part of our attention on our experiencing, we can work to retain surroundings that offer richly nourishing experiences, making sure that we maintain for ourselves a planet capable of helping us toward the next boost in our understanding.

Conscious noticing of what we're experiencing, once we get back the hang of it, can be a common denominator, a language of connectedness between social, environmental, and economic concerns—just as Central Park in New York pulls people together for an outdoor concert on a summer night, and gives songbirds a stopover point every year on their spring migration north, and increases property values on Fifth Avenue. Using the things we know or sense about places but seldom put into words, we can bring all of our minds to bear on the problems of how our communities, regions, and landscapes should change. We each have a contribution to make.

So this book is also about making a new start together.

I
EXPERIENCING
CITIES

1 Simultaneous Perception

Just walking through the vast main concourse of Grand Central Terminal, in New York—something that over half a million people do every working day—almost always triggers in me a spontaneous and quiet change in perception. It alters what I know about my surroundings and about whatever is going on around me, and at the same time modifies my sense of what all these things mean to me. The change—one that is reasonably well known to all of us, or is at least lodged somewhere in our memories—lets me gently refocus my attention and allows a more general awareness of a great many different things at once: sights, sounds, smells, and sensations of touch and balance, as well as thoughts and feelings. When this general kind of awareness occurs, I feel relaxed and alert at the same time. In addition, I notice a sort of unhurried feeling—a feeling that there's time enough to savor all the sights and sounds and other sensations coming in.

Our habitual style of thinking, it is often said, is a stream of consciousness pouring and pushing its way through the present; but this feeling, which I call simultaneous perception, seems calmer, more like a clear, deep, reflective lake. Both the pinpoint focus of ordinary perception, which lets us shut ourselves off from our surroundings, and the broad-band focus of simultaneous perception, which keeps us linked to our surroundings, are inherited skills built into each of us. People sometimes get so good at blotting out the sights and sounds and smells around them that simultaneous perception, when it resurfaces, can catch them by surprise. But because this ability is always in operation, it's constantly available. And whenever we summon it, it's richly informative. Simultaneous perception helps us experience our surroundings and our reactions to them, and not just our own thoughts and desires.

The main concourse of Grand Central—an enormous room, with fourteen entrances—is only one part of an intricate structure that was opened to the public in February of 1913 and is justly famous as a crossroads, a noble building, an essential part of midtown Manhattan, and an ingenious piece of engineering that can handle large numbers of trains, cars, and people at once. You can buy a ticket and get train information in the concourse—and these days you can also buy a flower or a drink or a meal—but the main purpose of the room is to move people through it. It was designed to handle huge crowds and to impress people with the immensity and the dignity of enclosed public places in a modern city. From the accounts left by its builders, however, it was not designed to provide the experience actually available there today. That experience is one of the unplanned treasures of New York.

The concourse is 470 feet long and 160 feet wide, and it is 150 feet—fifteen stories, perhaps—from the floor to the peak of the vaulted ceiling. The room has arched windows 33 feet wide and 60 feet high, which are deep enough to have corridors running through them—a series of walkways built between the outer glass and the inner glass in each window—and it has constellations painted on the ceiling, with sixty of the stars really glowing, because they are small light bulbs. A balcony 30 feet wide and 20 feet above the floor runs along every wall except the south one. From the west balcony a marble staircase pours down and then divides in two to flow around steps that lead from the concourse to a lower concourse for suburban trains. The main concourse is bigger than the nave of Notre Dame, and it is sometimes called awe-inspiring or referred to as an American cathedral, but the experience it offers has to do with day-to-day urban living: It's a sort of introductory course (or, for old-timers, a refresher course) in how to join the choreography of New York City.

The experience of the concourse seems to have changed very little in the last seventy-seven years. At least, what I find there now is substantially true to the continuing experience I found there forty-three years ago, when I was six and a newcomer to the city. Two major attention-grabbing additions to this huge room since the late 1940s—a big illuminated clock and stock ticker on the south wall and an oversize illuminated Kodak photograph on the east wall—have recently been removed, and the gigantic windows have been washed. These days, though, there are much sadder sights in the concourse than there used to be: In the mid-1980s, Grand Central became a principal hangout for large numbers of homeless people, as well as for some of those who prey on the homeless.

One recent weekday afternoon around three-thirty, I entered the concourse from the east, through one of the two long, nearly straight passageways that lead in from Lexington Avenue. I came out of the East Side IRT subway into the more southerly of the two straightaways and immediately found myself part of a stream of people, four and five abreast, all of them looking straight ahead and moving at a fast New York clip toward the concourse along the right-hand side of a tunnel only twice the width of the stream itself. Toward me along the left-hand side of the corridor—which is well lighted, has a low white ceiling and a beige marble floor, and is lined with convenience stores—came a second stream of people, just as wide, and moving at the same speed and with the same look. Though I could hear my own footsteps, nearby footfalls and normal tones of voice registered as loud but blurred, indeterminate noises, and although no one was touching me, or even brushing past, I kept feeling that I was about to be bumped into. People sounded closer than they looked, and they seemed closer still, because my eyes and ears couldn't determine whether the people I was looking at were the people making the sounds I could hear.

I felt hurried along. My breathing was shallow and slightly constricted; my neck and shoulders were tight. I could smell cookies and pizza baking in the shops around me, but it seemed difficult to look to either side. I could see maybe twelve feet ahead of me—a view consisting entirely of backs of heads and oncoming faces. There was nothing in any of the faces to suggest that they had just come from a different kind of place. The only alternative to hurrying forward seemed to be to swerve right at random and come to rest in front of a shop.

Then these two streams of people crossed a second pair of streams, running at a right angle to them. The stream I was in entered a space with a slightly higher, cross-vaulted ceiling, and I had a moment to feel alarmed in retrospect, wondering why no one had bumped into anyone else during the crossing. The whole journey so far had taken something like fifteen seconds. Crossing this new space in the next five or six seconds, I was aware of a slight diminution in the noise around me, felt a slight lightening in my shoulders, noticed that the stores on either side were a vitamin shop and a snack bar, and saw in front of me a different light: grayer, clearer, brighter, less intense. I felt that something in me and near me was about to change.

In another step, I was in the concourse. I knew this first not by sight but by body sensation, sounds, the absence of a smell, and breathing. I felt as if some small weight suspended several feet above my head that I had not till then even been aware of, had just shot fifteen stories into the air. I straightened up, my breathing slowed down, and I noticed that the scentless air around me was warm. I was walking at the same fast clip, and

The main concourse in Grand Central Terminal, New York City. *Photograph courtesy of Frank English*

on the same kind of marble floor, but now, and for the rest of the minute it took me to walk the length of the concourse, I could no longer distinguish the sounds of my own footsteps. All the sounds that reached me seemed to have been fused into a single sound. Vast and quiet, it seemed to be evenly distributed throughout the great room. This sound, pleasant in all its parts, regular in all its rhythms, and humorous and good-natured, seemed also to have buttoned me into some small, silent bubble of space. I felt that I wasn't quite walking but was paddling—or somehow propelling—this bubble across the floor. I became aware that my pace had slowed.

This sound was produced by five hundred or more people talking and walking on marble through the bottom part of eleven million cubic feet of air. Within two or three feet of where I stood, I could hear separate voices: ''Take care, now'' and ''Yep, see you tomorrow" and "All 'board!" And quite often, and from quite far away, I could hear laughing. The rest of what I heard was just the single commingled sound. I could see, quite clearly, two things: an unmoving framework made up of marble floor, tall piers, arched windows, high barrel vault, daylight, and faint electric stars; and the swirling, living motion of five hundred people walking, two and three abreast, from and toward the fourteen entrances and exits of the concourse. Moving silently, as it seemed, within that sound, I noticed once again that no one was bumping into anyone else—that every time I thought I myself might be about to bump into people near me, both I and they were already accelerating slightly, or decelerating, or making a little side step, so that nobody ever collided. On top of this, the weightless sensation in my head gave me the feeling that I could look down on all this movement, in addition to looking out at it. I had a sense that the cooperation I was a part of kept repeating itself throughout the vast room around me and the vaster city beyond it.

I thought, as I have many times in the concourse, that if I were a stranger to this overwhelming city, it would be helpful to me to know that something in me and in everyone around me already knew how to fit in with all the people circulating through the city and going about their business. After emerging onto Vanderbilt Avenue, I found that when I crossed over and walked along the south side of Forty-third Street, I could for a while keep with me this awareness of the cooperation that makes a city possible. It lasted about a block and a half—until, as I was standing at a stoplight at Fifth Avenue, a screaming ambulance and the rest of the traffic brought me back to a more ordinary sense of separateness and disjointedness. At the same time, waiting for the light to change, I could see that even though I no longer felt it, some form of cooperation was continuing to govern the movements of people near me on the sidewalk. People moving in four different directions passed one another without colliding, and in each minute, hundreds of accidents never occurred. Still, the overall level of cooperation seemed diminished, because there was no sense of connectedness between the people on foot and the people in vehicles.

———————

Several overlapping kinds of evidence—among them work by public safety and public health investigators; research findings about the human mind and brain; and a host of personal experiences in a wide variety of settings—have in recent years been opening up our understanding of many of the complex and subtle ways in which we commonly interact with our everyday surroundings: train stations, parks, office towers, shopping arcades, and all the other settings of our lives. Far from constituting a kind of backdrop that we can ignore at will—as long as it permits us to see and breathe adequately—such things as the kind of light around us, the chemical composition of the air, and arrangements of rooms, hallways, and staircases affect not only physical health and mental grasp and agility but our sense of humanity's pressing problems and unfinished business.

The same evidence that has been showing us how much of their ordinary environments people respond to is also leading us to the idea that people have within them various brain-body mechanisms that react to different aspects of their surroundings. An example: Dr. Gary E. Schwartz, a Yale professor of psychology and psychiatry, has found that some scents produce changes in blood pressure comparable to those achieved through meditation; the smell of spiced apple is particularly effective in reducing blood pressure. Another example: Experiments by a bacteriologist and public health biometeorologist have shown that unscented air, if it contains a certain quantity of small-air ions—clusters of molecules with a negative electrical charge— can also have the effect of a drug, lowering the amount of serotonin in the midbrain; high levels of serotonin are associated with sleepiness.

The structure of another brain-body system we use for responding to the environment has been traced in some detail: A research psychiatrist has found that some of the light that enters our eyes when we're outdoors in bright sunlight bypasses the cortex and finds its way, in sequence, to the hypothalamus, the spinal cord, a nerve center in the neck, and, finally, the pineal gland, where it suppresses the production of a hormone called melatonin, which may affect mood and also fertility and many other body functions. And preliminary research in the new field of photobiology, or color therapy, indicates that a bubble-gum color called passive pink may have an almost immediate effect on aggressive behavior. When a berserk sixteen-year-old is placed in a four-by-eight-foot passive-pink cell at the San Bernardino County Probation Department, he is calmer within a few minutes. After ten minutes or so, he's sometimes lying on the floor, nearly asleep.

Some people may wonder why, if we've always been responding to light and air and colors and smells, we're only now beginning to notice these things often enough to have suddenly acquired a lot of information on the subject. Probably, such investigations have taken place in the postwar period because it has been during the past forty-five years that almost everyone in the Western world has for the first time moved indoors—away from bright sunshine, sealed off from the mountains, forests, and streams that, for instance, naturally have an abundance of small-air ions. In the words of Dr. Richard J. Wurtman, a professor of brain and cognitive science at the Massachusetts Institute of Technology, "We are all unwitting subjects of a long-term experiment on the effects of artificial lighting on our health." Speaking solely about the brain-body systems that respond to light, he has made this interim recommendation: "Until much more is known, we should design indoor lighting to resemble as closely as possible what the sun provides."

In all the millennia since our human ancestors descended from the trees of the forest and learned to roam upright across the savannas of East Africa, we have never before made changes capable of impairing the workings of our particular internal systems that rely on light or scent or other aspects of the environment. Now, all of a sudden, it has happened: In America today, almost all of us spend almost all of our time inside, breathing recycled air and absorbing artificial light. And as our internal systems begin to react—badly, more often than not—to this new environment, we become aware of their existence. All the time they were unknown, they functioned beautifully, but now that we do know about them, we have to take conscious responsibility for creating man-made environments that won't further diminish the healthy performance of these systems.

Brain-body systems have thus become a public health matter—a health need that whole communities have to think about collectively, because the health of individual people will be determined by the workings of large-scale environments. Modern public health knowledge got started when nineteenth-century doctors, studying urban diseases, realized that as more and more people lived closer together in cities, local springs and wells would no longer automatically flow clean and pure. People got sick more often in these new cities than they did in villages; that was the first fact. Then it was noticed that people took sick in certain areas within the new cities. Eventually, investigators discovered that bacteria that had entered specific wells could cause cholera in anyone who drank the water from the wells. Discoveries like these led to today's extensive systems of reservoirs and legal watershed protection; we try to protect from development the land whose streams feed a city's reservoirs.

Nineteenth-century public health officials were modern pioneers of the inadvertent, after-the-fact research method that is still being used to uncover various brain-body systems. The basic tool is an ability to be alert to correlations between two different kinds of unintended changes: fluctuations in people's

health or mental functioning that point back to specific alterations of the environment. And what makes the search possible
is a realization that changing the environment—whether care-
lessly or in good faith—can disastrously change the information
that our surroundings feed to some unsuspected internal mechanism. Now that the universal need for clean water has been so
clearly demonstrated as to seem almost self-evident, we have to
remind ourselves that it took almost a hundred years to make
the point. Decades followed the doublings and triplings in size
of English cities and the subsequent alarming increases in the
death rates in those cities before it was possible, through the use
of maps that showed both the sites of wells and water pumps
and the block-by-block spreading of various diseases, to prove
the connection between communicable disease and filth in the
environment. And forty years more went by before bacteriolo-
gists, working in the last decades of the century, began to be
able to identify the specific microorganisms that could cause
specific diseases.

But that wasn't the end of it. Public health researchers have
discovered in just the last few years that a twentieth-century use
of water—in the systems that cool centrally air-conditioned
buildings—has helped cause infections and may contribute to a
set of symptoms known as the sick building syndrome (the
symptoms range from headache to sore throat, wheezing, and
shortness of breath). Both can be transmitted to occupants of
modern high-rise buildings through a process that is simultaneously waterborne and airborne.

Many modern office and residential buildings are tightly sealed
structures, their windows permanently closed. Such buildings
were at first widely applauded as energy savers, because their
integrated heating, ventilating, and air-conditioning (or HVAC)
systems reduced heating and cooling expenses by using the same
air over and over. The stale air that accumulates in sealed buildings can contribute to outbreaks of sick building syndrome, in

part because it contains contaminants—fungi, bacteria, and gases produced by many of the man-made materials found inside sealed buildings. Fabrics for rugs and upholstery, for instance, are increasingly made from man-made materials. These materials and the adhesives used to apply them can release what Dr. Jan A. J. Stolwijk, an epidemiologist and a public health specialist at the Yale School of Medicine, calls "a variety of volatile organic compounds," which can cause eye and upper-respiratory irritation.

Sometimes the problems of sealed buildings are compounded by the presence in the air of cooling-tower drift—water droplets so fine they can penetrate unnoticed deep into a person's lungs. In an HVAC system, excess heat is vented through cooling towers, and the water in the towers can be invaded by microorganisms, just like the water in a well. Often the fresh-air intake for one sealed building is close to the cooling tower of another sealed building. Drift transmits any bacteria that may be growing in cooling-tower water, and transmits them so efficiently that the possibilities of infection are considerably greater from breathing the drift-laden air than from breathing outdoor air. One of the serious infections brought about by drift is already well known: Legionnaires' disease.

Stolwijk estimates that most sealed buildings are in a sick condition at least part of the time. All this information is changing professional attitudes toward the value of the sealed modern tower. According to a paper that was read at the Third International Conference on Indoor Air Quality and Climate, in Stockholm in 1986, these buildings may have to be regarded as "a failure." We know now that the study of how contaminated water affects human health has not yet been completed.

An equally long-running environmental experiment on people has to do with simultaneous perception—the system we use to experience our surroundings. Since simultaneous perception is the only internal mechanism we know about that can combine the responses of all our senses, any change in our surroundings which our senses can register—in the light, in colors, in sounds, in smells, in anything else we can detect—alters the information that this mechanism receives. But what kinds of changes, large or small, or what combinations of changes, will actually alter its workings? Beginning with the nineteenth-century cities and continuing through our postwar reshaping of cities, suburbs, and countryside, we have been making changes in the environment at an unprecedented rate. Today's world not only looks very different from the eighteenth-century world but also sounds very different and smells very different. Whatever else these changes have brought us in the way of human benefits or environmental degradation, they have offered us an unparalleled chance to look at how our health and well-being are affected by changing what we can experience in a place.

Surprisingly, this particular inquiry is turning out to be both more extended and more compressed than the long investigation into the need for clean water. Even in the mid-nineteenth century, public health advocates could present a strong empirical case for clean water—that, for some reason then unknown, it was dangerous not to have it. And they were able to convert this insight into public policy within only a few years; in New York, for example, the old Croton reservoir, a multimillion-dollar project, began sending pure upstate drinking water to the city as early as 1842. In some cases, the more comprehensive understanding of water contamination that was finally provided by late-nineteenth-century researchers only confirmed the validity of major actions taken years before.

While many of the links that connect places and experiences and health have yet to be traced, some people have started treating their own experiences of places in a mid-nineteenth-century clean-water fashion, by taking action to protect experiences that are important to them—for example, fighting to prevent the demolition of places like Grand Central Terminal. Over the past

two decades or so, organized citizen efforts like these have resulted in the creation of official municipal landmarks preservation commissions in hundreds of American cities, towns, and
suburbs.

The people involved in this work speak, often, not just of
architectural beauty but of the character of a place, or its essential spirit, or the quality of life there, or of its livability, genius,
flavor, feeling, ambience, essence, resonance, presence, aura,
harmony, grace, charm, or seemliness. These are probably al-
lusions to an actual direct experience of some place. And mention of "people places," or of the individuality of a specific
place, or the urban or rural or wilderness quality there, or its
scale, or human scale, or visual charm, or beauty, or scenic
quality, will most likely be an attempt to convey some specific
component of an experience. The language of the laws that set
up landmarks preservation agencies sometimes makes it clear
that such experiential considerations are at work. It's part of the
job of the eleven commissioners of the New York City Landmarks Preservation Commission, for instance, to make experiential judgments whenever they have to weigh the merits of a
proposal to set up a possible historic district in the city. New
York City's Local Law No. 46 of 1965, the Landmarks Preservation and Historic Districts Law, defines for the commissioners
the criteria that an area of the city must meet in order to be
eligible for designation as a historic district. Historic districts,
the law says, "have a special character or special historical or
aesthetic interest or value."

In a similar spirit, Christopher Alexander, an architect in
Berkeley, California, and five associates spent eight years studying their own and other people's reactions to buildings and cities
in order to find out why certain places "make people feel alive
and human." In their 1977 book, *A Pattern Language,* they
identify 253 elements, or aspects (they call them patterns), of
rooms, streets, and districts that seem somehow to have definite

links with joyful experiences. Eighty-four patterns, or just over
a third of those discussed, get two asterisks in the book—the
equivalent of three stars in a *Guide Michelin*—to denote connections between place and experience so strong and so consistent
as to form what the authors call an "invariant" and also a "deep
and inescapable property of a well-formed environment." Some
two-asterisk patterns are Identifiable Neighborhood, Sunny
Place, Pedestrian Street, Warm Colors, Old People Everywhere,
and Four-Story Limit to the height of buildings. ("There is
abundant evidence to show that high buildings . . . can actually
damage people's minds and feelings.") One two-asterisk pattern, Accessible Green, is based on research by the authors in a
Berkeley park which showed that although people derive great
benefits from a neighborhood park, they tend not to use it if it
is more than about 750 feet—about three blocks, that is, or about
three minutes' walk—from their doors. "Apparently, there is a
threshold . . . where the distance prevents them from meeting
their need," the authors report.

In three years of careful observations of how people use or
avoid public plazas in New York City, William H. Whyte found
such precise and demonstrable correlations between what he
called "amiable" design—"the quality of experience" available
in a plaza—and the fullness or emptiness of that plaza that in
1975 the city redrafted its open-space zoning provisions to in-
corporate his discoveries. Two interconnected elements of amiable design, Whyte learned from standing outside Paley Park,
are shallow steps and low flights of steps. Paley Park is a vest-
pocket park on East Fifty-third Street that occupies the site of
the old Stork Club, and there are four steps up from street level
to park level. In his book *The Social Life of Small Urban Spaces,*
Whyte writes:

Many people will do a double take as they pass by, pause, move a
few steps, then, with a slight acceleration, go up the steps. . . . Watch

these flows and you will appreciate how very important steps can be. The steps at Paley are so low and easy that one is almost pulled to them. . . . You can stand and watch, move up a foot, another, and then, without having made a conscious decision, find yourself in the park. . . . A slight elevation, then, can be beckoning. Go a foot or so higher, however, and usage will fall off sharply. There is no set cut-off level—it is as much psychological as physical—but it does seem bound up with how much of a choice the steps require. One plaza that people could be expected to use, but don't, is only a foot or so higher than two comparable ones nearby. It seems much higher.

The New York City zoning code now specifies: "The level of an urban plaza shall not at any point be more than 3 feet above nor 3 feet below the curb level of the nearest adjoining street."

Studies by BOSTI, the Buffalo Organization for Social and Technological Innovation—one of the first firms in a new field called workplace-design research—are also making it clear that there is a relationship between how people experience the offices they work in and their productivity level on the job. "The environment seems to act in nontrivial ways," says Michael Brill, an architect who is BOSTI's president. A seven-year examination by BOSTI of the conditions in some seventy offices around the country strongly suggests, Brill says, that there are at least seventeen different aspects of office design—ranging from how enclosed an office is to how noisy it is—that can affect job performance, job satisfaction, people's abilities to communicate with other workers in an office, or their satisfaction with their surroundings. Job satisfaction (an index that has to do with turnover, absenteeism, lateness, and grievances) has always been important to workers, but unlike job performance (a measure of things like rates of error and the meeting of deadlines), it was until recently not a factor that many employers paid much attention to—largely because there was no way it could be translated into monetary terms. Now, however, a new discipline known as human-resources accounting can calculate job satisfaction as a cost of doing business. It's a real cost: According to BOSTI, in a well-designed office, workers will get from five to nine percent more work done in a year's time. And, says Michael Brill, "The economic benefit could go as high as fifteen percent if the office were planned and designed to be a perfect fit for the work."

No one has yet made a compilation of all the reliable empirical findings now available about experiences of places—or of how widely the findings have been acted upon. But already, as even a small sampling can show, the information is so extensive that just by putting it together we can start to see in detail some otherwise shadowy features of the way people relate to their surroundings. One such feature has to do with how close different types of surroundings need to be for people to take advantage of them. Alexander's discovery that Berkeley residents will walk about three blocks to reach a park is closely paralleled, it turns out, by a finding of Whyte's about how far New York City office workers will walk to sit in a public plaza at lunchtime. "Commuter distances" to and from plazas, Whyte says, "are usually short; for most plazas, the effective market radius is about three blocks." This suggests that office neighborhoods function much as residential neighborhoods do, and that the two have much the same size: If people will walk three minutes to reach a central gathering point, then a neighborhood is, in effect, about six minutes' walking time wide—or, in linear terms, five or six blocks, which is between fifteen and sixteen hundred feet.

Corning Glass Works, a few years ago, according to Philip Langdon, writing in *Metropolis,* a design magazine, had two goals: a new engineering building in Corning, New York, and increased productivity from its engineering and support staff, eight hundred strong. Dr. Thomas J. Allen, a professor at the Sloan School of Management, at the Massachusetts Institute of Technology (and now Director of the International Center for

Research on the Management of Technology), who was hired by
Corning as a consultant, found that more than eighty percent of
an engineer's ideas come from face-to-face contact with colleagues, but also that engineers won't walk more than about a
hundred feet from their own desks to exchange thoughts with
anyone. The cutoff point in this case is a walk that takes more
than half a minute, so conversation has to be available almost
next door. Engineers attend conventions reluctantly, he found,
and they completely reject any of the technological substitutes
for personal encounter. They hate asking for information on the
phone, and they get even less out of reading technical journals.
Accordingly, the William C. Decker Engineering Building, in
Corning, is equipped with twelve separate discussion areas (each
one with a coffee machine and wall-size blackboards), and the
building's three floors are connected by seven sets of open stairs,
two escalators, a double bank of elevators, and several ramps.
Corning Glass says it is satisfied with the increase in productivity that has resulted.

Landmarks preservation commissions, zoning code changes,
productivity programs, are having their effect, but there's something else at work here as well. Even while we're still opening
up the empirical, or mid-nineteenth-century, phase of examining
our experiences of places, we're starting to realize that scattered
all around us—in places, books, and people—is more than
enough information to begin putting together a twentieth-century
body of knowledge of simultaneous perception that can in some
ways resemble the late nineteenth century's understanding of
clean water. In part, this knowledge stems from all our empirical
research on the brain and the various internal systems, but we
can expand the empirical discoveries about our reactions to
places by reading about such subjects as aesthetics, art appre-

ciation, wilderness and nature, and the history of the city and
the countryside. And beyond this, we can expand our knowledge
by the most powerful means of all—our own observation of local
places worth looking at.

One of the things that simultaneous perception can do, as the
experience available at Grand Central shows, is to pick up what
we could call cross-sensory, or multisensory, patterns of information—things or events we can recognize only when information from two or more senses is taken all together. I began to
develop an understanding of how people cooperate as they walk
through Grand Central when my mind took in two pieces of
information at the same time: I could see how other people were
changing their pace as I got closer to them, and simultaneously
I could feel in my legs and body and arms the moment-to-
moment adjustments in motion I was myself making in response
to their approach. Cooperation, the force that coordinated my
own actions with those of other people nearby, is something we
can actually see—that is, we see it in outline as this outline
moves across the senses. It's like seeing the shape of the wind
through your eyes, ears, and skin: hearing it slap against a distant flagpole, and then watching it curl through the branches of
a nearby tree, and then feeling it land softly on your face and
shoulders.

We can detect cross-sensory patterns like the cooperation in
a moving crowd because of three other processes in simultaneous perception—processes that have been the object of research.
According to Anton Ehrenzweig, an art historian at the University of London, his work with artists shows that people have an
innate capacity that he calls "utter watchfulness": We can pay
equal attention to everything at once, omitting nothing and at
the same time emphasizing nothing. Ehrenzweig also considered
the speed with which we can put together and respond to the
information made available by "utter watchfulness" and concluded that people's thinking then shows "split-second reaction

to innumerable variables.'' Another process that assists this kind of cooperation is the gaining of a relaxed sense of our own outside edge—the place where we stop and everything else begins. Dr. Arthur Deikman, a California research psychiatrist who has looked into this aspect of our thinking, calls this border a "fluid body boundary," which can lead to "diminished self-object differentiation"—that is, a point at which we divide our attention equally between ourselves and things outside ourselves. The diminished differentiation makes it easier to move in concert with other people: Fluid body boundaries can turn what might amount to getting through an obstacle course into something as easy as dancing across a ballroom.

Thus, simultaneous perception, putting at our disposal an evenhanded, instantaneous, and outward-looking flow of attention, acts like a sixth sense. Without one of the more familiar senses, touch, we couldn't register things like heat and cold; if I scalded my finger in hot water, I might find it out afterward by seeing my finger turning pink, but in the meantime the heat would be imperceptible to me, and I wouldn't react to it. Without the help of simultaneous perception, multisensory patterns would be hidden from us, and we might bump into everyone in Grand Central Terminal. And when simultaneous perception shows us a pattern like cooperation in a moving crowd, something else appears that's normally invisible: a different sense of who, or what, we are.

Ordinarily, we seem to be completely separate from everything and everyone in our surroundings, and our sense of external things (if not of other people) is that they are waiting around until we can find something for them to do. At moments when the boundaries flow together, perhaps even disappear, a different sense emerges. Walking through a landscape, we have the sense that the plants and animals around us have purposes of their own. At the same time, our sense of ourselves now has more to do with noticing how we are connected to the people and things around us—as part of a family, a crowd, a community, a species, the biosphere. Since the quantum revolution in physics, sixty years ago, it has become relatively easy to think that at the submicroscopic level an electron or a photon of light can be both a particle and a wave. In the last couple of years, researchers have found that peptides in the human immune system—substances large enough to be seen through a microscope—can also show both particle behavior and wavelike behavior. And now we're finding that the same thing is true of our perceptions of ourselves. Through one system of perception we see ourselves as observers of an environment composed of separated objects, but at the same time, through another system of perception, equally active, we look for ways in which we are connected to or are part of our surroundings.

We seem to use simultaneous perception constantly to monitor our surroundings on a subconscious level for information that helps us maintain ourselves and go about our business. According to William M. C. Lam, an architect and writer in Cambridge, Massachusetts, who investigated one aspect of this activity—our "fundamental and universally shared human needs" for visual information—we are always, "regardless of the specific activity which holds our attention at any one time," on the lookout for information that has to do with "orientation, defense, sustenance, stimulation, and survival." Lam, who specializes in lighting design and is perhaps best known for designing ceiling lights with a cathedral-like glow for the stations of the Washington Metro subway system, has worked for years to establish a comprehensive biological and psychological basis for the lighting codes that are used as industry standards by American builders. It's Lam's discovery that what satisfies people usually is not the quantity of light present but whether they can see things they must know about in order to fill needs that are "essentials of human nature." If we can see those things, as Lam says in his book *Perception and Light as Formgivers to Architecture,* we then "judge an environment to be cheerful . . .

attractive . . . sparkling . . . comfortable and reassuring.''
This is the link between "a good luminous environment" and
"physical, intellectual, and emotional well-being.''

Lam's ideas about lighting needs got him in trouble for a
number of years. When he started his research, oil prices were
so low that electric utilities around the country were merchan-
dising light like a commodity and looking for new ways to stim-
ulate light consumption. The lighting codes of the day, largely
drawn up by utility engineers, specified gargantuan quantities of
light in almost every situation—every square inch of surface in
an office, for instance, was supposed to have enough light to let
you read a fifth carbon copy. And this even though photocopiers
were already replacing carbon paper! When Lam began ques-
tioning the human need for this much light, the power and light
companies began to treat him somewhat the way General Motors
first treated Ralph Nader. They sent vice presidents and other
high-level speakers to denounce him at every meeting he addressed. Then came the oil crisis, and the vice presidents were
called off.

What kinds of things enable us to meet our biological needs
for visual information? Many of them are conveyed by daylight.
Outdoors, the position of the sun in the sky helps us orient
ourselves to the time of day and works to set a series of internal
clocks. That is not the simple act it seems, because information
about the sun's position comes to us in several ways. If we're
standing out in the sun, the sense of touch is involved: We react
to the strength of sunlight falling on our skin. But even when
the sun isn't directly on us, we're still dealing with complex
information, because when we look at where the sun is in the
sky, we're also looking at the brilliance of the light coming from
it, which varies during the day. And we're looking at the color
of the sunlight; it's bluer in the middle of the day and more
orange-red in the morning and evening. How much of this information can we do without before we no longer have access
to our daytime sense of orientation? Some two-foot-by-four-foot

openings designed by Lam give us a first answer to this question. The openings are high up in the walls that separate bedrooms from dressing rooms at the Hyatt Regency Hotel in Cambridge. (Lam designed the hotel's lighting.) The openings convey natural light to the windowless dressing rooms. You can't actually look through the openings—they're too high up—but they do bring in to an inner room the color and some of the brilliance of the daylight outside. The result, as I found out staying at the Hyatt Regency, is that a perfectly ordinary little nook becomes a friendly place that has, if only faintly, the relaxed and spacious feeling of a room in a resort.

So we don't always need to feel the sun or look at it in order to stay oriented, which means we can, if we have to, get by, at least for a while, on about half the information that natural environments provide about orientation. It does seem that the experiences of a place may have a certain amount of give to them, but we're also learning that there are real limits to the amount of experiential diminution we can tolerate. If the Cambridge Hyatt Regency decided to install heavily tinted glass in its bedroom windows, for example, that would distort both the brilliance and the color of the light coming in and might do real damage to the experience available there. The design principle here is that any change made to our surroundings has the potential to affect the way we experience a place, and that the cumulative effect of a number of changes may be at some point to alter the experience entirely.

People are often drawn to places that offer rich experiences: beautiful landscapes, glittering theater districts, tranquil neighborhoods. But changes made over the years to such places which fail to consider the experiential impact produced by physical alterations can turn pearls into paste and convert the real into a mirage. In Gertrude Stein's celebrated remark about Oakland, California, when you get there, there isn't any ''there'' there— no richness of experience. If we're ever to reach the goal of a man-made environment that nurtures human beings, we need to

proceed with caution; otherwise, the act of getti
take away any "there" there.

Orientation is just one component of our ever
scious use of simultaneous perception. According (
German research, when we approach or move thr(
or a park or a railroad station, we are alert for infc
has to do both with our immediate physical safety
general sense of how welcoming these new surroι
prove to be. We let the layout of a place give us
reading on such things as whether we can linger th
to keep on moving, how relaxed we'll be if we sta]
whether we'll feel comfortable about talking to peo
there. Though we may not notice it, we're taking i
information through simultaneous perception that it's
if we were receiving two different messages from our
ings at all times. Normally, preoccupied by some ι
action, we notice very little about our surroundings ar
be getting only one message: No immediate danger he
thing's in its usual place.

Something we don't realize is how much energy it
for us to maintain this routine ignoring of our surrc
depending on the contents of the second message. Sc
the second message may be telling us that something's
At other times, the second message may actively contr;
first. Last year, while I was waiting for a friend in the ε
garden court of IBM's midtown Manhattan skyscraper—
added to the building as a public amenity—I found mysε
ing increasingly uncomfortable and ill at ease, for no r
could pin down. There was no one around who seemeι
acing, and nothing seemed out of place: the court was a
expanse filled with light, plants, and movable chairs. ΄
began to pay more attention to everything around me,
noticed that the entire floor was built on a slight slant, lε
down to one corner—apparently for drainage purposes. ΄
eye, the floor seemed level, but my internal senses and the

:les in my ankles were telling me I was off balance. The sen-
ation was as if gravity had shifted slightly to one side. All
around, tables and chairs and overarching bamboo plants invited
people to stay, but the floor seemed to say, "Keep moving!"

Small, unnoticed changes in level play a larger organizing role
in our activities than we suspect: In Manhattan, the right-angle
street grid, which keeps people's eyes focused straight ahead,
and the uniform paving of streets and sidewalks, together with
the solid blocks of buildings on both sides, tend to keep New Yorkers from noticing the natural contours—or what's left of the natural
contours—beneath their feet. The nineteenth-century Manhattan
developers who covered midtown fields and meadows with
brownstones did such a good job of lopping off the tops of hills
and filling in valleys that a hundred years or so later, as Christopher Gray, a New York historian and preservationist, has pointed
out, no one really knows what the original topography was.

Descriptive names still exist—Murray Hill, Lenox Hill, Car-
negie Hill, Mount Morris—but we don't often associate them
with climbing or descending. Nevertheless, almost every block
has some rise or dip to it, and these hints of elevation do help
people define certain districts. The upper part of Fifth Avenue
as a shopping street, for instance, stretches from Forty-second
Street to Central Park, but the part of this expanse that people
tend to identify in their minds as the historic heart of this district
runs uptown from about Forty-sixth. If you look up the avenue
from Forty-second Street, say, you can see that Forty-sixth is at
the bottom of a small hill that has St. Patrick's Cathedral, at
Fiftieth Street, on its crest. The hill seems to have a certain
holding power, even today.

Because people can get many kinds of messages from each
place they encounter, any building or piece of land used or seen
by more than one person has a public-use component that always
needs to be managed in ways that take simultaneous perception
into account.

2 Connectedness

Simultaneous perception takes on another aspect when it becomes conscious. Some places, like Grand Central, seem to help us become aware of our own experiencing. How do they do this? Normal waking consciousness and our sense of separateness from the world protect us from harm by allowing us to focus instantly on any source of danger. And we're alerted to sources of danger by sudden and rapid movement or loud noises or strong smells. So for simultaneous perception to emerge, we need a place that seems safe, where the information presented to each sense is complex but not overpowering. If louder signals appear, they will tend to drive simultaneous perception underground. That is why we lose touch with it when we leave Grand Central and walk over to Fifth Avenue.

Grand Central not only is easy to experience but also offers a special kind of experience—one that seems to amplify our perceptive reach, allowing us to notice aspects of our mental activity that are normally veiled. Of all the ideas that may form part of a late-twentieth-century understanding of simultaneous perception, this one is probably the most startling—that particular places around us, if we're wide open to perceive them, can sometimes give us a mental lift. It's one thing to find out that a railroad station could be converted into a school and another thing to realize that a mere room can function as a teacher.

Since just glancing at a building or a room, or knowing what its ordinary function is, can't tell you what its subtler experiential capacities may be, it will obviously take some time to do extensive experiential mapping of the places we've already made for ourselves and, from it, to decide what experiences, at a minimum, any place needs to provide. Still, we do already have a couple of yardsticks we can apply to the experiences of a place: whether it provides richness of information reaching all the senses, and whether there is an absence of alarm signals. We also have an obvious place to look at first—our own national experiential heritage, shaped for us and bequeathed to us by America's nineteenth-century park designers, and still largely intact, even when our parks are no longer cared for on an experiential basis.

There's one place in New York—a small part of a major city park—that's almost a physical analogue of the rearranging of one's expectations that occurs whenever one wants to experience an area. This place—a short path just inside Prospect Park, in Brooklyn—also seems to be able to trigger something in people who walk down it into the park, something that makes many of them begin almost automatically to experience everything around them, whether they've come there with that intention or not. Since this path, which was built one hundred twenty years ago, was designed—by the landscape architect Calvert Vaux and his more famous partner, Frederick Law Olmsted—to produce just such an effect, a walk down it is probably the best sort of introduction to our country's experiential heritage.

The path, which is about eighteen feet wide, is paved with hexagonal asphalt blocks—a familiar sight in New York City parks. It leads south into the park from Grand Army Plaza, an enormous oval traffic intersection that is fed by two busy streets and a roadway through the park and is dominated by a huge classical arch built as a memorial to the Union dead of the Civil War. There are more classical ornaments immediately in front of the park itself: two little temples and four fifty-foot columns topped by eagles. The plaza is not a place for simultaneous perception: The traffic noise is a constant you need to tune out, and in order to reach the beginning of the path you have to keep an eye out for cars turning onto the park drive. But once you're inside the park you can give your full attention to the path.

Even at a slow pace, a pedestrian can walk the length of this path in three or four minutes. It's not a strenuous walk: The path runs straight for a bit, goes through a few gentle curves, and then straightens out again, and after about five hundred feet it's all over. When you first step onto the path, you may feel that there isn't very much to see—just a small, self-contained scene that is pretty and, after the monuments and the traffic of the plaza, certainly relaxing. And in a sense, there actually isn't a great deal to see here, for this is the one narrow part of the park. Directly ahead of you as you start down the path is a small grassy hillock with a few trees on top. The path curves right to avoid it, and at the turn there's a cast-iron lamppost. To the right and the left are pine trees and other evergreens, a beech tree, shrubs, and more grass, and behind them are hills that seem to be rising to run parallel with the path. Also on the right is a statue of James Stranahan, a Brooklyn man who worked for twenty-two years to get the park built. The only things that tug at your attention or seem likely to lead beyond the immediate are two things that can't quite be seen: It looks as though there might be a large tree and some sort of stonework behind the little hill, and you can't be sure where the path is heading, for the hill conceals the next stretch.

The last time I was there—it was a weekday afternoon in the fall, and there were very few people in the park—I noticed after my first few steps how quiet everything was in front of me. There were, though, small sounds in that quiet. Even while fire engines roared across the plaza behind me, up ahead I could hear a blue jay. I realized, too, that the city had already become almost invisible. Unless I turned around, I could see no sign of buildings or streets or construction or demolition. A few more steps, and I had a much clearer view of what was behind the little hill. The biggest thing was a taller and more rugged hill— a continuation of the hill already rising on my right. There was a large beech tree, and what had looked like stonework of some kind was in fact several different things—some boulders near the beech and, behind them, a large opening into what looked like a good-size cave. I could now see a little farther along the path too: After its first right turn to skirt the little hill, it made a left to go behind it. But where it went next, and whether it would take me anywhere near the mysterious-looking cave—that I couldn't make out.

I found I was walking a little faster, and as I followed the first curve of the path at this new pace, the scenery on either side of me seemed to be swinging slowly around itself and around me in an orderly sequence, like the moons and planets in a model of the solar system. The cave—which I now thought might possibly be man-made—disappeared as the beech tree moved in front of me to eclipse it, slowed to a stop, and then gradually reversed course. Shortly after the path turned left, I could begin to see the cave again, and when I caught sight of it, I turned to look behind me and realized that the small hill now blocked my view of the park entrance and the plaza beyond. Almost all there was to see was parkland and sky. A few more steps, and I could see that the path did lead to the cave—and that it led also to another path, which wound its way up a long hill to the left and vanished into some trees at the top. Then I drew abreast of the great beech and in that moment became aware that the cave was not a cave after all but a straight, dark tunnel with bright daylight at the far end. And while I was looking at this patch of light, I found that the path had turned right again to bring me closer to it.

When I got near the tunnel, I could see that it led to more

The Long Meadow in Prospect Park, Brooklyn, seen from Endale Arch. *Photograph courtesy of Mary Cregg*

parkland, with a path winding through it. The tunnel entrance was a wide Gothic arch of big stone blocks, some of them carved to show leaves and flowers. When I was closer still, I thought there might be a small meadow just on the other side of the tunnel. And then I was inside the tunnel and realized that it was vaulted and was as wide as the path had been. The air in there was cooler, and I could feel a breeze on my face and hear the echo of my steps and the brush of leaves blowing toward me along the tunnel floor. The tunnel was more than a hundred feet long, and the only light was what came into it from either end. Before the light from behind me faded, I could see that the tunnel was lined with brick and had niches in its sides, which might once have held benches for waiting out a sudden shower. As I got closer to the light up ahead, I began to think that the small meadow outside might lead off to the right for a short distance. Around me I could now see bits of wood paneling still fastened to the tunnel walls. I felt that in this restricted setting, where only diminished information was available to me, I had become alert to all small changes around me: I could see the grain in the battered old slabs of wood; I could hear my footsteps getting fainter as I walked through the last few yards of the tunnel.

When people emerge from the tunnel—its official name is Endale Arch—and walk straight ahead, they cross a small paved area that serves as the end of the original entrance path and the beginning of two winding paths that branch off left and right. If you were to come with me along the entrance path, through Endale Arch, and a dozen steps beyond it, you would find the surroundings changing dramatically in those final few paces, and what you experienced of these surroundings might change in an even more spectacular fashion. We would have just reached the north end of the beautiful, undulating Long Meadow—one of Prospect Park's three major features. (The two others are a sixty-acre lake and a wooded ravine which originally resembled a portion of the Adirondack Wilderness.) The Long Meadow covers seventy-five acres—it is six times the size of the more famous Sheep Meadow, in Manhattan's Central Park—and is thought to be the longest continuous open space in any urban park in the United States. On the entrance path and in the tunnel, all views are foreshortened, extending no farther than a couple of hundred feet. The edge of the meadow, by contrast, is one of the very few places in the park—in the *city*—where someone can look straight ahead for almost a mile and all there is to see is grass and the sky above it. To either side are the long, curving lines of two wooded hills that approach each other half a mile away and almost enclose the meadow. A paved walk heads up the hill to the left; a second walk wanders away to the right. Straight ahead, there is only the grass.

Remarkably, no buildings are to be seen in this whole expanse; even the horizon, which seems a long way off, beyond the far end of the meadow, shows only trees. Just as remarkably, on almost any day of the year the whole area is flooded with light. The light seems almost to be converging on the meadow from all directions—tumbling onto the grass nearby and also glowing through the trees beyond the meadow. At the other end of the meadow, where the two hills move toward each other, the hill on the left bends to the right and forms a point. A line of trees marches out from the hill on the right to approach this point but stops short, leaving a gap. A patch of meadow grass fills the gap and spreads beyond it; and above the line of trees a far crescent of meadow makes a looping swing to the right and is lost to sight. It looks very much as if the meadow might extend around a bend and continue for some unknown distance in that direction. Back near the entrance of the park, just inside Grand Army Plaza, where the path disappeared off to the right in less than two hundred feet, one got an impression, just strong enough to draw one on, that it probably kept going, left or right, for at least two hundred feet more. Now, standing up at the north end of the Long Meadow, a stroller may feel that a much vaster scene perhaps repeats itself many times over, distance upon distance.

The experience that this striking transition can offer is of being overtaken by a sense that in the midst of a crowded and confining city you can be present in and a part of a serene and endless world. People feel that they are being pulled forward into the meadow and, sometimes, that everything around them has become more vivid. There can also be feelings of welcome, of safety, of wonder, of exhilaration. I find that what stays with me after I leave Prospect Park is a sense that our two ways of responding to the world—ordinary perception and simultaneous perception—are both within easy reach and that moving from one to the other is simple.

Although there is no formula for experiencing places, the

landscape changes along the entrance path provide a rough anal-
ogy of the changes involved in any shift of perceptive state. One
part of experiencing places, for instance, has to do with changing the way we look at things, diffusing our attention and also
relaxing its intensity—a change that lets us start to see all the
things around us at once and yet also look calmly and steadily
at each one of them. The scenery right at the beginning of the
entrance path undergoes this sort of change: Streaming traffic
and fifty-foot-high columns give way to a short stretch of rather
ordinary-looking countryside. No single object in this setting
seems either threatening or thrilling, but I notice that something
in me is already responding to my new surroundings, slowing
down my pace and realigning the focus of my sight. The shape
of the entrance path and of the land around it are certainly part
of this process. The hills that rise on either side quickly blot out
the traffic noise. The continuing noises of the park, softer and
much more varied—wind rustling the leaves of a tree, a squirrel
chattering at another squirrel—can now be detected. These little
sounds come from all directions, and being able to take in sounds
from all over, even in this narrow neck of the park, immediately
contributes to one's sense of openness and of distance—a feeling
that the horizon is pulling back. A quiet place that offers no
threat seems to invite people to redistribute their attention, and
any number of subtle perceptual cues can then come into play.
For instance, the winding course of the entrance path makes
people lean very slightly first to one side and then to the other,
and this bit of a tilt and small shift of weight can in this quiet
place prompt an awareness of the inner-body senses that register
equilibrium and momentum—information that seldom reaches
full awareness.

Like Grand Central Terminal, Prospect Park is a place that
seems to welcome experiencing. Like Central Park, New York's
other large Olmsted and Vaux park—they thought of Central
Park as only a semisuccessful prelude to their work in Brook-

lyn—Prospect Park is in the middle of an ambitious restoration
program. It is now, once again, a secure place, as well as a
quiet place, and a place with a rich variety of things to look at,
listen to, and otherwise interact with. Such places offer simultaneous perception an enriched kind of stimulation and offer us
a chance to intensify such perception by making it conscious.
But then we have to choose what to do: whether to keep our
attention on our own thoughts and plans or accept whatever our
surroundings have to give us—whether to experience ourselves
or what's around us. That choice—made once or made many
times—determines in the long run how well we get to know a
place and whether we ever get the full benefit of the experiences
it makes available.

A third part of experiencing a place, then, involves taking our
attention away from the conversation that so much of the time
goes on inside our heads. Some routine assumptions and expectations—that we know all we need to know about what's going
on around us and what's likely to happen next—are disrupted by
a walk through Endale Arch. This may be because such ideas
operate to a large extent on visual information. Sight has been
our most important sense ever since our hominid ancestors stood
upright, away from the abundance of scents along the ground,
and found that they could see for long distances. Many of the
perceptions of ordinary consciousness evolved in this visually
dominant world. The tunnel that the entrance path leads through
is not an alarming place—everyone sees the other end of it for
a minute or so before entering—but once someone steps inside,
there is a sudden and drastic diminution of visual information.
Whenever I've walked through the tunnel, my thoughts have
trailed off, so that as I emerge I no longer have the ordinary
feeling of certainty about what's happening or what will happen.

In this situation, I find that all my senses are wide open to
absorb whatever information they can get. This sensory alertness
and the very pronounced contrast between the gloom of the tun-

nel, where there's no view at all, and the bright, bright light and endless view in the meadow certainly help to explain why the change of scene between tunnel and meadow has such a strong initial impact on people. But how do we account for the sustained power of the experience that people receive on that four-minute stroll down a path, through a tunnel, and out into a meadow? Why does it seem so complex? How is it that people can take a succession of meanings from it?

Two different kinds of information, put together, may help us answer these questions. We can look at the design techniques that Olmsted and Vaux evolved for large city parks and at some comments that Olmsted made on how parks affect people and why city people need them. And we can also look at current research into people's innate responses to such things as grass, the sky, winding paths, caves and vistas, beautiful and ugly surroundings, and an enriched environment. It may be more enlightening to consider this research first.

Dr. John H. Falk—an ecologist and a former special science assistant at the Smithsonian Institution, now president of MindVentures, an education company in Columbia, Maryland— is *the* expert on how human beings respond to grass. Early in his career, Falk became fascinated by the fact that Americans have consistently had such a liking for lawns that there are now twenty-five to thirty million acres of cultivated lawn in the country—an area the size of Indiana. This vast reshaping of the environment and the time and money needed to achieve it seemed far enough removed from earning a living and raising a family to require some kind of explanation. Falk, who holds a joint doctorate from Berkeley in biology and education, spent fifteen years researching landscape preferences, working first with Americans of all ages and later with people from Africa, India, and other countries, whose backgrounds represented every kind of human habitat, from rain forest to desert.

Falk's subjects looked at photographs of different landscapes and told him which ones they liked best. He discovered, not surprisingly, that they liked the environments they were used to—a response that could be explained as a purely cultural phenomenon. Less predictably, Falk also found a "deep, innate preference for a grass landscape," even among people who had never been in a grassland setting in their lives. Among the most extensive grasslands in the world are the savannas of East Africa, where human beings first evolved, and it is Falk's conclusion that human beings may have a genetically transmitted predisposition for the surroundings of the species' birth and early development.

"The logic of it seems pretty strong," Dr. Falk told me. "So much of what defines humanness relates to that savanna—bipedalism, and advances that walking upright made possible, like the apposable thumb and the use of the hands for carrying and as tools. Habitat preference may be tied into our basic anatomy. It would explain, for instance, why, although we've developed the technology to design any kind of floor covering, we continue to put carpets—a turf analogue—on our floors. We evolved to ambulate across grass, so a spongy sort of footing is easiest to navigate. Every vertebrate has a genetically transmitted habitat preference: Knowing what constitutes home has good survival value, so it's hard-wired—that means the animal doesn't have to think about it. We may no longer need this sense for day-to-day survival, but since it remains as a guide to behavior, we can still turn it to our advantage: Once we know that there are environments where people from all cultural backgrounds can come together and feel comfortable and relaxed, we are in a better position to address stress in modern life. This innate preference for grass may protect us in another way as well: by giving us a built-in reading of our optimal level of environmental stimulation, which is to say, of the kind of complexity we need—in the things to look at, listen to, sniff, and otherwise interact with—in order to be at our best. Any reduced or raised level of stimulus may impair our functioning."

This last idea of Falk's ties in with two other research areas:

one that connects the development of the mammalian brain—in shape, size, structure, and function—with sensory experience, and one that links the beauty of human surroundings to our behavior and job performance. Some of the best-known work having to do with environmental influences on the brains of mammals has been carried out at the University of California at Berkeley by the neuroanatomist Dr. Marian Diamond and her colleagues. They showed that when a young rat is placed in what they called an enriched environment—one that has more toys and playmates—its cortex begins to thicken in just a few days, while the cortex of a young rat confined to an impoverished environment actually diminishes in size. "The brain," as Drs. Robert Ornstein and David Sobel put it in their book *The Healing Brain,* like a muscle, "shrinks and grows in response to certain experiences."

Even old rats—rats that are the age equivalent of people seventy-five to ninety years old—grow bigger brains when they are transferred to an enriched environment. Yet greater increases in brain size occur when rats are placed in a "super-enriched environment"—two large cages connected by a bridge. The brains of rats raised in a "semi-natural outdoor environment" get bigger still. Outdoors, one researcher notes, "the ambient lighting, noise and odors . . . all appear to influence the observed behavior." And Dr. Diamond reports that an enriched environment does more than make brains bigger: It also increases a rat's intelligence; rats raised in such an environment are more adept at running mazes. "The main factor is stimulation," she says. "Nerve cells are designed to receive stimulation."

In the 1950s, Dr. Abraham H. Maslow, who is celebrated as one of the fathers of humanistic psychology, and Dr. Norbett L. Mintz, a colleague of his at Brandeis University, conducted one of the first known experiments on the effect of beautiful surroundings on human mental functioning. In this experiment, the two researchers, assisted by Mrs. Maslow, rigged up three rooms—a "beautiful" room, an "average" one, and an "ugly" one. The ugly room was fitted out to look something like a janitor's room and storage closet, with a hanging light bulb, torn window shades, battleship-gray walls, and a profusion of boxes, trash cans, mops, brooms, and dust, along with an old box spring. The beautiful room had large windows, indirect light, a Navajo rug, paintings, sculpture, beige walls, a bookcase, a soft armchair, and a mahogany desk. The average room, according to the experimenters, "gave the appearance of a clean, neat, 'worked-in' office in no way outstanding enough to elicit any comments."

Volunteers were told that they were studying photographs of people to see whether the faces displayed "energy" and "well-being." The volunteers were supervised by three examiners, two of whom were themselves unaware that the real purpose of the exercise was to look at people's reactions to their surroundings. The results showed that people found energy and well-being in faces when they looked at them in the beautiful room and found fatigue and sickness in the same faces when viewed in the ugly room; setting had a real impact on judgment. The behavior of the two examiners unaware of the project's intent also varied from room to room: They consistently rushed through interviews conducted in the ugly room, and also showed "gross behavioral changes" when they worked there, and complained of "monotony, fatigue, headache, sleepiness, discontent, irritability, hostility, and avoidance." Surprisingly, although their job performance and their job satisfaction were over and over again affected by where they were, neither of the examiners noticed this fact even once. The experimenters reported: "They evidenced surprise at the whole procedure. . . . *They were not aware that their activities were in such close relationship to the room conditions,* though they both realized that they did not prefer to test in the downstairs [ugly] room." And reactions to the average room more closely resembled those to the ugly room than to the beautiful room. So even an average room is a diminished room.

Dr. Falk, the grass expert, thinks that we may have inborn responses to several other parts of the natural landscape. "I'd be amazed if the preference for water in the landscape doesn't prove to be innate," he told me. "We've learned that we have to avoid having water in any of the pictures we show subjects. It's so highly preferred that its very presence will raise preference by an order of magnitude."

Drs. Stephen and Rachel Kaplan, a husband-and-wife team of research psychologists at the University of Michigan, think that we may have an inborn preference for winding paths, which provide what they call "mystery": Landscapes exhibit "mystery" when they "give the impression that one could acquire new information if one were to travel deeper into the scene." According to the Kaplans, who have looked at how people respond to a diversity of environments, "mystery . . . is a factor of great power in predicting preference for scenes of the outdoor environment."

In a recent book, *Cognition and Environment: Functioning in an Uncertain World,* the Kaplans relate the power of mystery to early man's life on the savanna, where human beings ranged over territories of up to a hundred square miles and had to be able to decide quickly whether a place they were seeing for the first time deserved further exploration:

Although [mystery] is a familiar concept in the context of landscape architecture and has long been used in the designs of Japanese gardens, it is somewhat unexpected in the context of psychology. Perhaps for this reason there has been an inclination to translate it into some more familiar concept, such as "surprise." A critical difference between mystery and surprise, however, is that in a surprise the new information is present and it is sudden. In the case of mystery, the new information is not present; it is only suggested or implied. Rather than being sudden, there is a strong element of continuity. The bend in the road, the brightly lighted field seen through a screen of foliage—these settings imply that the new information will be continuous with, and related to, that which has gone before. Given this continuity one can usually think of several alternative hypotheses as to what one might discover. The mind-filling . . . experiences of entertaining a few fairly strong alternatives at once should yield a high level of preference; research . . . suggests that this is in fact the case.

The Kaplans think that we also have an innate preference for open spaces, which provide what they call "legibility." "Just as one can imagine oneself somewhere in a scene acquiring new information, one can imagine oneself somewhere in a scene getting lost," they write in *Cognition and Environment*. "Legibility . . . is characteristic of an environment that looks as if one could explore extensively *without* getting lost. Environments high in legibility are those that look as if they would be easy to make sense of as one wandered farther and farther into them. Enough openness to see where one is going, as well as distinctive enough elements to serve as landmarks, are important here."

And Jay Appleton, a geographer at the University of Hull, in northeast England, has identified two more human preferences in landscapes: "prospect" and "refuge." Both, he says, are aspects of the environment that support human functioning and make survival more likely. "Prospect" means a long, sweeping vista—a place where viewing is unhindered and we can take in information from miles around. "Refuge" means a hiding place where, from concealment, we can see without being seen, and gain information without giving away information about ourselves.

All these factors that modern research has shown to be part of the human response to landscapes are present along the entrance path to Prospect Park: The Long Meadow provides savanna, prospect, and legibility; the path itself affords mystery; the tunnel gives refuge; there is plenty of sky, natural light, and information we can use to orient ourselves. Were these factors incorporated deliberately? Scholars of the work of Olmsted and Vaux tell us they were. But how could Olmsted and Vaux have known what we're just finding out about? There appear to be two answers to this question. One is that they were retransmitting ideas discovered by much older cultures. The other is that Olmsted had a clear personal understanding of the need for simultaneous perception, even if he lacked a late-twentieth-century vocabulary with which to describe it.

There is now a large-scale revival of interest in Olmsted and his works. He is widely acknowledged to be the father of landscape architecture in this country, and of regional planning as well, and he has become the subject of scholarly biographies. Many of his works survive, including—besides Central and Prospect parks—major city parks in Chicago, Louisville, and Montreal, landscaping around the Capitol in Washington, D.C., park systems in Buffalo and Boston, estates, campuses, planned communities, cemeteries, and hospital grounds. He founded the firm of Frederick Law Olmsted in 1858, a full forty-five years before his death, in 1903, and he left a son and a stepson who carried on his work, as Olmsted Brothers; a successor firm, the Olmsted Office, is still in business in Fremont, New Hampshire, and the extant works by Olmsted and his family and other successors—landscapes that are now collectively identified by park officials as "Olmsted legacy parks"—number in the thousands. New York State alone has more than a hundred Olmsted legacy parks and public spaces; Connecticut has identified two hundred fifty; Massachusetts claims three hundred. Prospect Park and Central Park have been designated as both New York City and

National Historic landmarks, and Olmsted's home and office in Brookline, Massachusetts, are a National Historic Site. He and Vaux are jointly credited with establishing a number of important park design principles: These were sketched out in Central Park in the 1850s and perfected in Prospect Park in the 1860s. They include:

1. The use of natural forms—lakes, streams, woods, winding paths, turf meadows dotted with trees—whether the area already provided them or the materials for providing them had to be brought to the park site. The Long Meadow of Prospect Park had no antecedents in that part of Brooklyn and is pure Olmsted and Vaux. It was created, according to one book, "on a low swampy plain bisected by a ridge."

2. The separation of parks from the city. This is done by planting the edges of the park thickly and by forming berms, or hills, just inside the edges of a park and planting the berms with trees. A berm to the left of the Prospect Park entrance path sets it apart from Flatbush Avenue and shuts out the Flatbush Avenue traffic noise.

3. The separation of different pathways within a park, keeping pedestrian paths apart from both bridle paths and roads for vehicles. The hill that Endale Arch passes through carries the principal road in Prospect Park.

4. The efficient use of space to create the maximum amount of openness and light within a park. When you walk out of Endale Arch, you can see farther than you can along any open-space vista in Central Park, even though Prospect Park is less than two-thirds the size of the Manhattan park; this view is possible because the Long Meadow runs down the axis of a triangle that constitutes the top half of the park, and the view out beyond the bend in the meadow encourages the eye to look straight through the triangle and on down the longer diagonal in a squashed rectangle that forms the rest of the park, below the triangle. This line of sight has also been so oriented that it faces

almost due south. In our hemisphere, south is where the sun sits
and where the sky is brightest. The result, as two Olmsted scholars, Jeffrey Simpson and Mary Ellen W. Hern, noted in a 1981
book, *Art of the Olmsted Landscape,* is that when you leave the
arch you walk straight into "as dramatic a flash of light as the
nineteenth century—lacking electricity—ever saw, the golden
white sun of the meadow."

Olmsted's supporters, who cherish his writing about parks,
celebrate him chiefly for creating natural environments, for creating works of art, for enhancing cities, and for providing recreational opportunities. Their principal interest is in preserving
and restoring his works, yet although their aim is to be faithful
to his original choices of what trees and shrubs to plant, many
restoration plans have not so far incorporated Olmsted's most
fundamental discovery about park design—that parks exist in
order to be experienced. In an 1870 address to a group of Boston
social scientists who had met to consider what sort of park that
city needed, Olmsted spoke about how the word "park" is really just an abbreviation for the phrase "the park experience."
"We want a ground to which people may easily go after their
day's work is done," he said, ". . . where they may stroll for
an hour, seeing, hearing, and feeling nothing of the bustle and
jar of the streets, where they shall . . . find . . . the greatest
possible contrast with the restraining and confining conditions
of the town, those conditions which compel us to walk circum-
spectly, watchfully, jealously, which compel us to look closely
upon others without sympathy."

Olmsted was convinced that access to simultaneous perception was nowhere available in the heart of nineteenth-century
cities. He told the Bostonians: "Whenever we walk through the
dense part of a town, to merely avoid collision with those we
meet and pass upon the sidewalks, we have constantly to watch,
to foresee, and to guard against their movements. This involves
a consideration of their intentions, a calculation of their strength

and weakness, which is not so much for their benefit as our own. Our minds are thus brought into close dealings with other minds without any friendly flowing toward them, but rather a drawing from them. . . . If we had no relief from it at all during our waking hours, we should all be conscious of suffering from it. It is upon our opportunities of relief from it, therefore, that not only our comfort in town life, but our ability to maintain a temperate, good-natured, and healthy state of mind, depend. . . . Men who have been brought up, as the saying is, in the streets . . . generally show, along with a remarkable quickness of apprehension, a peculiarly hard sort of selfishness. Every day of their lives they have seen thousands of their fellow men, have met them face to face, have brushed against them, and yet have had no experience of anything in common with them."

To counteract this, Olmsted said, "what we most want is a simple, broad, open space . . . the beauty of the fields, the meadow, the prairie, of the green pastures, and the still waters . . . to gain . . . tranquillity and rest to the mind." And this space should be surrounded by "depth of wood enough . . . not only for comfort in hot weather, but to completely shut out the city from our landscapes." He concluded, "The word *park,* in town nomenclature, should, I think, be reserved for grounds of the character and purpose thus described."

Olmsted was equally specific in his speech about both the social benefits and the health benefits that are conferred by the park experience. "There are certain forms of recreation," he said, citing the promenade, or walking about in company, "the attraction of which must, I think, lie in the gratification of the gregarious inclination, and which . . . are so popular as to establish the importance of the requirement." He continued:

I have never been long in any locality, south or north, east or west, without observing a *custom* of gregarious out-of-door recreation in some miserably imperfect form, usually covered by a wretched pretext of a wholly different purpose, as perhaps, for instance, visiting a grave-yard. I am sure that it would be much better, less expensive, less harmful in all ways, more health-giving to body, mind, and soul, if it were admitted to be a distinct requirement of all human beings, and appropriately provided for.

At another point in his speech, Olmsted said:

Consider that the New York Park [Central Park] and the Brooklyn Park are the only places in those associated cities [Brooklyn was then a separate city] where, in this eighteen hundred and seventieth year after Christ, you will find a body of Christians coming together, and with an evident glee in the prospect of coming together, all classes largely represented, with a common purpose, not at all intellectual, competitive with none, disposing to jealousy and spiritual or intellectual pride toward none, each individual adding by his mere presence to the pleasure of all others, all helping to the greater happiness of each. You may thus often see vast numbers of persons brought closely together, poor and rich, young and old, Jew and Gentile. I have seen a hundred thousand thus congregated, and . . . I have looked studiously but vainly among them for a single face completely unsympathetic with the prevailing expression of good nature and light-heartedness.

Is it doubtful that it does men good to come together in this way in pure air and under the light of heaven, or that it must have an influence directly counteractive to that of the ordinary hard, hustling working hours of town life?

Another idea of Olmsted's that has not yet been championed by many of his followers is that even a park that fits his own definition in every way is not a place that can completely serve people's need to have access to simultaneous perception unless it forms part of a connected citywide—or even regionwide—park system. "It is a common error to regard a park as something . . . complete in itself," he said. On the contrary, "it should

. . . be planned . . . with constant consideration of exterior objects, some of them quite at a distance.'' The linking system he
proposed was a network of what he called ''parkways''—and he
was quite specific about how they should be designed: ''narrow
informal elongations of the park,'' he called them, ''varying say
from two to five hundred feet in width, and radiating irregularly
from it.'' And ''they should be so planned and constructed as
never to be noisy.'' And ''they should be branched or reticulated
with other ways of a similar class, so that no part of the town
should finally be many minutes' walk from some one of them.''
In proposing these parkways, Olmsted seems to have remarkably
anticipated Christopher Alexander's recent finding that people
will not make regular use of a city park if it is more than about
750 feet, or three minutes' walk, from their doors. And Olmsted
also seems to have anticipated an even more recent conclusion
by the President's Commission on Americans Outdoors—that the
country needs a national system of ''greenways,'' linear parks
and scenic highways that provide a direct physical link between
downtown city centers and existing national parks.

Olmsted and Vaux took their major design elements for city
parks—meadows, groves, lakes—from the country parks maintained by eighteenth-century English gentlemen, park designs
that were adapted for city use by nineteenth-century English
landscape architects. These country parks have an ancient design
history: They derive from medieval deer parks—fenced-in meadows and groves where deer were allowed to roam—and those
parks, in turn, were continuations of Roman deer parks that were
designed to be both beautiful and useful and were placed,
throughout the empire, where their owners could see them from
their homes. The Roman parks are thought to have carried forward traditions of beautiful landscapes that date back at least
2,500 years, to Achaemenid Persia—''if not,'' as one scholar
says, to ''the Garden of Eden itself.'' And there are scholars
who equate the Garden of Eden with the savannas of East Africa.

Since we have not yet constructed an Olmsted system of parks, we have so far inherited only half the experiential legacy he bequeathed us. But Olmsted himself stopped short of reintroducing to Western culture the ancient idea of designing whole cities so that every place in them offers a full measure of experiencing, and therefore we are probably working with, at best, only a quarter of the experiential heritage that could be ours. "Openness is the one thing you cannot get in buildings," Olmsted said once; and "tranquillity and rest to the mind," he added a second later. We are only just now beginning to realize that a building—even a skyscraper—may be able to exert an Olmstedian influence on our thinking, by helping us to sense what it is we have in common with all of the life around us. But it turns out that a new perspective on our planet is now continuously available in lower Manhattan.

A number of American astronauts report that the experience of looking back at the earth from the black vastness of space changes their lives: It shows them, for the first time in their lives, that being human means being connected to a small and beautiful planet that is both vulnerable and precious, a "blue pearl in space" that needs our care and understanding. Some of the astronauts have said—wistfully, of course—that they wished great numbers of people could be boosted into space to be filled with this vivid sense of environmental awareness, so that back on earth they might then start to pay more attention to the many urgent warnings from leading ecologists and biologists, among others, that the planet's basic life-support systems are in trouble. I can recommend one alternative to such a massive airlifting of humanity, an experience now accessible in New York at street level right next to the base of the two giant, 110-story towers of the World Trade Center, in downtown Manhattan.

The flat-topped identical twin towers, currently coholders of the runner-up distinction of being the second-tallest buildings in the world, are square-shaped and rise straight up without orna-

ment to a height of 1,350 feet. Although in good weather they
can be seen from up to fifty miles away, standing on the horizon
like chimneys or milk cartons or salt and pepper shakers, depending on the distance, the towers are more tolerated than admired by New Yorkers, and the large plaza at the base of the
towers is generally avoided in any weather. The two buildings
create strong winds that buffet passersby, and when you get close
to them they seem to loom over you in a way that sometimes
makes me think of the colossal ruined statue encountered in the
middle of a trackless desert in Shelley's poem "Ozymandias":
"Two vast and trunkless legs of stone" somehow survived where
"Nothing beside remains."

When you come near to the two towers, you can see that
although, at a distance, they look as square as four-by-four fence
posts, each one is in fact eight-sided. Every corner edge, on top
as well as on the sides, has been flattened or blunted or
trimmed—if the buildings were blocks of wood, you might think
that someone had been sandpapering the sharpness off the edges.
The result is that on both towers, the four huge walls, each one
just under 200 feet wide, don't meet directly but instead are
connected by tiny corners that are a full 1,350 feet high but only
about 10 feet wide. It's these little aluminum-covered corner
walls (which were added solely for structural reasons, the building's designer, Minoru Yamasaki, once assured me) that provide
an equivalent for an experience available only in outer space.

Because most people mind their own business in New York,
you can walk straight up to one of these corner walls—let's say
one of the ones on Liberty Street, down at the southern end of
the Trade Center—and stand there facing it from a distance of
one or two feet for five or ten minutes or more, without attracting even a glance. If you put yourself in this position, you'll
find that because of the angles of the walls, this narrow strip is
all you can see of the tower; the main walls on either side are
now hidden from your view. The wall in front of you has a shape

A side wall of one of the two towers of the World Trade Center, New York City. *Photograph courtesy of Dorothy Alexander*

something like a one-lane country road. That is to say, in the aluminum panels there are two parallel grooves or ruts that run straight up the wall like cart tracks or tire tracks on a dirt road. And near each edge of the little wall there's a sort of hump in the aluminum that seems to suggest a shoulder by the side of a road. If you lean your head back, you'll find that you're looking straight up the entire length of this piece of empty, gray metal road.

Now, by some strange trick of perception that I haven't seen described in textbooks, if you let your head stay tilted back for a minute or so, in a short while you start to feel curiously weightless, and suddenly, instead of feeling that you're standing on the *ground* looking *up* at a stretch of road, you feel that you're standing on the *road* looking *down* it, or along it. And then the funny thing is that all you can see at the other end of

A one-lane country road, Plainfield, Massachusetts. *Photograph courtesy of Harry L. Dodson*

the road is sky or clouds—or stars, if it's a clear night. The feeling that this produces is unique—you have the sense that you've somehow wandered onto one end of a road that crosses the sky and doesn't stop until it reaches the very top.

After that, there's another realization: If I can see clear across the sky, then the other end of the atmosphere isn't so very far away. I always thought of the world as vast, but really it's paper thin. There's some sort of life—a kind of mollusk—down at the bottom of the ocean, five and a half miles below the surface of the water. And there's some sort of life—a kind of red alga—up near the summit of Mount Everest, five and a half miles above sea level. When we think of the difficulties involved in our getting to the ocean floor or all the way to the top of the world's highest mountain, they both can seem worlds away. But when we are given a chance to measure the depth of the sky, the same picture comes together to form a different pattern. And what we see then is that all the organisms we know about—meaning five and a third billion of us added to the total numbers of individuals from all the other thirty or more million species of living beings—plus all the air, water, and earth that sustain all of us, are wedged inside a single long, low room with the strangest of shapes. It stretches almost twenty-five thousand miles from front to back or side to side but runs only about eleven miles at the most between its floor and its ceiling—and that's shorter than the length of Broadway. Looking up this narrow wall, you can experience the biosphere around us.

3 The Possibilities of Planning

Several new planning tools allow us to work directly with our experiences of our surroundings. One of the most innovative of the tools is a recently developed technique called environmental simulation, which enables planners to look at an area facing development—New York's Times Square, say, or the hundred-plus city blocks constituting San Francisco's downtown office and shopping district—and make a short movie that immediately shows people how changes being proposed there will affect their experiences of the place. If the changes under consideration—new buildings, new uses—will damage or diminish the experiences already available in that place, the movie can also show how the changes may be redesigned to protect or enhance people's experiences.

Five years ago, twenty-three major sites around Times Square, where most of the buildings dated from before the Depression, were being looked at for immediate redevelopment with huge office buildings and hotels, up to seventy stories high. A simulation film of the Times Square plans which was made in 1985 by Peter Bosselmann, director of the Environmental Simulation Laboratory at the University of California at Berkeley—the first research facility of this kind in the country—was able to show that the still-existing overall experience in this world-famous place, despite its long, slow decline, continued to have great strength and vitality. And then the movie demonstrated that it would make both economic and social sense for the city to redevelop Times Square by building on that eighty-year-old experience. At the same time, Bosselmann's Times Square movie made it clear that unless the zoning rules in effect for this area could be changed in three different ways by late summer or early fall of 1987—before construction began on any of eleven new buildings already in the planning stage—the classic experience of Times Square faced almost immediate extinction.

Despite repeated urgings by New York civic groups, led by the Municipal Art Society, the New York City Planning Commission responded favorably to only two of the zoning changes proposed in the Bosselmann film: In late 1986, it voted a requirement that all new buildings around the Square be festooned with bright, festive, gaudy lights and signs, and mandated a setback at about sixth-floor height to accommodate giant signs. And in a separate move, the commission later directed Times Square developers to set aside work space for the businesses that support the theater industry, such as costume makers and set makers. But the film pointed out that new buildings must meet another minimum requirement in order to preserve the existing Times Square experience—they need to have their bulk restricted, a large part of which could be accomplished by including a second setback, at about the twelfth floor, so that sunlight and sky could continue to be seen from the Square. And the Planning Commission, which was supposed to have produced a comprehensive plan for the redevelopment of Times Square by 1983, has never acted on this final must item.

Some of the buildings now being placed around Times Square contain stack upon stack of huge open floors to accommodate computer operations—such structures have been called "factory offices." All of the new buildings can be expected to remain standing for twenty or thirty years, if not longer, and it's costing billions of dollars to put them up. It cost almost a million dollars just to draft an environmental-impact statement for the area in 1984. Bosselmann's movie, which also surveys the whole area, was made in two months and had a total budget of $25,000. Environmental simulation, I learned five years ago from working as an unpaid and uncredited assistant to Bosselmann on the narration of the Times Square film, can provide a quick, low-cost analysis of development decisions that gives you an unforgettable picture of otherwise unforeseeable effects, adapting for planning purposes a discovery about human visual perception that was made years ago by Hollywood special-effects experts (and by cost-conscious Hollywood producers).

Scale models make excellent stand-ins both for imaginary monsters and for real locations that are hard to get to or are expensive to replace after they have been flattened by monsters. Just as the human eye, watching a movie, accepts a succession of still pictures as a single continuously moving picture—providing the stills go by fast enough, at a rate of twenty-four every second—the eye will also respond to full-size pictures of miniatures (even, as *King Kong* showed, an eighteen-inch ape doll covered in rabbit fur and clinging to the top of a tiny Empire State Building) as if it were reacting to real-life events. This taking of one thing for another is familiar to every moviegoer and has even been known to deceive Academy Award judges, who reportedly once refused to nominate for a special-effects Oscar a search scene with model helicopters from *Close Encounters of the Third Kind* because the judges thought the helicopters were real.

The power of simulation to evoke undistorted experiences of a place has been confirmed by almost two decades of testing at the Berkeley Simulation Laboratory, or Sim Lab, as it is often called. In one experiment, volunteers were asked, "Would you consider buying a home in this neighborhood?" A third of the volunteers were then shown a film of a trip through some Bay Area locale—one that they were all unfamiliar with and so had no strong opinions about. Another third saw a film that explored a model of the same area. And the rest were taken in a van for a drive through the neighborhood itself. Going over all the different reactions later, researchers found it hard to tell who had been looking at what, because the three different methods of viewing a place seemed to produce almost uniform responses. Volunteers liked this or that house, or they reported that such and such a street seemed unsafe, and these experiences seemed to occur to all of them, whether they spent time in a place, watched a movie of it, or watched a movie that only showed them a model of the place.

A simulation movie's ability to give us accurate samples of our experiences of different places comes partly from getting both the lighting and the camera angles right, tricks of the trade that filmmakers mastered long ago. Another part of it, one the Berkeley Sim Lab has been exploring, has to do with the fact that with the proper presentation, a seemingly simple model, something that looks like a toy, can convey a "terrific amount of information about a place," as Peter Bosselmann puts it, "that hooks right into the experiencing of it."

Proper lighting is a technical business—a matter of grouping studio lights so that a model seems to be flooded with natural light and all the shadows fall in the right places. At the same time, it's equally important to make sure that a camera moves past a model at what seems to be eye level. When people stand up or walk around, their eyes are generally five feet off the ground, and this vantage point, although we may seldom notice it, is one of the few visual constants in the experiencing of all kinds of places. If this eye-level requirement is ignored, we no longer respond quite the way we would in a real-life setting. But simulating eye level can be tricky, because on a model built at the commonly used sixteen scale—where one inch equals a distance of sixteen feet—eye level is pushed down to about a quarter inch off the ground. And of course most movie cameras are much taller than just a quarter inch.

The Berkeley Sim Lab solves this problem by using a movie camera suspended from an overhead crane. Hanging from the camera is a long lens based on a periscope originally developed for American tanks in the Second World War. This lens can quite easily hover a quarter inch above the base of a model, and it can also swivel around, left and right. There's even a computer-operated motor attached to the camera, which lets the lens swing smoothly and majestically past a model in order to simulate the experience of walking by. At an ordinary strolling pace, we cover about four feet of ground every second, so to achieve a comparable speed alongside a model built at sixteen scale, camera and lens have to move forward an inch in just over three and a half seconds. Pull the lens sideways so it's a little farther from a model, lower it an eighth of an inch, and then boost its forward speed to about two inches a second—and the camera can simulate the experience of driving through a site at a careful twenty miles an hour, a good sightseeing speed.

Peter Bosselmann calls his equipment "low to mid tech," at least in comparison to the capabilities of a Hollywood special-effects group like George Lucas's Industrial Light and Magic, which uses superimposed shots to blend together stationary models, moving models, background paintings, live actors, and animations in order to show things like a DeLorean car heading back to the future, or a figure coming out of a stained-glass window to attack a clergyman.

But Bosselmann doesn't need all of ILM's technological improvements, because he's not trying to provide novelty or even excitement; all he has to do is get in touch with something that's already operating in us, our ability to experience our surroundings. Sim Lab films accomplish this, according to Bosselmann, by simulating simultaneous perception. He has found that simply by moving the camera around, he can make the eyes engage more than one sense. When we can see ourselves not only in a place but also moving through it, things loom up and recede, and we begin to get an internal physical sensation of being near

The unimproved West Side Highway along the Hudson River in New York City. *Photograph courtesy of Tom Fox*

An environmental simulation of a landscaped boulevard and esplanade to replace the old West Side Highway. *Photograph courtesy of Peter Bosselmann*

some of the objects we're looking at and distant from others. It seems our body sense of being placed in space makes use of different kinds of information. While it's based partly on the sense of touch—feeling air pressing on our skin as a way of knowing about the volume of the space around us—it's also based partly on visual cues.

So Sim Lab movies keep everything moving. At the same time, the seemingly ordinary stationary objects in the movies— the models themselves—are passing on to people a large part of the detailed visual information that is absorbed during the experiencing of a place. The models of various buildings may be nothing more than photographs pasted on sheets of cardboard, supplemented by cutout photographs of moving crowds of people, tiny trees, and toy cars built for model-train layouts—in fact, just such objects were used in Bosselmann's Times Square film—but what you can take from such bits and pieces once they've become part of a Sim Lab movie is an understanding of such things as how much sunshine and shadow there is in a place; how much sky can be seen; how the place looks at night; whether you can orient yourself in the place; the height, shape, scale, and density of all the buildings in the area; the kinds of uses provided by these buildings; the number of people and the amount of traffic in the vicinity; whether there's a sense of openness, any views or vistas or places to stop and just look around; whether there's an overall sense of security, or perhaps a sense of welcome or delight; how many reasons there seem to be for spending any time at all in the place.

Quick contrast, another standard Sim Lab movie technique, sometimes jolts people into realizing how much they value the continuing experience a familiar place offers, by taking it away from them unexpectedly before giving it new life a minute or two later. A simulation movie often presents something of a fast shuffle through alternative views of a place, showing current conditions followed by pictures of two different tomorrows. The

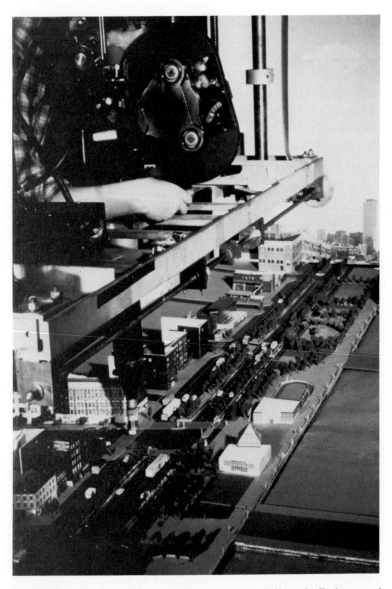

The simulation process: a periscope camera lens—or "probe"—at the Environmental Simulation Laboratory, Berkeley, California, hovers over a model of the proposed West Side Boulevard and Esplanade in New York City. *Photograph courtesy of Peter Bosselmann*

first tomorrow sets forth the zoning "build-out," as it's called: This is an image that telescopes time by superimposing on the initial scene all of the new buildings permitted by the zoning now in force in an area, at the same time making each of these buildings exactly as tall and as bulky as the law allows. It's like beginning a book and then flipping immediately to the last chapter to see how the plot will turn out.

Since our existing zoning regulations in almost every zoned community are still nonexperiential for the most part—failing to protect, say, the amount of sunlight that reaches a street—the first future depicted in a Sim Lab movie is usually not a happy ending and shows people a much darker and more somber experience than the one they know. The second tomorrow presented, on the other hand, often makes the first tomorrow look insubstantial, no more than a hallucination. What's shown here is an "experiential build-out"—new development based on an amended zoning code sensitive to experiential needs, so that all new tall buildings, for instance, have enough setbacks to let the sun shine on through. This time people are looking at a future that still has strong ties to the present. It's an unusual, and sometimes disquieting, way of bringing simultaneous perception into full awareness—one that almost amounts to living backward for a few moments. It lets us see an existing experience fresh, by getting us to look back at it, as if, like Ebenezer Scrooge, we could step down into it from an era in which it had already become only a memory.

Some architects—those with an unusual combination of abilities—have always been able to feel the experience of a new building before it goes up. Previsualization, as this ability is called, is not something that is taught in schools, and it's often treated as a sort of minor gift that can make work go faster— similar in some ways to a musician's possession of perfect pitch or a politician's ability to remember names and faces. With those architects who have it, previsualization seems to be a matter of doing two things at once: They must be sensitive to their own experiences of places, and they need well-developed powers of visualization. People equipped in this way can look at the plans for a new building and conjure up the completed structure in their minds. They can see themselves standing in front of the building and can note their own responses. Not every architect can previsualize. Several years ago, Peter Bosselmann took drawings that a number of Berkeley architecture students had been working on, built models based on these drawings, and then photographed the models in the Sim Lab. When he invited the students to look at the Sim Lab pictures, they all failed to recognize the buildings they had themselves designed.

But probably no one—not even architects who can visualize their own work, and certainly not mayors or planning commissioners—can previsualize the effects that large-scale rebuilding will have on the experiencing of an area, because this means trying to previsualize the cumulative effect on a place of years of change and redevelopment. And so most predictions about the results of full-scale rebuilding are largely guesswork. When the guesses turn out badly, as they frequently do, there is likely to be widespread distress—after the fact—about the loss of a valued experience. People who lived in New York in the early 1960s, for instance, can still remember the shock they felt when Pennsylvania Station, a railroad station bigger than Grand Central, was torn down for a new station, underground. "Until the first blow fell no one was convinced that Penn Station really would be demolished or that New York would permit this monumental act of vandalism," a 1963 *New York Times* editorial said in summing up reactions throughout the city. Penn Station, which covered two city blocks, was a gargantuan but exuberant structure—half greenhouse and half Roman arches, and both halves full of light—that made you feel glad you had arrived in New York. The replacement station, cramped and shabby, makes people pull into themselves and hurry through.

The loss of Penn Station and its experience led directly to a new government program in New York. Within a year and a half, the city, responding to popular pressure, established the New York City Landmarks Preservation Commission as a permanent city agency, to give some protection to important buildings. In the 1970s, because of the existence of the Landmarks Commission, efforts to tear down Grand Central, which had been designated a city landmark, were thwarted, and so that building and its experience are still available.

Most American communities now realize that it's possible to have a special concern for older buildings and their experiences without taking attention away from economic and social goals. It has taken far longer to develop the techniques that will let us deal directly with another vulnerable community resource—the experiences that our surroundings provide. But today action can be taken in this field too: We can identify the important experiences in a community and then maintain and enrich them through successive waves of rebuilding.

One American city, San Francisco, has already taken on the job of looking after its own experiences. A series of films about San Francisco development options that the Berkeley Sim Lab produced over a six-year period for the San Francisco Department of City Planning—films that were shown to San Franciscans on television—helped lead in 1985 to a new plan for downtown San Francisco, which limits the height, the bulk, and the number of new buildings, as well as the amount of shade they can cast, in order to preserve the existing experience of the area by maintaining its views, its openness, its sunshine, and its low wind speeds. Using models and quick contrasts, the films let people from all parts of the city experience in advance the effects of each development option. The resulting plan makes it San Francisco's responsibility to think about its economy, its social programs, its environment, and its experiences, all at the same time. The intent, according to a draft of the plan, is "to make possible appropriate growth but to manage vigorously its effects," by "maintaining San Francisco's renowned environment and character" and "preventing building where change would diminish the city's character or livability but accommodating development that would further the city's economic and social objectives." One San Francisco planning commissioner has said, "It was the simulation films that let us see what would happen to the city if we stayed with the old zoning—and what kind of zoning we need to get the city we want." Other experiences, in different communities—Times Square among them— lack this kind of care and safeguarding.

———

Times Square, the "crossroads of the world" and the place where Broadway opens up to become the "Great White Way," has performed three overlapping functions in the life of metropolitan New York for more than eighty years: It is where people come together, where people go out on the town, where they head just to take a look around. It is the heart of the city: a centrally located open space that is a transportation hub (transit lines feed in from all the boroughs, and the Lincoln Tunnel brings cars and buses from New Jersey), is big enough to hold crowds of several hundred thousand people, and has enough light—more than two hundred miles of neon tubing—to illuminate gatherings day and night.

Times Square is also New York's central entertainment district. The world's largest concentration of legitimate theaters is supplemented by support activities that, historically, have been tucked away on side streets or upstairs—dance studios, rehearsal halls, recording studios, costumers, script services, theatrical agents, ticket agents, hardware stores, paint stores, musical-instrument shops. The theaters, most of which went up during the first three decades of the twentieth century, are themselves a major part of New York's inheritance. The designers of these buildings came up with something new, as contemporary architectural historians are now pointing out—a modern form of urban-entertainment architecture. The idea was to build lavishly, colorfully, and gaudily everywhere, inside and out, as a way of extending the atmosphere of the drama beyond the stage—of bringing it through the auditorium, into the lobby, and out onto the street. The effect of these designs is to surround both audiences and passersby with a festive glow.

Many of the theaters are also individual national treasures, with the sight lines of an arena and the acoustics of a concert hall, in addition to their exuberant decoration. Broadway performers have compared these theaters with great musical instruments, with Stradivarius or Guarneri violins, for their special ability to fuse the energy of audiences and the emotions of actors into the kind of focused force that only live entertainment generates. At the old Broadway legitimate theaters, memorable performances have been a continuing reality since before the First World War: Fred and Adele Astaire danced at the Winter Garden, where *Cats* is now playing, and Jolson sang there, and Fannie Brice, and Barbra Streisand *as* Fannie Brice. Sarah Bernhardt, the Marx Brothers, Judy Garland, Bette Midler, and Diana Ross have all played the Palace. The Broadway theaters pull eight million people to Times Square every year all by themselves, and crowded in among the theaters are the area's many other entertainment activities—bars and restaurants, discos and dance halls, nightclubs, jazz clubs, a concert hall, hotels, shops and shopwindows, amusement parlors, street musicians, gigantic flashing signs, and twenty-one first-run movie houses, which, according to figures gathered three years ago, sell more tickets than all the other movie houses in the city put together. Many of Times Square's businesses are family-owned and have been around almost as long as the theaters. Manny's Music Store, where Jimi Hendrix and the Beatles bought guitars, is more than fifty years old, and so is the Broadway Arcade, a meticulously maintained pinball parlor that draws fathers and sons, businessmen, mailmen, Broadway stars, and the best pinball players in the world.

Most of the established businesses in the Square still cater to a middle-class and family crowd, and an increasing number of these middle-class customers are black families, Hispanic families, and Asian families. In the mid-1980s, New York City became what's known as a "majority minority city" for the first time in its history, meaning that it has a population with a majority—54 percent—of nonwhite people. One of the still largely unnoticed benefits of this change has been that Times Square is now on its way to becoming the first fully integrated American entertainment center.

Times Square is the tourist and visitor center of New York— a function that is rapidly taking on increased importance now that tourism, an industry growing steadily nationwide, has become the largest industry in the city. More than seventeen million visitors now come to New York in a year, and while they're in the city they spend more than two billion dollars and provide work for four hundred thousand people. Because Times Square is one of the most widely recognized place names in the world, it's the city's biggest tourist attraction—even though at the moment, once it has attracted its visitors, it doesn't do much about recognizing their existence. The only visitors' center in the area is a trailer on Forty-second Street. New York does not offer tours of the area or backstage tours of the theaters, and there are no signs laying out a tourist trail to link Times Square to other nearby attractions, like Central Park, Fifth Avenue, St. Patrick's Cathedral, Radio City Music Hall, or Macy's.

All three of these principal uses of Times Square have so far managed to survive two periods of urban change—first, decades of decay and neglect, which hit Times Square with as much devastation as afflicted any downtown district in the country;

then, in the late 1980s, a sudden surge of speculative rebuilding.
A long drought followed by a drenching flash flood. One reason
traditional uses of Times Square have shown such resilience is
that the experience of the area, a dynamic one, is still, despite
everything, almost intact: Many of its chief components and
ingredients remain in their original positions. The experience
there has been reduced, it is off balance and calling for help,
and increasingly it's now also hemmed in, fenced off, loomed
over, and belittled by the new buildings going up around the
Square. The taste there is more bittersweet than the taste at
Grand Central or in Prospect Park; but if Times Square has been
brought close to the breaking point, it is as yet unbroken. People
can still walk through Times Square and day or night pick up a
feeling of being in contact with the energy of a whole city.

The first thing I noticed on a mid-afternoon visit to Times
Square late last year was the sun pouring down on me and filling
both ends of the intersection. Times Square is not really a square,
of course; it is made up of two long triangles touching nose to
nose—the triangles formed by the crisscrossing of Seventh Avenue and Broadway. Manhattan's one long diagonal street, Broadway follows Indian trails, colonial wagon roads, and a fault line.
It predates the right-angled Manhattan street grid, and it provides
midtown with a series of wedge-shaped open spaces—bow-tie
intersections, planners call them—as it angles past the successive
north-south avenues. South of Central Park, Broadway's slicing
through has created not only Times Square but also Columbus
Circle (which has actually been scooped out to form a complete
circle), Herald Square, Madison Square, and Union Square.

On city maps, the two Times Square triangles now have separate names: The southern triangle, the one near Forty-second
Street, is the official Times Square, while the northern triangle
has been renamed Duffy Square, in honor of Father Francis P.
Duffy, an army chaplain and Times Square pastor whose bravery
under fire made him a hero of the First World War. But people

continue to use the name Times Square for both triangles, and as a neighborhood, Times Square is even bigger: It includes Forty-second Street between Seventh and Eighth avenues, a movie-theater block that has at times been almost overwhelmed by social problems, including drug dealing, vagrancy, prostitution, con games, pickpockets, teenage runaways, homeless families put up in welfare hotels, and small groups of unemployed young men, mostly black and Hispanic, with nowhere to go and nothing to do. The Times Square area also takes in Restaurant Row, on Forty-sixth between Eighth and Ninth, and all the operating legitimate theaters on the side streets off Broadway and Seventh starting at Forty-first Street and stretching up as far as Fifty-third. But the experience of Times Square is generated primarily in the open space in the middle: in the bow tie.

Walking along Forty-fourth Street and emerging into the full sunlight in the Square, I was surrounded by a mixture of warmth, activity, noise, bright colors, and neglect, with openness all around and blue sky and white clouds to my left and overhead. Taxis, cars, buses, and trucks thundered by; large numbers of people moved past busily; a breeze picked up pages from an abandoned newspaper and pushed them along the sidewalk near my feet; and there were bright flashing signs up ahead of me. But for a few moments my attention was elsewhere. Simultaneous sensations of flooding sunshine, extensive openness, and a chunk of blue sky reaching down almost to eye level are so rare in Manhattan outside a park or a penthouse that I glanced up toward the sun to see how long the sunshine part of this could last.

This is one kind of celestial calculation that many New Yorkers learn to make automatically; it amounts to an astronomical equivalent of looking at a parking meter or checking the fuel gauge on a car's dashboard—only, instead of looking at an arrow moving through a semicircle on top of a parking meter to see how many minutes you've got left before the EXPIRED sign flips up, you look up at the sun to find out how big a piece of open sky it can still arc through before a building somewhere on the skyline blocks it and throws a shadow over you. Tall, bulky buildings can cast broad shadows for surprising distances, influencing the experiences of people who never go near them. Right now, the New York developer Donald Trump wants to put up the world's tallest building on Manhattan's upper West Side—a 136-story skyscraper that would be the centerpiece of a new development to be called Trump City. This building, if it ever goes up, will create shade on the far side of the Hudson River, in New Jersey, more than a mile away.

There are now four modern high-rise towers near the center of Times Square to cast shadows over the area. Two are right in the middle of the west side of the Square: One Astor Plaza, a block-long office building rising fifty-four stories straight up, sits next door to a block-long hotel, the New York Marriott Marquis, which rises fifty stories straight up. On the east side, there's a block-long office building that rises thirty-three stories straight up, and One Broadway Place, a brand-new, forty-four-story, blue and green glass, block-long office building (with a sixth-floor setback to conform to the city's new Times Square signage requirement). Still, last year when I looked up to check the Square's sun-supply gauge, I could see that the tank was brimming: In the extreme southwest corner of the Square, down by Forty-second Street, two blocks of low buildings, mostly four and five stories high, would continue to let afternoon sun stream into the Square for several hours. I turned north to walk through this protected light, with a feeling that I had a wealth of sunshine to spend. Only two years before, whenever I made this same walk, I could look around and see that old four-story and five-story buildings of walk-up height were still the norm in Times Square, as they once had been all over the city. Up at the north end of the Square, two key adjacent blocks of these modest buildings, small-scale commercial structures more than half a century old, have since disappeared—one's become a 500-foot-high hotel; the other's now a 685-foot-high office building with bulky, "factory office"–size floors. But four blocks of small buildings remain standing, almost by accident—because down the years, things have seldom gone altogether according to plan in Times Square. There are just enough small old structures left to make it clear that it was very low-rise buildings which anchored the classic experience of Times Square for several generations of New Yorkers.

Until the theater arrived in Times Square, just after this century began, the district was, like other New York neighborhoods, a nomadic operation. While the city's most fashionable residential neighborhood migrated up Fifth Avenue from Washington Square toward Central Park during New York's great nineteenth-century expansion, the theater district flowed north along Broadway, lighting up one bow tie after another: Union Square in the 1860s, Madison Square in the eighties, Herald Square in the Gay Nineties. Even during the boom years of theater construction in Times Square, it seemed reasonable to assume that after a few years the business would again pick up stakes and head north, this time to Columbus Circle. And one theater did get built near the Circle—the New Theatre, a beautiful white marble structure designed by Carrère and Hastings, the architects of the great white marble palace that serves as the main branch of the New York Public Library, at Fifth Avenue and Forty-second Street. But the New Theatre was a commercial failure—first as a theater and then as an opera house. The economy changed, and then the world, the city, and entertainment itself; rebuilding stopped during the Depression and the Second World War. When building started up again after the war, the island was for the first time full: There were no empty areas in which to relocate. Consequently, the upper East Side continued to be the best address in town, and the theater district stayed on in Times Square. And there wasn't much money for putting up

new structures even there, because a lot of people had moved
to the suburbs and now spent their evenings watching television.

A number of the older buildings around Times Square—office
buildings and hotels—are twelve to sixteen stories high. There's
also a medium-size skyscraper, dating from the 1920s—the Paramount Building, reaching thirty-one stories after seven setbacks. But up until the late 1980s, it was the very low-rise
buildings that predominated. Thanks to them, for most of the
twentieth century the main architectural feature of New York's
entertainment district, day and night, was light.

In their old unity, the small buildings created a bowl of light,
a mixture of natural light and the bright lights of Broadway.
Building heights that let the sun pour in are also just low enough
so you see a great sweep of sky and clouds without having to
tilt your head back. At the same time, these buildings proved to
be just the right size to serve as the supporting framework for
the gaudy—and expensive—advertising signs that Times Square
is famous for: There are still huge flashing neon signs fastened
on the fronts of Times Square's remaining small buildings, covering their top two or three stories, and neon signs and bill-
boards, equally huge, if not bigger, up on their roofs. Almost
all the rooftop signs are set at angles to the buildings and streets.
This special placement justifies their expense, because angling
a roof sign that says MITA, JVC, or CANON—Japanese companies
are now a major presence in Times Square advertising—gives
the name much more visibility: You see the sign long before you
walk in front of the building it's on top of.

In Times Square, the angling of the signs has another kind of
impact as well; three years ago, at night, there were thirty-one
big signs around the Square reaching for people's attention—so
many signs, in so many places, that in the end they seemed to
band together and surround the area with an unbroken ring of
light. Some of this three-dimensional system of light has stayed
in place, and until earlier this year you could see the hugeness

of it at the northern end of Times Square, where a sloping stack of roof signs reached gradually up and away from the Square, over the space of a couple of blocks. First, there was a red-and-white COCA-COLA sign, on top of a low building at Forty-seventh Street. Above and behind it, a red, white, and gold SUNTORY ROYAL sign (Suntory Royal is a Japanese Scotch) hovered over the back of the same building, at a greater height. Finally, in the next block north, a 250-foot-high all-white SONY sign rises high above a ten-story building, almost like a snow-capped peak in the distance. This dramatic sequence of cascading signs frequently appears on postcards of the Square.

Three years ago, on one springtime walk through the Square, I found myself ducking out of the moving crowd just north of Forty-sixth Street to stand beside the statue of George M. Cohan, the dancer-actor-producer-playwright who wrote songs—"I'm a Yankee Doodle Dandy," "Give My Regards to Broadway"—that still resound with the energy and bounce and beat of Times Square. I had a feeling that day that I wasn't yet in touch with all the sensations reaching me, and although I had no sense of danger, I could see that I couldn't just do what is so easy to do in a place like Grand Central Terminal or Prospect Park—that is, slip almost automatically into a greater awareness of how the major ingredients of a place work together and what they bring to people. It took me a while, as I stood beside the statue, to realize that this was because here in Times Square I was getting a first lesson in how to repair damaged experiences. Last year, when I came back to the statue, I found a second lesson in the same place—about banding together to become the guardians of an experience, rescue it, and convoy it through rapid or long-term changes.

The statue of Cohan, which shows him carrying his straw hat and his cane, is on a traffic island, a concrete triangle in the middle of the northern end of the Times Square bow tie. The statue is near the southern point of the triangle, and on the rest

of the traffic island are a couple of flagpoles, a statue of Father
Duffy, some concrete tubs holding flowers and small trees, the
TKTS booth for half-price Broadway theater tickets, and several
rows of metal stanchions, used to organize the people who line
up for tickets. A few of the stanchions have been placed so that
they also fence off the Cohan statue from the sidewalk, and an
unintended result of this is to make the two or three feet of space
right around the statue the closest thing Times Square has to a
sheltered, quiet spot.

You can't sit down—there's no public seating anywhere in
Times Square—and you have to scramble around the stanchions
in order to get close to the statue. But once you're there you've
moved a full two steps away from all the activity swirling through
the Square—enough of a distance in this kind of space to confer
a feeling of privacy. Every so often when I'm there, I have to
step sideways for a few moments, so that people on the other
side of the stanchions can take pictures of the statue. The rest
of the time, I'm not in anybody's way, and then I have a chance
to take a long look at whatever I'm experiencing—at my reactions to my surroundings.

As recently as three years ago, you could see a lot of light
and openness from the Cohan statue. The cascading signs of the
north end were a block away. Right across the street to the west
was the first of the four adjacent blocks of lower buildings along
Broadway, three of which extended beyond the Square to the
northwest. (That first block is still in place. The second block
has given way to the new 685-foot-high office building; and the
third block has become the new 500-foot-high Holiday Inn
Crowne Plaza Hotel. The fourth block, as ever, is dominated by
the eleven-story Brill Building, the original Tin Pan Alley building.)

On my initial visit to the statue, I found I could look straight
up Seventh Avenue as far as Central Park, which showed up as
a small blob of green more than half a mile away; when I turned

around and looked down Broadway, I saw a corner of the gar-
ment district. I could feel a slight breeze in my face, and the
breeze was also rustling the leaves of the little trees in front of
me. And sunshine continued to pour down on me pleasantly.
Standing in this warmth, I took a good look at the low buildings
along Broadway and realized that from the center of the Square,
these small buildings seemed to be much farther away than just
across the street. At this point, one part of what I was experiencing began to make better sense to me: Although Times Square
isn't as big or formal or as carefully planned an open space as,
say, the Grand Army Plaza in Brooklyn, it used to have an unusual feeling of welcoming spaciousness that wasn't to be found
at the Brooklyn plaza or at any other New York intersection. It
gave you a sense of being protected, because it gave the impression that there was room enough here for all. And it was
because of this feeling of roominess that tens of thousands of
people could jam into the two smallish triangles of Times Square
and yet not feel crowded.

Times Square's spaciousness, like Times Square's bowl of
light, was very much a product of small-scale buildings, light,
and sky. You could see how these three ingredients worked together to convey the impression of roominess by taking a walk
through the Square toward the end of a sunny afternoon—as I
did about half an hour later. By that time, I had picked up a
better understanding of some of the contributions that each one
of these elements could make to roominess. Standing at the
statue, I had begun to see, first, two things that sunshine by
itself does to make nearby buildings seem farther away. One of
them is a purely visual effect: Sunlight had made the actual
volume of space around me into a visual object. It's something
like the effect of throwing dye into a river in order to see the
shape of currents in the water. In this case, it was a matter of
sunlight reflecting off the dust in the air, making the air seem to
be charged with light and showing it as a three-dimensional

form. As I came to realize this, openness took on more of a presence, with the consequence that buildings, high and low, seemed to keep their distance; for now there was a sun-filled block of air between me and them.

At the same time, I was responding to the touch of the sunlight on my skin; I could sense both heat and something like weight, or pressure. Because this force from ninety-three million miles away can come right up to our own outsides, the sun can seem to be the closest thing around, and then everything else, even sun-filled air, begins to seem slightly farther away—somewhere on the other side of an enveloping glow.

Like the sun, the great expanse of open sky over the Square seemed to be putting me at my ease: It was giving me an enlarged sense of where I was. The small buildings around Times Square, in addition to not disrupting sunlight and views of the sky, reinforced the impression of roominess by encouraging in people a sense of buoyancy of the kind found on return visits to grade-school classrooms. It's a sensation, I would say, that's built out of three feelings: of self-confidence, of safety, and of being the right size. When I went back—as a grownup—to my fourth-grade schoolroom, my initial reaction was surprise: It's so small! And then came the sense of buoyancy. The words in my head were: I can handle this. Part of this response was just hindsight, a realization that if I'd known more—about people, about decimal points—I could have coasted through fourth grade (or some of it). I was also feeling reassured just because I was no longer being dwarfed by my surroundings.

This sense of buoyancy is deliberately evoked at Disneyland, where all the buildings are scaled down to something like seven-eighths size. This is not enough of a reduction to make the buildings look like miniatures, but I've noticed at Disneyland that even this slight shrinkage does have the effect of helping people relax and feel more in control of their circumstances. In Times Square, the sense of buoyancy complemented the effects produced by the sun and the sky, and together these made it possible for people to feel spaciousness within themselves as well as around themselves.

What would Times Square be like without its roominess? This question could already be answered three years ago. When I left the Cohan statue to walk back south through the Square, the center of the Square—the knot in the bow tie—was sitting in a late-afternoon shadow cast by the two modern fifty-or-more-story buildings on the west side of the Square that were put up before the recent surge of rebuilding. The shift in my attention as I stepped into the shadow, with the two high-rises straight ahead of me, was as striking as any engineered by an environmental-simulation movie. I hadn't been thinking much about the two big buildings as I walked toward them through the sun, because, like the small buildings in the Square, they seemed to be at some remove from me; my sense of them, before I reached their shadow, was that despite the long blank walls they presented to the street and their huge size—which was already cutting off a large part of my view of the sky—the Square could somehow absorb both of them.

As soon as I reached their shadow, however, the two buildings had almost all my attention: With the sunlight gone, they seemed to push forward, almost to lunge toward me, and at the same time I suddenly became aware of their height and weight up above me, hanging down over the Square. A few moments later, I was chilled by a sharp gust of wind pushed downward by the building nearer me, the Marriott hotel. This rough transition was then something new in Times Square—the Square had never had two adjacent skyscrapers until the hotel was completed, in September 1985—and both it and the hotel had already attracted harsh comments. "Walking north on Seventh Avenue from Forty-second Street, I felt the weather suddenly get warmer and brighter and the emotional temperature likewise improve: I'd just emerged from the shadow of . . . the Marriott," one New

Yorker wrote in a letter to the Municipal Art Society. And Paul Goldberger, the architecture critic of the *New York Times,* was even more severe: "The Marriott is a hulking, joyless presence, looming over the one part of New York that, whatever its problems, always used to walk with a spring to its step."

But at the time, most of Times Square still had sunlight—and the spaciousness and buoyancy that sunshine helps create—most of the day. And wherever light and openness were working together in the Square, it was possible to become aware of twin sensations of *I've got time enough to take a good look* and *I've got room enough to look around.* What happened if you accepted these standing invitations to stop, look, and linger—to experience Times Square? When I first stood at the Cohan statue and began to pay equal attention to everything I could see, I found that I was looking at hundreds of activities grouped into six different patterns, or streams, of motion. High overhead, a strong wind was pushing several lines of small white clouds from west to east. Down where I was standing, a different wind, a breeze from the north that had been tugging at my jacket and fluttering the leaves on the small trees near the TKTS booth, was now vigorous enough to stir a dirty, faded orange, white, and blue New York City flag near the trees and to shake a dozen yellow pennants that had been hung on streetlights around the Square to advertise the annual New York City Marathon. Halfway up to the high clouds—as it appeared—a vast flock of pigeons was wheeling in midair, and closer to hand, several smaller flights of pigeons were swirling up from the ground. One pack came to rest on the metal letters CIT in CITIZEN QUARTZ WATCHES, a large mid-1980s sign on a rooftop on the west side of the Square. Still more birds were strutting around near my feet, searching for crumbs. I had never before noticed birds in Times Square or thought of it as a pigeon center, but here was an assemblage of pigeons that was almost big enough to handle at least one end of the Piazza San Marco in Venice.

The flashing electric lights of the Times Square signs made another moving pattern. Although most of the major neon signs were dark—since it was still midafternoon—when I looked north I could see the lights of eleven different signs blinking or flickering or twinkling, and when I looked south I could see nine electric signs in motion at the same time, including the famous Times Tower "zipper," a long band or ribbon of 14,800 electric light bulbs that spells out news headlines. Originally installed by the *New York Times* to flash news of the 1928 elections, the zipper passed into other hands in 1961 and finally went dark in 1977, after years of fitful operation. But in 1986, a new city paper, *New York Newsday,* brought it back to continuous life.

The two other moving patterns in the Square—traffic and people—are constants, and both take place right at eye level. Twenty-five lanes of traffic roar into and squeeze through the Square, which, like the rest of midtown, is congested most of the day, now that eight hundred thousand cars a day are pushing into Manhattan—twice the daily number that entered the city at the end of the Second World War. On top of this, both Broadway and Seventh Avenue, each one of which is a major southbound artery, shrink down from a width of five lanes to only three lanes as they approach the center of the intersection (the knot of the bow tie encloses a bottleneck). The noise of taxi, car, bus, truck, limousine, and motorcycle horns, engines, brakes, tires, and rattling bodywork is a constant presence in the Square. Sometimes you can hear and feel a subway train rumbling past under your feet. Weaving through the traffic are the people in Times Square: workers, passersby, sightseers, pleasure seekers, hangers around, and the homeless—strolling, hurrying, dawdling, window-shopping, waiting for friends, standing on line for tickets, bunching up around food vendors, street peddlers, three-card-monte men, and street musicians.

The sight of all this energy in action has been, I think, the central experience Times Square has made available. It has of-

fered a sense that here in this one place, the energy of an entire
city has been put on display. It's been like a window overlooking
the engine room of an ocean liner, or a cutaway view of a dy-
namo. Thanks to Times Square's full supply of sunlight and
openness, this energy has not felt overpowering and threatening
but, rather, like an abundance, a surplus, readily available, constantly replenished, the city dweller's secret asset, and yours to
tap into and use—to walk a little more briskly, or whistle a tune,
or exchange a smile, or lift up your spirits, or what you will.

At night, when the patterns of motion are different in the
Square, the feeling of available energy has intensified. Then
there's no sun, no birds, no views of the working of the winds;
instead, the great neon signs have almost surrounded the Square
with flashing light. Even today, during the height of the theater
season, if you head for the Cohan statue just before curtain
time—at around a quarter to eight—and stand there for a minute
while taxis and theatergoers push past on all sides, you may well
feel the pulsing light of the signs already at work inside you. As
one New Yorker recently put it, "The switch that turns on the
lights seems to turn on a light within."

4 Picking Up the Pieces

Why, then, if there is such a strong, enduring, and invigorating experience still at the heart of Times Square, does it now take so much time and effort to get the full taste of it? Is there some kind of interference at work—apart from the Marriott hotel and the other new skyscrapers, which so far are having a mostly localized effect on the way the Square is experienced—and is it something that we could diagnose and deal with? Even three years ago, visitors to the Square could clearly see that the most common explanation of Times Square's troubles—the idea that the Square is awash in pornography and overrun by "undesirables"—provided only a small part of the answer, although it starts to suggest why some people now actively avoid the Square altogether. In the first place, there isn't much pornography left in Times Square: "Adult" bookstores, peepshows, and theaters showing hard-core pornographic movies, which did proliferate in the Square in the late 1960s, have been in decline over the past eight years or so, and today they account for just thirty-two, or 7.4 percent, of a total of 430 retail businesses in the Square. From the Cohan statue, for example, only one such place is visible.

Kevin Lynch, a highly regarded city planner who taught for many years at the Massachusetts Institute of Technology, was able to show, in an innovative book called *The Image of the City*

(1960), that the "mental maps" of our home towns which we all carry around with us have a lot more precision and detail if we live in places that offer us richly detailed and well-defined experiences. (In his famous example, a typical mental map of Boston was an intricate diagram, and a typical mental map of Jersey City was practically a blank.) That Times Square's reputation as a pornography center has lived on despite a quietly effective cleanup effort suggests that in times of rapid change, our mental maps of places quickly get obsolete. Certainly if we're not in the habit of checking up on the experiences around us, we will be slow to recognize either a deteriorating environment or one undergoing a process of renewal.

The question of the so-called undesirables is a little trickier. Many of the unsolved social problems that have always been part of the city spilled over into Times Square years ago: Derelicts, pickpockets, con artists, prostitutes, and gangs of unemployed young men all got there long before the upsurge of pornography shops, in the late sixties. People from newer problem groups, such as drug dealers and teenage runaways, got to the Square around the same time pornography did, and it was this combined arrival that gave Times Square the reputation of being a dangerous place. In the years since, members of still newer problem groups have reached the Square—homeless families being sheltered in the area's welfare hotels, and homeless mentally ill people, who wander the streets in unprotected distress. There are also crack dealers in Times Square these days, as in so many urban American neighborhoods. But despite a sudden increase in arrests brought about by the crack problem, there is now somewhat less crime in the Square than there was in the 1970s; the notion of danger, however, declined far more slowly than the danger itself.

Another social problem, race prejudice, has also worked to retard the rehabilitation of Times Square's reputation. Middle-class black and Hispanic families were beginning to make greater use of the Square in the same years crime and pornography were on the increase there—and racial tensions were becoming more jagged throughout New York and many other major cities in this country. Some easily frightened white people have been keeping away from Times Square ever since. (Blanks on mental maps may perhaps indicate avoided experiences, as well as under-developed ones.)

But if fear is only one part of the interference at work in Times Square, how do we get at the rest of it? Perhaps if for just one moment we could think of Times Square as a well-spring of liveliness, something that needs the careful tending given any wondrous object, it might help us see that there are three kinds of things that can interfere with our experience of this place: The experience can be diminished if spectacular or essential or well-liked components of it are taken away; it can be weakened or contaminated, or even poisoned, by the addition of inappro-priate elements; and it can get out of balance if some of the signals are very strong or raucous, because people will then have a hard time broadening the sweep of their attention to bring all of what they are experiencing into conscious focus.

If you stand at the Cohan statue right now and keep this kind of checklist in mind, you can see that Times Square has for years been suffering mightily from all three of these difficulties. For example, two of the gaudiest and most dramatic of the Times Square signs, the famous Pepsi waterfall and the equally famous Camel man, are gone, one of them replaced by a bright but plainer—and dry—sign, the other replaced only by a piece of wall. The Camel sign dated from the 1940s, the Pepsi sign from the 1950s. The Pepsi sign featured a three-story-high real waterfall, almost a block long, that constantly recycled ten thou-sand gallons of water. The waterfall was flanked by two five-story-high Pepsi bottles, and all three perched thirty feet over Broadway and were drenched with a million watts of illumina-tion. The Camel man, a block to the south, was only a gigantic painted head with a hat that was changed from time to time, but he had a round, perpetually open mouth that blew a perfect smoke ring of steam every twenty seconds around the clock. A publicity agent once calculated that this many puffs was the equivalent of smoking four cartons of cigarettes a day. (There is some continuity in Times Square's sign decline: The waterless new illuminated sign on the Pepsi site is a puffless advertisement for Camel Filters. There's flashing gold neon in the new sign, but its largest single feature is motionless—a 37.5-foot-high plastic camel's head lighted from behind by unwinking fluorescent lights.)

At the same time, Times Square is both filthy and dilapidated: The streets and the sidewalks are dirty, fences and trash baskets are dented or mangled, and many property owners, who have been waiting around for years to see whether the city will finally begin adopting and implementing a comprehensive plan for the future of the area, have simply abandoned any attempt at maintenance. Deliberate neglect, as a number of unscrupulous developers have discovered over the years, has a powerful perceptual effect: Dirty, broken, or boarded-up windows, peeling paint, and a sagging cornice are painful to look at; consider the word "eyesore."

The Times Square experience is also ill-balanced. The Cohan statue is just about the only place where you can stand still; the noise of the traffic batters at you constantly and distracts your attention, especially since there's no waterfall to drown it out with a more soothing sound. And in addition to all this, in front of several of the neglected or abandoned buildings on the edges of the Square—of world-famous Times Square, the center of the richest city in the Western Hemisphere—the stench of urine, until you hurry past it, is almost overwhelming.

The first of the new buildings in Times Square, high-rise towers designed with only a single setback, have been doing new damage to the Times Square experience—just as Peter Bosselmann's film predicted. While sunlight, for example, still pours into the north end of the Square for much of the day, the sense of openness there has now been badly obstructed. The new view north, except when you crane your head back at a sharp angle, is for the most part a blank view of glass, metal, and brick facades, so that the area no longer seems like an almost infinitely expandable outdoor room with walls and a ceiling made of vast stretches of sky. What used to be a bowl automatically brimming over with light now feels increasingly isolated from its sources and more like an oddly shaped bucket that's starting to drop down a well and sink away from the reach of the sun.

We have come close to losing the Times Square experience— which means New York is now in danger of being at least partially cut off from one of five urban experiences that together, according to one historian of cities, have helped shape modern America. In his book *City People,* Gunther Barth, a professor at the University of California in Berkeley, describes the intertwining influences of five types of city institutions which only began to flourish after the Civil War: apartment houses, newspapers, department stores, baseball parks, and vaudeville houses; four of these institutions represent place-based experiences. The idea Barth develops is that a hugely diverse population of European immigrants, most of them from small villages, only learned how to become citizens of a modern industrial democracy because, when they landed on American shores, nineteenth-century city life grouped them together at home, when they went shopping, and even during their time off. Baseball, for instance, exposed them to the idea that "freedom [exists] within fixed parameters," that the team of any city could win game after game only when everyone on each team acted in unison and with the same alertness. And in the heart of a city, "the timing, tempo, and high degree of organization that finally characterized circuit vaudeville" was almost a mirror in which people could see themselves taking part in their new lives in a new land. Over time, by participating again and again in such experiences, displaced Europeans became modern Americans, a unified and confident group of people—made up of "motormen, janitors, maids, waitresses, clerks, floorwalkers, newsboys, reporters, baseball players, hoofers, comics, ushers"—who understood each other well enough to work together as a nation.

Thirty-five years ago, New York City had seven daily newspapers and three major league baseball teams, as well as a healthy Times Square. It now has two major league ball teams (for a while it had one) and four daily papers (for a while it had three)—and a diminished Times Square. One of New York's four newspapers is a new start-up; on the other hand, Gimbels, one of the city's oldest department stores, famous as the great rival of Macy's ("Does Macy's tell Gimbels?"), closed its doors in 1986. And just last Christmas, B. Altman's, New York's best-liked department store, abruptly went out of business. At Altman's, both the building and the sales staff seemed equally welcoming. There were high ceilings and wide aisles on all floors, and the company made a point of treating employees with respect, so they would then make the store's customers feel at home. Even well into the 1980s, there were a doctor and several nurses in the store just to treat staff health problems; and in the employee cafeteria at lunchtime there was always at least one main dish that sold for only a quarter.

Gimbels' bankruptcy may lead directly to a further contraction of New York's portion of the fivefold modern urban heritage: There's repeated talk that the New York *Daily News* is in trouble because it can no longer rely on the ten million dollars of advertising revenue it took in every year from Gimbels. For many years, Altman's seemed to have found a unique solution to the urban heritage question—Benjamin Altman, when he died in 1913, left his business to a family foundation which continued his policies and practices. In 1985, however, the government made it illegal for foundations to run for-profit businesses, and two years later the store was acquired in a leveraged buyout by a Canadian development company, which drained Altman's assets when it couldn't afford its own interest payments.

What is the remedy for Times Square, or for any place where a valuable experience is threatened or needs repairing? Perhaps the first thing we need to do is simply to get used to the idea that, with the help of environmental simulation and several other new planning techniques—such as those being developed by Project for Public Spaces, a nonprofit New York City research and consulting group, and by Toni Sachs Pfeiffer, an American filmmaker currently working in Bonn—we now have enough basic understanding of people's experience of places to begin to be able to protect and enhance the experiences that mean the most to us. We can even salvage and rebuild them. Just as, earlier in the century, it was found that after the discovery of sulfa drugs and antibiotics people only gradually adapted themselves to the fact that doctors could now actually cure a whole range of diseases, so today most people—including most planners, architects, developers, and mayors—have not yet formed the habit of expecting cities to know how to care for the experiences of places.

A long-term solution to Times Square's problems could emerge from a new effort to regear the city's economic strategy so that it can give the same kind of emphasis to developing tourism that it does to the further development of the service economy: banking, law, insurance, financial services, and real estate. During the Reagan years, all American cities had to scramble to find new funds, because of drastic cutbacks in federal and state spending on urban services. New York's first attempt at solving this problem concentrated on assisting the service industries by putting up as many new office buildings as possible: more than eighty new office towers have gone up in

from shoppers to beggars. The passageway was crammed with huge "elephant feet" columns, as she called them, which were there to hold up the street above. The columns not only created a network of blind subspaces in very small alleyways but also were disorienting: You couldn't see the length of the space, and there was no way of telling where you were in relation to the street. Even the police got confused there. The physical layout of the space, in other words, made people feel insecure. But people didn't say this. What they said was "It's a very dangerous place." In reality, only three crimes a month took place in the Hauptwache, yet it began to be known as the second most dangerous place in town—next to the area around the railroad station. And this reputation began to attract new users, such as derelicts, the homeless, and lunchtime adventure seekers.

Pfeiffer and her team told Frankfurt's city planners that it was possible to help people to use the Hauptwache as the new center of the city—by making two sorts of changes: tearing open the roof around the main entrance, so that people downstairs in the subway station could see what was happening up above them on the street, and installing a color-coded orientation system in the station, so that people could always tell where they were. At the same time, they could devise all sorts of niches to accommodate all the people who had been using the passageway. When these changes were in fact made, the result was that shopping increased and the drifters stayed put, but now shoppers and drifters no longer felt intimidated by each other's presence. Frankfurt has a new and functioning city center, and the Hauptwache is also cleaner now that it is more heavily used: The heightened feeling of security seems to have permanently sapped any will to besmirch. "As soon as people begin to spend time regularly in a space, they begin to take care of it," Pfeiffer found.

A few blocks from Times Square in New York is a cheerful little public park, on the edge of Rockefeller Center, that is heavily used all day long, by office workers, shoppers, mothers and children, teenagers, and middle-aged and older people. It contains trees and flowers, tables, chairs and benches, a food stand, a security guard, and, along one wall, a waterfall. Thirteen years ago, Exxon Park, as it is known, had much the same kind of equipment—trees, flowers, seating, security patrols, food service, and a waterfall—but in those days the park was empty most of the time, and aside from some young men with loud radios, its two most frequent patrons were drug dealers, one of them up by the front gate and the other down by the back gate.

The primary difference between then and now is that in the late 1970s a team of space doctors, as they sometimes like to call themselves, from New York's Project for Public Spaces—three people who are by training a geographer, a city planner, and a landscape architect—studied the park for Rockefeller Center, shut it down for two months, and, in that interval, rearranged and redesigned its various components. "What we've found is that you can have all the necessary ingredients for a good park and still not generate any users," says Fred Kent, the geographer, who has served as the president of PPS for fifteen years—during which the firm has worked on projects in over a hundred North American cities and towns. "In fact, these wonderful elements can actually be repelling people. The trick is to arrange all the parts of a park so that people can see all of them and use them and also have spots that give them a feeling of privacy. When you do this, all of a sudden a place feels more comfortable to be in, and that feeling acts as a magnet. A healthy mixture of people doesn't just happen by itself anymore. But now we're capable of creating healthy mixtures in any kind of place."

Exxon Park is an L-shaped mid-block park west of Sixth Avenue that was built in the 1960s. In its original design, the long leg of the L, which stretches between Forty-ninth Street and Fiftieth Street, was left relatively open, and as a result it was used principally as a shortcut between the two streets, so people moved through it swiftly and didn't linger. The food stand was hidden in a corner behind the waterfall—you couldn't see it from either Forty-ninth or Fiftieth. Also, its prices were high, and it offered no quick takeout food. When the drug dealers first appeared in Exxon Park, Rockefeller Center tried to box them out by putting up heavy fences along both Forty-ninth and Fiftieth. Then you couldn't see into the park at all except through a narrow gate at either end, and still fewer people used it. One small area near the waterfall attracted a few mothers and children and older people, and their presence convinced the PPS team that there was a potential for a broader variety of park users.

The PPS analysts focused considerable attention on the park's two drug dealers and realized that these men had staked out for themselves the two spots in the park that were most visible from the street. So PPS decided to put a food-vending cart in the busier of those two spots—out by the front gate. That cart now does a roaring business. PPS also scattered tables and chairs throughout the park and put a second food cart in the middle. This served three purposes: It slowed down people who wanted to use the park as a crosswalk; it made tables and chairs something you could see from the street; and it created more pools of privacy.

PPS also opened up the fence by adding a second gate to it. This gave people walking by the park on Fiftieth Street two chances to look inside as they went past, instead of only one. Before the redesign, when people did glance inside the park all they got was a quick glimpse of a rather bleak expanse, and for the most part they just kept on going, without slackening their pace. Now, however, when passersby looked inside the first gate they saw greenery, two food carts, tables, chairs, and other people, and the result was that many of the walkers started to slow down to get a better view. And when they did this, often enough it brought them to a halt directly in front of the second gate—at which point a number of them would decide to go right on into the park.

William H. Whyte, who has studied this slowing-down process, calls it "window-shopping," because it's the same thing that happens outside a department store. In the case of a park or a plaza, he says, it serves as the mechanism that allows the life of the street to flow into an adjacent open space. And Fred Kent points out an additional reinforcing phenomenon that's at work—the "shill effect": When people see that other people have stopped to look at something, they tend to stop and look at the same thing, whatever it is. Exxon Park now draws crowds every day—a lunchtime crowd of office workers and a neighborhood crowd of older people who use it all day long.

A third new way to enhance the experience of an area is to provide a place with what Ronald Lee Fleming, an architect and planner in Cambridge, Massachusetts, calls "lovable objects," meaning unexpected extras that people can talk to each other about, or explain to strangers, or laugh at, or clamber over, or make a point of looking for every time they visit the area. The statue of Hans Christian Andersen's Little Mermaid, perched on a rock and looking out over the harbor in Copenhagen, is one such object; another is the bronze statue in Central Park of Balto, the heroic husky sled dog who braved a blizzard to deliver typhoid serum to Nome, Alaska—children admire this statue so much that its nose is always a glowing gold color from having been rubbed by loving hands. Just outside the Oyster Bar in Grand Central Terminal, there's a tiled archway that transmits sound beautifully—the "whisper arch." If you stand facing one corner of the arch and get a friend to stand facing the opposite corner—which is thirty feet away—the two of you can talk in whispers and hear each other perfectly: The sound scoots right up the tiles and bounces down into your friend's ears. No one will have any idea what you're doing.

The managements of privately owned public areas, like theme parks and shopping malls, see the maintenance of such areas as a routine part of day-to-day operations. At Disneyland, for example, no piece of trash spends more than fifteen minutes lying on the street. But so far there is no watchdog group to act full-time as the vigilant guardian of the experience of a public area not under single ownership. There is one analogous development in the theater, where the director and the actors are sometimes supplemented by a dramaturge. While the actors think about their parts and the director concentrates on shaping a performance, the dramaturge looks out for the play itself, and makes sure no one moves away from what the playwright originally had in mind. Similarly, the two largest Olmsted parks in New York City are served by groups of friends who have assembled to act on their behalf: The Central Park Conservancy and the Prospect Park Alliance are nonprofit organizations that raise money from corporations, foundations, and individual well-wishers to restore the two parks and to set up permanent endowments for the two park experiences.

A new kind of urban watchdog group—an organization called, let's say, the Friends of Times Square—might even go beyond the work of a dramaturge: by sending an experience, in this case the Times Square experience, back for rewrite. The Friends could take on responsibility for improving the experience of this world center and for monitoring any improvements made: One early task could be to compile an inventory of lost elements in the Times Square experience and work for their restoration—in addition to the lost rooftop signs, this list would include things like the spectacular low-cost restaurants that used to pull people to the Square, such as a giant Automat and a pancake house that kept a chef up in the front window flipping flapjacks. Another job of the Friends could be to scour the country for new ways of making illuminated signs—such as laser projections or light sculptures or billboard-size television screens—or new ways of making movie theaters more exciting (such as lobby projection units that can simulate a rain forest or a lunar landscape), and then see to it that these innovations receive Times Square installations. The friends could work with the theaters: Too many Times Square theaters are dark; too many ticket prices are out of reach. And early on, the Friends could help out with the dirty work. In Philadelphia, where a budget crunch has cut back the number of city sanitation workers by half, a group of downtown businessmen has organized the Market Street Marshals, a thirty-member uniformed brigade who sweep up litter in front of a mile-long stretch of shops and also assist visitors who have lost their way. According to a report in the *New York Times,* Bill Horton, one of the marshals, says he has a great job: "We help blind people across the street, you know, things like that. It's unique in the city. People have to take pride in Philadelphia again."

Occasionally, a single person will become the conscience keeping watch over a place. One of the most successful place-keepers I've ever met was the late Hattie Carthan, the "tree lady of Brooklyn," who lived in Bedford-Stuyvesant, a largely black neighborhood that in the 1960s became notorious as the nation's worst slum. When Mrs. Carthan's block on Vernon Avenue began to go downhill, she decided that it would cost too much to move, and that anyway she was tired of running away from problems. Mrs. Carthan was already sixty-five and about to retire when the idea of raising money to plant trees first hit her. By the end of the sixties, her Vernon Avenue tree planters had inspired the founding of seventy-five different block associations in Bedford-Stuyvesant dedicated to planting and taking care of trees. And then she saved a hundred-year-old, forty-foot-high magnolia grandiflora tree in the heart of Bedford-Stuyvesant by getting it designated an official city living landmark.

The magnolia grandiflora, a beautiful tree with dark-green leaves and creamy yellow flowers, is a native of the American South and by rights shouldn't be found growing anywhere north of North Carolina. The Brooklyn magnolia grandiflora, brought north as a sapling around the time of the Civil War, had somehow survived because it was planted in a front yard across from a small city park. The tree's roots spread under the street until they reached the soil of the park, and the houses behind the tree protected it from the winter winds. The only way to save the magnolia was to save the brownstones behind it. And once the buildings had been saved, it made sense to Hattie Carthan to use them for something worthwhile. So she launched the Magnolia Tree Earth Center, a still-flourishing nonprofit environmental workshop where children, even in the middle of the inner city, can learn about the importance of trees and how things grow.

———————

Every experiential watchdog group will have to make sure that none of the corners of an experience get inadvertently knocked off by a city crisis. Periodically, New York, like many cities, hatches an emergency plan to cope with some shortage or head off some danger, and because such a plan usually doesn't include assigning someone to put things back to rights when the emergency has passed, supposedly temporary procedures are in many cases extended indefinitely. In the past, without any advocacy group available to assure the continuity of the experiences of places, people have often started to forget that some experience is still crying out for repair, and newcomers to a city, people who have arrived after the damage was done, may never even get to know that something is now missing. For instance, in the mid-1970s, during the oil crisis, New York City cut back on energy consumption, and one casualty was the small electric time and temperature sign on top of the *Newsweek* tower, on

Madison Avenue at Forty-ninth Street, which now was shut down at eight p.m. instead of flashing twenty-four hours a day. Later, as oil prices fell, skyscrapers uptown and down that had never before been anything but black silhouettes all night became bathed in ornamental floodlights until midnight or beyond—but for years afterward the *Newsweek* sign still clicked off at eight.

In 1965, during a major drought, the New York City water commissioner ordered city restaurants not to set a glass of water in front of any customer unless specifically requested to. Up to that time, it had been a custom in New York restaurants to give everyone just sitting down a glass of ice water. But after the drought, many restaurants in the city never bothered to resume the practice of dispensing unasked-for water.

At the beginning of the Second World War, the city ordered that skylights in public buildings be tarred or painted over so that any enemy planes that might fly over North America couldn't see lights leaking into the sky. The Metropolitan Transportation Authority, which inherited Grand Central Terminal from its Second World War landlord, New York Central Railroad, through several intermediaries, only recently got around to scraping the black paint off all Grand Central skylights. Patrons of the Palm Court at the Plaza hotel haven't been so lucky. Once the Tiffany-stained-glass skylights there had been covered over, the management installed a central air-conditioning unit overhead, permanently blocking off all natural light from the room. The Palm Court ceiling is now lighted by concealed fluorescent bulbs.

In our culture, people are so used to ignoring their experiences of the places around them that working with these experiences as a part of our procedure for taking care of our cities and landscapes may mean that we'll have to get rid of a few long-held habits of thought. One tendency that I have found to be a strong part of my own makeup appeared a few years ago in a *New York Times* article about Rockefeller Center's decision

Manhattan just since 1980, which is like adding downtown Dallas to downtown and midtown New York. These new buildings have increased the city's tax base for the time being, but one problem with this solution is that tourism is now the largest industry in the city—and also the fastest-growing industry in the city—and tourists don't like to visit office districts. Their interests, as planners like to point out, are in seeing safe, beautiful, interesting places—places that afford vivid and memorable experiences. The gradually dawning realization in the financial community is that unless New York starts to safeguard and polish its experiences of places, the New York City tourism industry won't have a product to offer visitors.

All the new planning techniques can play a part in maintaining and enriching the experience of Times Square as part of a revamped New York City economic development strategy. Peter Bosselmann's environmental-simulation movie about the Square was one start, making it plain how vulnerable the experience is to any unsympathetic zoning changes. And the experience can also be redesigned and then actively managed in ways that go far beyond simple rezoning.

Toni Sachs Pfeiffer, who is known, among other things, for design improvements that have dramatically increased the numbers of people who flock to the Hauptwache, one of the major central public spaces in the city of Frankfurt, says that there are two basic needs to meet in order to enhance the experience of a public open space. First, she has found that people's sense of security in a public space is "spatially anchored": Each user has to be able to find some space within that place—a little niche where he or she can stand or sit without being bothered by other people and without getting in anyone's way. (For me, in Times Square that space is next to George M. Cohan's statue.) If you can't find such a space, she points out, you'll start to feel insecure and as a result threatened by the other people around you, whatever they are doing or not doing. Second, she says, people need reasons for going to a place, and the more reasons they

have, the more secure they feel and the more time they'll spend
there; they'll visit more often, and they'll make longer visits.
For Pfeiffer, there are two sorts of reasons for spending time in
a public space: passive reasons, like standing and looking around
at people, or sitting and reading and eating a sandwich; and
active reasons, like talking to people, or asking for information,
or buying a book or a sandwich or a drink, or taking a photograph, or meeting a friend. When Pfeiffer works on a space, she
tries to cram in as many niches and as many reasons for being
there as she can.

While other West German cities have spent substantial sums
on neighborhood rehabilitation, the city of Frankfurt has concentrated on upgrading its major public open spaces. In the process, the city has changed radically. From being a stodgy,
uninteresting banking and industrial city—and barely a city, at
that—it has come to be generally considered a real city, with a
complex metropolitan character and with a certain dash. Perhaps
as a result, Frankfurt is growing, and retail sales in its downtown business district have been increasing. "People want to
come in regularly to cities, not just once," Pfeiffer says. "That
is, they want to have a reason to come in regularly. And if you
can get them to come and spend time, they'll start to spend
money too. Each time they visit, they'll buy something—a lip-
stick or a T-shirt—and then they'll go eat."

Pfeiffer's understanding of how public places function is a
product of a unique observing technique she has worked out—
one that, for the first time, allows people to study the totality of
uses and experiences that occur in a public place. Pfeiffer's technique, which she sometimes describes as "becoming a space"—
she means getting to know a place as well as it could know
itself—was developed in the 1970s, when German National Rail-
ways hired her to make a study of how six of its main center-
city stations were being used. Train ridership was decreasing,
and railway officials were worried that this might be connected
to a growing feeling that "undesirables," which meant primar-

ily Turkish, Yugoslavian, and other foreign workers living in German cities, were loitering in the stations, and perhaps even taking them over. Pfeiffer's approach was to photograph comprehensively events and interactions in the stations over a period of several months. She and her co-workers took sixty thousand photographs, and ten people then worked for two and a half years analyzing them.

The results were astonishing. In the first place, it was found that the Turks and other foreign workers posed no threat to anybody. Although they had been thought of as dominating the stations, their actual numbers there, as a percentage of the total number of people, were exactly the same as their actual numbers as a percentage of the population of the city—which they were not thought to be dominating. The reason for the misperception in the stations was this: The foreign workers were poor and lived in old buildings downtown, where the stations were; they had few meeting places of their own, so they used the railroad stations—the nearest public spaces—as places to wait for friends; the best place to wait for people was inside, next to the main doors; unlike travelers, who hurried through the doors, the foreign workers had to stand around until their friends got there; consequently, the only people that travelers noticed as they entered the stations were foreign workers, and they also noticed that the foreign workers were not moving, so to them the stations were full of loitering Turks, Yugoslavs, Greeks, and Portuguese.

But that wasn't the big news. Careful examination of the photographs showed that many of the presumed travelers were not travelers at all but people who had nothing else to do with their time and spent their days, week after week, walking in and out of the railroad stations. Pfeiffer called these people the "profis," for "professional railroad station users." No one—not travelers, station attendants, or railroad officials—had ever noticed the profis, because they kept moving, just like real travelers. According to Pfeiffer, at least 25 percent of the people in the stations stayed there between six and sixteen hours every day.

Since this pioneering study, which revealed the existence of a large, hidden population of isolated and lonely people, Pfeiffer has refined her research techniques to include extensive interviewing of people who use the spaces she's concerned with and asking them to draw or take photographs of what they find important about these spaces. In studying a variety of places, among them working-class residential neighborhoods and major downtown plazas, Pfeiffer has turned up a vast amount of material indicating that the organization of space organizes people's experiences and much of their behavior—including, startlingly, whether they feel that they are allowed to interact with one another and with their surroundings, and whether they will assume responsibility for maintaining some part of the places they use, by watering a street tree, say, or weeding a planter. Pfeiffer continues to discover hitherto unknown phenomena, like the "third skin," which is the sense that she says many German housewives have of their neighborhoods. (The first skin is their own; the second skin is their family; the third skin is the area in which they know everybody.) She hopes ultimately to show how we can design places that will encourage people to take on purposeful behavior—so that they will spend their days caring for their streets and planting trees instead of entering and leaving railroad stations.

When the city of Frankfurt hired Pfeiffer to look at the Hauptwache, a major intersection in a sparsely used commercial district at the center of the city, with a subway station and a large underground pedestrian passageway lined with shops—"a hole with staircases," Pfeiffer has called it—her initial assignment was quintessentially German. Because city officials had noticed litter in the Hauptwache passageway, she was asked to investigate the *Subjektive-Schmutzbereitschaft* of the Hauptwache—the "subjective willingness to make dirt" of its users.

Pfeiffer took time-lapse photographs throughout the hole and spent months identifying and interviewing all its user groups, from shoppers to beggars. The passageway was crammed with huge "elephant feet" columns, as she called them, which were there to hold up the street above. The columns not only created a network of blind subspaces in very small alleyways but also were disorienting: You couldn't see the length of the space, and there was no way of telling where you were in relation to the street. Even the police got confused there. The physical layout of the space, in other words, made people feel insecure. But people didn't say this. What they said was "It's a very dangerous place." In reality, only three crimes a month took place in the Hauptwache, yet it began to be known as the second most dangerous place in town—next to the area around the railroad station. And this reputation began to attract new users, such as derelicts, the homeless, and lunchtime adventure seekers.

Pfeiffer and her team told Frankfurt's city planners that it was possible to help people to use the Hauptwache as the new center of the city—by making two sorts of changes: tearing open the roof around the main entrance, so that people downstairs in the subway station could see what was happening up above them on the street, and installing a color-coded orientation system in the station, so that people could always tell where they were. At the same time, they could devise all sorts of niches to accommodate all the people who had been using the passageway. When these changes were in fact made, the result was that shopping increased and the drifters stayed put, but now shoppers and drifters no longer felt intimidated by each other's presence. Frankfurt has a new and functioning city center, and the Hauptwache is also cleaner now that it is more heavily used: The heightened feeling of security seems to have permanently sapped any will to besmirch. "As soon as people begin to spend time regularly in a space, they begin to take care of it," Pfeiffer found.

A few blocks from Times Square in New York is a cheerful little public park, on the edge of Rockefeller Center, that is heavily used all day long, by office workers, shoppers, mothers and children, teenagers, and middle-aged and older people. It contains trees and flowers, tables, chairs and benches, a food stand, a security guard, and, along one wall, a waterfall. Thirteen years ago, Exxon Park, as it is known, had much the same kind of equipment—trees, flowers, seating, security patrols, food service, and a waterfall—but in those days the park was empty most of the time, and aside from some young men with loud radios, its two most frequent patrons were drug dealers, one of them up by the front gate and the other down by the back gate.

The primary difference between then and now is that in the late 1970s a team of space doctors, as they sometimes like to call themselves, from New York's Project for Public Spaces— three people who are by training a geographer, a city planner, and a landscape architect—studied the park for Rockefeller Center, shut it down for two months, and, in that interval, rearranged and redesigned its various components. ''What we've found is that you can have all the necessary ingredients for a good park and still not generate any users,'' says Fred Kent, the geographer, who has served as the president of PPS for fifteen years—during which the firm has worked on projects in over a hundred North American cities and towns. ''In fact, these wonderful elements can actually be repelling people. The trick is to arrange all the parts of a park so that people can see all of them and use them and also have spots that give them a feeling of privacy. When you do this, all of a sudden a place feels more comfortable to be in, and that feeling acts as a magnet. A healthy mixture of people doesn't just happen by itself anymore. But now we're capable of creating healthy mixtures in any kind of place.''

Exxon Park is an L-shaped mid-block park west of Sixth Avenue that was built in the 1960s. In its original design, the long leg of the L, which stretches between Forty-ninth Street and Fiftieth Street, was left relatively open, and as a result it was used principally as a shortcut between the two streets, so people moved through it swiftly and didn't linger. The food stand was hidden in a corner behind the waterfall—you couldn't see it from either Forty-ninth or Fiftieth. Also, its prices were high, and it offered no quick takeout food. When the drug dealers first appeared in Exxon Park, Rockefeller Center tried to box them out by putting up heavy fences along both Forty-ninth and Fiftieth. Then you couldn't see into the park at all except through a narrow gate at either end, and still fewer people used it. One small area near the waterfall attracted a few mothers and children and older people, and their presence convinced the PPS team that there was a potential for a broader variety of park users.

The PPS analysts focused considerable attention on the park's two drug dealers and realized that these men had staked out for themselves the two spots in the park that were most visible from the street. So PPS decided to put a food-vending cart in the busier of those two spots—out by the front gate. That cart now does a roaring business. PPS also scattered tables and chairs throughout the park and put a second food cart in the middle. This served three purposes: It slowed down people who wanted to use the park as a crosswalk; it made tables and chairs something you could see from the street; and it created more pools of privacy.

PPS also opened up the fence by adding a second gate to it. This gave people walking by the park on Fiftieth Street two chances to look inside as they went past, instead of only one. Before the redesign, when people did glance inside the park all they got was a quick glimpse of a rather bleak expanse, and for the most part they just kept on going, without slackening their pace. Now, however, when passersby looked inside the first gate they saw greenery, two food carts, tables, chairs, and other people, and the result was that many of the walkers started to slow down to get a better view. And when they did this, often enough it brought them to a halt directly in front of the second gate—at which point a number of them would decide to go right on into the park.

William H. Whyte, who has studied this slowing-down process, calls it "window-shopping," because it's the same thing that happens outside a department store. In the case of a park or a plaza, he says, it serves as the mechanism that allows the life of the street to flow into an adjacent open space. And Fred Kent points out an additional reinforcing phenomenon that's at work—the "shill effect": When people see that other people have stopped to look at something, they tend to stop and look at the same thing, whatever it is. Exxon Park now draws crowds every day—a lunchtime crowd of office workers and a neighborhood crowd of older people who use it all day long.

A third new way to enhance the experience of an area is to provide a place with what Ronald Lee Fleming, an architect and planner in Cambridge, Massachusetts, calls "lovable objects," meaning unexpected extras that people can talk to each other about, or explain to strangers, or laugh at, or clamber over, or make a point of looking for every time they visit the area. The statue of Hans Christian Andersen's Little Mermaid, perched on a rock and looking out over the harbor in Copenhagen, is one such object; another is the bronze statue in Central Park of Balto, the heroic husky sled dog who braved a blizzard to deliver typhoid serum to Nome, Alaska—children admire this statue so much that its nose is always a glowing gold color from having been rubbed by loving hands. Just outside the Oyster Bar in Grand Central Terminal, there's a tiled archway that transmits sound beautifully—the "whisper arch." If you stand facing one corner of the arch and get a friend to stand facing the opposite corner—which is thirty feet away—the two of you can talk in whispers and hear each other perfectly: The sound scoots right up the tiles and bounces down into your friend's ears. No one will have any idea what you're doing.

The managements of privately owned public areas, like theme parks and shopping malls, see the maintenance of such areas as a routine part of day-to-day operations. At Disneyland, for example, no piece of trash spends more than fifteen minutes lying on the street. But so far there is no watchdog group to act full-time as the vigilant guardian of the experience of a public area not under single ownership. There is one analogous development in the theater, where the director and the actors are sometimes supplemented by a dramaturge. While the actors think about their parts and the director concentrates on shaping a performance, the dramaturge looks out for the play itself, and makes sure no one moves away from what the playwright originally had in mind. Similarly, the two largest Olmsted parks in New York City are served by groups of friends who have assembled to act on their behalf: The Central Park Conservancy and the Prospect Park Alliance are nonprofit organizations that raise money from corporations, foundations, and individual well-wishers to restore the two parks and to set up permanent endowments for the two park experiences.

A new kind of urban watchdog group—an organization called, let's say, the Friends of Times Square—might even go beyond the work of a dramaturge: by sending an experience, in this case the Times Square experience, back for rewrite. The Friends could take on responsibility for improving the experience of this world center and for monitoring any improvements made: One early task could be to compile an inventory of lost elements in the Times Square experience and work for their restoration—in addition to the lost rooftop signs, this list would include things like the spectacular low-cost restaurants that used to pull people to the Square, such as a giant Automat and a pancake house that kept a chef up in the front window flipping flapjacks. Another job of the Friends could be to scour the country for new ways of making illuminated signs—such as laser projections or light sculptures or billboard-size television screens—or new ways of making movie theaters more exciting (such as lobby projection units that can simulate a rain forest or a lunar landscape), and then see to it that these innovations receive Times Square installations. The friends could work with the theaters: Too many Times Square theaters are dark; too many ticket prices are out of reach. And early on, the Friends could help out with the dirty work. In Philadelphia, where a budget crunch has cut back the number of city sanitation workers by half, a group of downtown businessmen has organized the Market Street Marshals, a thirty-member uniformed brigade who sweep up litter in front of a mile-long stretch of shops and also assist visitors who have lost their way. According to a report in the *New York Times*, Bill Horton, one of the marshals, says he has a great job: "We help blind people across the street, you know, things like that. It's unique in the city. People have to take pride in Philadelphia again."

Occasionally, a single person will become the conscience keeping watch over a place. One of the most successful place-keepers I've ever met was the late Hattie Carthan, the "tree lady of Brooklyn," who lived in Bedford-Stuyvesant, a largely black neighborhood that in the 1960s became notorious as the nation's worst slum. When Mrs. Carthan's block on Vernon Avenue began to go downhill, she decided that it would cost too much to move, and that anyway she was tired of running away from problems. Mrs. Carthan was already sixty-five and about to retire when the idea of raising money to plant trees first hit her. By the end of the sixties, her Vernon Avenue tree planters had inspired the founding of seventy-five different block associations in Bedford-Stuyvesant dedicated to planting and taking care of trees. And then she saved a hundred-year-old, forty-foot-high magnolia grandiflora tree in the heart of Bedford-Stuyvesant by getting it designated an official city living landmark.

The magnolia grandiflora, a beautiful tree with dark-green leaves and creamy yellow flowers, is a native of the American South and by rights shouldn't be found growing anywhere north of North Carolina. The Brooklyn magnolia grandiflora, brought north as a sapling around the time of the Civil War, had somehow survived because it was planted in a front yard across from a small city park. The tree's roots spread under the street until they reached the soil of the park, and the houses behind the tree protected it from the winter winds. The only way to save the magnolia was to save the brownstones behind it. And once the buildings had been saved, it made sense to Hattie Carthan to use them for something worthwhile. So she launched the Magnolia Tree Earth Center, a still-flourishing nonprofit environmental workshop where children, even in the middle of the inner city, can learn about the importance of trees and how things grow.

Every experiential watchdog group will have to make sure that none of the corners of an experience get inadvertently knocked off by a city crisis. Periodically, New York, like many cities, hatches an emergency plan to cope with some shortage or head off some danger, and because such a plan usually doesn't include assigning someone to put things back to rights when the emergency has passed, supposedly temporary procedures are in many cases extended indefinitely. In the past, without any advocacy group available to assure the continuity of the experiences of places, people have often started to forget that some experience is still crying out for repair, and newcomers to a city, people who have arrived after the damage was done, may never even get to know that something is now missing. For instance, in the mid-1970s, during the oil crisis, New York City cut back on energy consumption, and one casualty was the small electric time and temperature sign on top of the *Newsweek* tower, on

Madison Avenue at Forty-ninth Street, which now was shut down
at eight p.m. instead of flashing twenty-four hours a day. Later,
as oil prices fell, skyscrapers uptown and down that had never
before been anything but black silhouettes all night became
bathed in ornamental floodlights until midnight or beyond—but
for years afterward the *Newsweek* sign still clicked off at eight.

In 1965, during a major drought, the New York City water
commissioner ordered city restaurants not to set a glass of water
in front of any customer unless specifically requested to. Up to
that time, it had been a custom in New York restaurants to give
everyone just sitting down a glass of ice water. But after the
drought, many restaurants in the city never bothered to resume
the practice of dispensing unasked-for water.

At the beginning of the Second World War, the city ordered
that skylights in public buildings be tarred or painted over
so that any enemy planes that might fly over North America
couldn't see lights leaking into the sky. The Metropolitan Transportation Authority, which inherited Grand Central Terminal
from its Second World War landlord, New York Central Railroad, through several intermediaries, only recently got around
to scraping the black paint off all Grand Central skylights. Patrons of the Palm Court at the Plaza hotel haven't been so lucky.
Once the Tiffany-stained-glass skylights there had been covered
over, the management installed a central air-conditioning unit
overhead, permanently blocking off all natural light from the
room. The Palm Court ceiling is now lighted by concealed
fluorescent bulbs.

In our culture, people are so used to ignoring their experiences of the places around them that working with these experiences as a part of our procedure for taking care of our cities
and landscapes may mean that we'll have to get rid of a few
long-held habits of thought. One tendency that I have found to
be a strong part of my own makeup appeared a few years ago
in a *New York Times* article about Rockefeller Center's decision

to close the observation deck on top of the RCA Building. The observation deck was a lovely spot, absolutely quiet, generally almost empty, a sort of picnic ground halfway to the sky. The reporter who covered the story obviously loved the place, but in writing about it he implied that the experiences we cherish have to be relinquished sooner or later. The *Times* headline over this piece read: A QUIET PLACE AT RCA'S SUMMIT DRIFTS ONTO THE PAGES OF THE PAST.

In my case, I had the good fortune of learning at an early age that experiences of places can be a valuable part of life, but it took me years to learn the next lesson: that these experiences are under our control; they are a rainbow well within our grasp. From an early age, I savored the experiences that New York then had to offer—double-decker buses and Checker cabs and two-way avenues and double-red stoplights (when all the traffic at an intersection came to a complete halt for a few moments) and movie palaces and small midtown cafeterias and second-hand bookshops. But like many other people, I assumed that experiences were only a by-product of other, more important purposes. When they disappeared—and they did, faster and faster—I mourned them but thought, like the *Times* reporter, that it was their nature to vanish.

No American city has as yet set up either a Department of Experiential Protection or an Urban Experience Development Corporation. But we can already begin to recognize that because we have built into us two different systems for organizing our perceptions—the narrowing focus of ordinary consciousness and the more inclusive approach of simultaneous perception, which responds to whatever the senses can detect—we need continuing contact with a rich variety of experiences in a place if we are to stay connected with our environment and with other people. We already know that these experiences can be very complex. A single experience may have a number of universal elements in it, common to everyone, like our response to grass, say, or to winding paths. At the same time, that experience may contain certain culturally conditioned components that will be common only to people from the same society. Arabs, for instance, the anthropologist Edward T. Hall has pointed out, like to stand close enough to their friends to be able to smell them; Americans don't. And still other elements of an experience may be purely personal—we all use long-lasting and familiar buildings, for instance, as a mnemonic device that can organize and prompt our memories: That's where I went on my first date; that's a place where my father once worked.

In addition to all this knowledge, we already have an abundance of tools for cultivating and enhancing these complex and composite experiences: We can simulate them; we can previsualize them; we can redesign them; we can manage them; we can add on new awarenesses. We're finally in a position to get on with the job of making sure that all places are worth experiencing.

II
ENCOUNTERING THE COUNTRYSIDE

5 Working Landscapes

Even though I know it's there, and can see it in my mind, and can even remember the fresh smell of its damp earth, when I go visit the old Klein farm, out in a residential part of northeastern Queens—it's about eleven miles almost due east of the Empire State Building, and at the moment it's the only working family farm within New York City—the initial sight of the place always catches me by surprise. The first time I went there was by New York public transportation—a long ride on the subway followed by a long bus ride along Union Turnpike. The final leg of this route was a short hike north on 195th Street, a quiet, two-block-long, tree-lined stretch of neatly spaced, self-contained single-family houses, garages, driveways, and front lawns with crew cuts, where in the early afternoon the only moving vehicles were driving-school cars.

Then I got to the corner of Seventy-third Avenue, and there, on the other side of the street, was the Klein farm. What stopped me in my steps was that the place looked huge—an appearance that made no sense, because John Klein, the third-generation Queens farmer who runs the place, had told me on the phone that he had only two acres; his family had started selling most of their farmland, one hundred forty acres, over fifty years ago. But the place seems to be made of elbowroom, scope, leeway, and room to spare: There's a big brick house on the side of a

hill, with a brick barn behind it, and even a second house—a
little two-story brick house with a pitched roof—tucked neatly
into one corner of the property. There are big trees near the big
house, and sloping cropland behind it, pushing up row after row
of vegetables, and in front there's a wide, rolling lawn that comes
right down to the sidewalk.

There is also a farm stand—a large, deep, sturdy, open-sided,
maple-shaded structure, overflowing in season with baskets and
crates of fresh fruits and vegetables—and it has plenty of
standing-around space for squeezing tomatoes or catching up on
events with Barbara Klein, John Klein's wife. The placement of
the Klein farm stand, it eventually occurred to me, is what gives
the farm such a sense of amplitude: It's not right up front, and
it isn't exactly set back; it looks as though it had just nosed up
next to one of the big maple trees in the middle of the lawn and
then spread out under the tree's shade.

The next time I visited the Klein farm, I had a car and came
at it from the north and west, dropping off the Long Island
Expressway at the Fresh Meadows exit and driving slowly south
and east through the twisting narrow lanes, crescents, circles,
and ovals of Fresh Meadows—a hundred-seventy-acre garden-
apartment rental community built by the New York Life Insurance Company shortly after the Second World War. One of the
Fresh Meadows crescents brought me out to Seventy-third Avenue, where I made a left, and there was the Klein farm. I realized that in terms of square footage, the Klein farm is only a
little bite of land that didn't get swallowed by New York Life
forty years ago; there is a three-story Fresh Meadows walk-up
right next to the west side of the Klein place, and an almost
identical Fresh Meadows building in back of the farm, on the
north. As I got out of the car, I began to feel something that I
had also noticed when I walked up to the farm on my first visit:
a kind of welcome.

This time, John Klein, a strong, sturdy, quiet-talking man in

The Klein Farm, Queens, New York City, at harvest time. *Photograph courtesy of Tony Hiss*

his mid-forties, who was wearing blue jeans and a blue T-shirt, was taking a rest from weeding and harvesting and bagging groceries for farm stand customers, and he had time to invite me up onto the back of the farm. Klein's two-hundred-year-old back field, carefully safeguarded by his family ever since they bought it from the descendants of the first farmers in the area, turned out to be a tiny, complex, satisfying, and eye-opening piece of property. Our walk took us up a cracked concrete driveway behind the farm stand, past a small old gray-and-red Ford tractor, past a holding area for handcarts and extra crates and baskets, and past the big house—a sturdy, roomy three-story red-brick farmhouse John Klein's grandfather built for his family in 1930, when the Kleins were still farming one hundred forty acres in this part of Queens.

There's an enormous kitchen in the basement of this house—

it doesn't see much use these days—which was built so that the Kleins could accommodate as many as fifty farmhands at meal-time during the growing season. The farmhouse, like the farm stand, is maple shaded, because Adam Klein, John Klein's grandfather, planted nine five-foot maples next to the house when he built it, to keep the place a bit cooler in the summer, and seven of them survive. The house has a small front porch with a roof and two white columns; two small white wooden benches, facing each other, flank the front door. Past the farmhouse, the driveway ends, and you have to follow a narrow dirt path that runs next to a long, ground-hugging greenhouse covered by a loose-fitting, hoop-shaped plastic roof and ends at parallel lines of beet greens and cucumber vines. When I've stood out here for a minute or two, whatever the season, I've found that after taking a stroll of no more than a few hundred yards I've reached a place that surrounds me with a strong sense of having traveled somewhere deep into the open countryside.

Part of this has to do with Public School 26. In the 1950s, the New York City Board of Education bought from the Klein family part of the land in back of the farm, to the north, and all the remaining family land on the east side of the farm, to build a new grade school for the children of Fresh Meadows. The city's engineers chopped off all the east side of the Klein's hill to put in a large, level asphalt playground, but they apparently never figured out a use for the land they had acquired just north of the farm. As a result, this bit of land is still hilly; the school building itself is down at the bottom of the hill, to the northeast of the farm. And because this bit of land hasn't been paved or farmed, or even played on much, during the last thirty years, it's begin-ning to revert to woodland: There's now a shady patch of oak trees behind a chain-link fence at the back of the farm.

Beyond still seeming like open country, John Klein's back field transmits a feeling I used to think existed only in children's books or in science fiction: My sense of community and connection is stretched and extended in several different directions at once, so that "now" seems to be a time that began many generations ago and has no foreseeable ending, while "here" becomes a place that stretches far beyond the horizon, and even "we" seems to involve both the land itself and the people living on it. I think this is because the Klein farm isn't just somewhere out in the open country; it's the surviving representative of a specific territory. And that makes it possible for you to feel in this particular place that, whatever has happened to the world in the last half century, right here you're still standing inside the boundaries of an ancient and abundantly productive region of working countryside covering thousands of acres: a landscape that set the pattern for all of this part of Queens until change overtook it and, shortly after the end of the war, obliterated it forever.

This region was rural Flushing: a wide expanse of big truck farms, with immense, rolling fields that stretched on and out in all directions—fields a lot like the vast potato and cauliflower fields that are still being farmed seventy miles east of Flushing, on the North Fork of Long Island. In its peak years—starting, say, in the second half of the nineteenth century and extending through most of the first half of this century—rural Flushing was renowned chiefly for its long growing season, made possible by the nearness of the Atlantic Ocean, which holds off the frosts that strike upstate farms not long after Labor Day and sets up an Indian summer. Often Flushing farmers were able to harvest Kieffer pears, the last fruit to ripen in the fall, as late as the week after Thanksgiving.

Old rural Flushing was also characterized by its gusting winds, deep snowdrifts, and salmon-colored sunsets in the winter; by lines of old stone walls; by a loosely woven network of dirt lanes bordered by wild violets in the spring and wild purple phlox and Queen Anne's lace in the summer, with hedges of blackberry bushes and blackcap bushes (blackcaps are berries that are smaller, and more tender, than raspberries); and by an abundance of rabbits, pheasants, meadowlarks, crows, and soaring hawks.

Up on the North Shore, along Long Island Sound, were a few factories turning out tinware and ironware and—in the early years—goods made of whalebone and India rubber. Near the factory settlements were some small fishing and oystering and clamming villages. To the northwest of rural Flushing, along the east side of Flushing Bay, was the village of Flushing, which by the 1880s had become an affluent, city-oriented community of commuters—an hour to Manhattan on a weekday morning, either by steamboat or on one of three different railroad lines.

Early-twentieth-century rural Flushing still had a few, much cherished late-seventeenth-century apple orchards and cherry orchards, which had been set out by a group of Huguenot families who moved into the area for a few years after fleeing France, and then moved on; it also had several highly prized groves of tall specimen trees and elegant shade trees—copper beeches, elms, lindens, cedars of Lebanon—which had been planted either by a celebrated local eighteenth-century nurseryman, William Prince (George Washington visited Prince's nursery) or by an even more celebrated nineteenth-century nurseryman, Samuel B. Parsons (Parsons helped design the grounds of the New York Botanical Garden in the Bronx, and supplied both Central Park and Prospect Park with some of their original trees and shrubs). One of Parsons's trees, a sixty-foot-tall weeping beech in the village of Flushing, with a great overhanging canopy, eighty-five feet across, still flourishes and, in fact, has been showered with attention in recent decades: It sits in the middle of a small city park enclosed by a cast-iron fence, Weeping Beech Park, and in 1966 it became the first tree ever named an official living landmark by the New York City Landmarks Preservation Commission. (Mrs. Carthan's magnolia grandiflora in Bedford-Stuyvesant was the second.)

Here and there throughout rural Flushing—on the hilltops, or surrounding some freshwater ponds or creeks, or patches of wetlands that had never been drained—sizable silent clumps of deep oak woods and maple woods survived, sheltering deer and even a few porcupines. Except for these woods, the land of rural Flushing was given over to open fields, acre after acre of them, planted every summer to potatoes, spinach, rhubarb, beans, lettuce, corn, parsnips, tomatoes, carrots, beets, kale, and savoy cabbage—crops that got loaded onto trucks and hauled into big public markets in lower Manhattan or Brooklyn or to a smaller market down near the summer resorts that had sprung up in Canarsie, where one of the selling points of the new hotels was the "farm-fresh food" on their bills of fare.

It's hard to find an early photograph of these old Flushing fields—there were so many of them they seemed too ordinary to point a camera at. Several early landscape painters, whose works, slightly darkened by coats of varnish, now hang in local historical societies, tried to convey on canvas something of the peaceful, rustic, lush, timeless quality they found out in the Flushing fields. No famous American novelist ever wrote about these fields—although Edith Wharton did set one scene in her book *Old New York* on an 1840s mid-Manhattan farm turned country seat, filled with flowers—a place "at a convenient driving distance" from her hero's town house on Canal Street— where, on a midsummer afternoon, mosquitoes hummed by now and again, and "hay, verbena, and mignonette scented the languid July day."

You can sometimes see just a corner of an old Flushing field behind the principal subject that did attract the attention of the first Queens photographers—the trucks themselves. "Truck," in its old sense, had nothing whatever to do with motors: It meant a farm wagon as tall as a person which could be loaded to more than twice its own height with up to five tons of hay or vegetables (such marketable produce was itself then known as "garden

truck'') and then hauled away by a pair of big work horses—
although it usually took four horses to get a truck up the side of
a hill that had any steepness.

Since a truck could get into Manhattan from eastern Queens
in two to three hours, including the time it took to cross the
East River on a ferryboat—farmers began this trip in the early
evening, had dinner at a chophouse, and made most of their
sales to dealers and wholesalers sometime between midnight and
six in the morning—generations of New Yorkers held on to the
idea that good-tasting, fully ripened local produce from close-
at-hand farms, such as the thriving farms of rural Flushing, was
one of the benefits that went along with life in a modern city.
After the Civil War, the close-to-the-city Long Island farmers
had to compete with produce shipped north by rail from the
South, as well as with local-area farmers from the counties up
the Hudson River or over on Staten Island. But Queens farmers,
thanks to the freshness of their wares, generally had an edge.

All over rural Flushing, in the years when it flourished, you
would have found a sprinkling of good-size farmhouses, some
of stone and some of wood, a number of which dated back as
far as the Revolution. Many of the earliest houses had been built
by English farming families, and some of these had eventually
been sold to Dutch farming families from down in Brooklyn;
Dutch farmers tended to have big families and often outgrew
their original settlements. A final wave of Queens County farmers—German farming families, for the most part, and some Polish farming families—arrived in rural Flushing in the 1870s and
1880s. After a few years as farmhands or tenants, they had often
acquired enough money to buy out their employers or neighbors
and move into the big old farmhouses, with their shade trees up
close, and generally a small stand of fruit trees within walking
distance; a cluster of stables, barns, and sheds, for the draft
horses; a couple of dairy cows, for the family; some chickens,
for their meat and eggs; and at least one or two guard dogs. A

well-run family of ten kept three dogs: one in the yard, one in the stable, one in the barn.

The majority of the rural Flushing farms dated back to the years just after the Revolution. For almost all the present post-glacial age—the period that began when the last North American and European glaciers receded north, eighteen thousand years ago—what is now northern Queens had been heavily forested and only very lightly settled. The hills of the area are the work of the glacier, which, at its greatest reach, extended from the Arctic to a point about a mile south of the Klein farm. The rich, dark soil of the area is also a legacy of the glacier: The ice scraped the topsoil off preglacial New England and carried it to northern Long Island. South of the point where the glacier stopped, the land is sandy, gravelly, and much flatter.

Between 1776 and 1783, almost all the Long Island woods disappeared. English troops occupied Long Island throughout the American Revolution, and as soon as the English military regime took over, British authorities instituted a policy of stepped-up resource extraction. In addition to requisitioning chickens and cows from Long Island farmers, the British shipped out huge quantities of timber. Black Stump Road, as Seventy-third Avenue in Flushing was originally called, probably dates from around that time, and the name may reflect the land-use policies of the British troops. By the time the Americans got the Island back, most of the postglacial hardwood forests, dominated by great chestnuts and huge oaks, had been cleared. What woods remained went through further changes: A great blight destroyed nearly all the chestnut trees on this continent around 1900, and during the First World War many of the surviving walnut trees on Long Island were felled because the wood made good gunstocks.

When farmers arrived in force to cultivate the Long Island land that had been deforested by the British, the greater part of the Island's West End, as it was then called, became fields, orchards, meadows, and pastures. (The West End—a term no longer used—took in all of Brooklyn, Queens, and what is now Nassau County, a county formed in 1898 by three old Queens County townships that refused to join the new, five-borough City of New York, because they wanted to remain permanently rural.) Although no one seemed to pay much attention to the fact, the clearing of the forests had created a continuous band of openness the length of Long Island—the first such line of open land since the Island's early postglacial tundra period. This line had five main links: the West End fields; the Hempstead Plains; the Oak-Brush Plains; the Pine Barrens; and the East End fields, on the North Fork and the South Fork.

The cleared fields of Flushing stood just north and west of the Hempstead Plains, which was the only naturally occurring prairie east of the Alleghenies—a tract of rolling grassland, some twenty miles long and five miles wide, that was admired by eighteenth- and early-nineteenth-century visitors to Long Island. The Plains, which were originally held as a common—they were owned jointly by all the farmers who pastured livestock on them—received their greatest number of visitors during the first two weeks of May, before the grasses grew tall, at the time of the flowering of the bird's-foot violet. So many billions of these five-petaled prairie wildflowers blossomed at once that the Plains presented an unbroken vista of purple haze—a blend of deep purple, lavender, lilac, and white that one naturalist called "a celestial hue due to thousands of bouquets."

The shape of the Plains could still be seen until 1947, when William J. Levitt, a Long Island builder, began constructing Levittown on what was left of them; 17,447 houses went up over the next four years. To the east of the Plains—in the Island's line of open space—came the Oak-Brush Plains, 60,000 acres of dwarf oak trees under a few widely scattered pitch pines. Then came the Pine Barrens, covering a quarter of a million acres, 40 to 45 percent of which remains open today and, in its hillier regions, affords spectacular panoramic vistas. And beyond the Barrens was the East End, and you were back among farming families, many of whom by the end of the Revolution were old-time Long Islanders: Several East End towns had been established by New Englanders who sailed across the Sound in the seventeenth century.

By the time the Kleins arrived in rural Flushing, about 1895, the countryside around their place had been farmland for over a century and had been specializing in market gardening for seventy years. Adam Klein's father, a Brooklyn farmer, had decided to stake his son to a big place out in Queens. The son's neighbors were the Skillmans to the north, a couple of Polish farmers east, an Italian farmer west, and two Bohemian florists, who raised flowers on a tiny plot next to the Skillman place. To the south of the Klein farm—in an area now partly occupied by Cunningham Park, a large park which the city established in the 1920s—were wooded hills: the hills where the glacier stopped moving south. Adam Klein got married about two years after coming to Flushing, had seven children, and gradually, as the children grew up, acquired more property in the area: a farm to the west of his original holding and even some land to the north, across Black Stump Road. The Klein farm that exists today is the last little piece of this fourth neighborhood farm bought by the family.

Rural Flushing was wonderful country in the days when the family first moved there, especially for children, according to Margaret Klein Pfaff, one of Adam Klein's daughters, who still lives on the farm, in the little house at its east end. "That was a great childhood we had," she recalls. "The air smelled fresher than nowadays, especially after a nice dew. The wind whistled good when snow was coming, and in the summertime you could see a thunderstorm coming a long ways away. At the back end of the farm were the wild dogwood trees, pink and white—they were special every spring. It was a beautiful place, and we loved it, and our big old farmhouse, painted gray with white trim, and heated only with wood-burning stoves, was where all the children in the area loved to gather. We had so much space to race around in, so many places to play hide-and-seek in, so much company, so many things to learn about, kindling to bring in, corn to pop, cherries to jar, cookies to make—a dishpanful of chocolate-chip or raisin-filled sandwich cookies lasted two days at most.''

Rural Flushing was the last section of the city's Long Island farmland to disappear, and some of the first nonfarming uses to reach the area, during the 1920s, did little to change the character of the region: The city bought some of the southern woods just beyond the Klein land and created Cunningham Park; the Fresh Meadows Country Club bought up the Skillman farm and laid out an eighteen-hole golf course. The great crash of 1929 wiped out the cut-flower business, and the Kleins themselves started hauling their produce to market in a motorized truck—after that, they used horses only for plowing—but rural Flushing was still open country: a broad belt of everyday rural landscape, or working countryside, within the City of New York.

———————

Working countryside; working landscape; managed landscape; humanized landscape; historic landscape; ancient landscape; cultural landscape; heritage landscape: These are all terms that have been coined over the years by botanists, landscape historians, sociologists, historical ecologists, and other specialists who have studied both the history and the future of the countryside in order to distinguish two different kinds of terrain—natural landscapes, which, in this very broad definition, are those parts of the countryside that human beings haven't altered or interfered with; and landscapes whose function and look, or character, or feel, have been shaped over time by sequential, ongoing human activities as much as by natural processes. The latter are perhaps most commonly referred to as working landscapes.

Some of the oldest working landscapes we are aware of are now about six thousand years old and started to take form when groups of early Neolithic, or New Stone Age, settlers arrived in what are now England and France. These settlers began clearing the local postglacial wildwood forests, first to create pastures for grazing animals, and later for fields and gardens. Over time, these early Europeans learned that abundance in an area can be tickled into being, as we might call it: Their great discovery, as Martin Holdgate, a former director of the Institute of Terrestrial Ecology in England, has explained, is that "all living species have a potential reproductive capacity far beyond that needed to sustain a stable population." Predators can survive only "because of the crop of 'extra' young produced by prey." So if natural predators can be kept away from any region, a crop of "extras" becomes available for human consumption. With careful management, this plentiful yield can be sustained by a settled human population, year after year, like a cup you can rely on to keep running over.

The working landscape/natural landscape distinction is admittedly a slightly tricky one. It doesn't necessarily mean just talking about open country, on the one hand, and tangled, overgrown, impenetrable country, on the other. Some landscapes that might at first glance look like natural landscapes, such as our national forests, are really either working landscapes, where all the trees are planted crops, or a blend of natural and working landscapes; and conversely, some large areas of completely open countryside—the Hempstead Plains before Levittown, say—are naturally occurring countryside formations.

Despite this complexity, the idea of discussing countryside under two different headings has helped turn people's consideration toward some special qualities maintained by rural regions that aren't wild and aren't always spectacular, and might other-

wise have seemed to be only plain, ordinary countryside. It's an
idea that is still not fully formulated; a new college-level landscape architecture textbook points out: "The profound importance of the rural and agricultural landscape has only recently
received much attention." Some of the environmentalists who
have started studying working-farmland landscapes take a special interest in the soil itself; they remind Americans that, for
instance, only eleven percent of the surface of the earth is rich,
productive farmland, and that, as a recent Sierra Club book,
Soil and Survival, puts its, "an exceptionally large part of this
eleven percent exists here in the United States." The book quotes
Hans Jenny, the dean of American soil scientists, who has discovered that on productive farmland there are more creatures
living under the ground than on it and above it—"the equivalent
of twelve horses per acre." Jenny concludes: "Hence, I desig-
nate soil as a living system." Just-completed research now being
featured in American newsmagazines indicates that there may
be more horses under our feet than even Jenny ever suspected:
At the very bottom of the subsoil in South Carolina, more than
a third of a mile below ground, biologists have now uncovered
three thousand previously unknown species of microorganisms,
which may have been living down there for up to seventy million
years. "It's a new environment, a whole new biosphere," David
White of the University of Tennessee recently told a *Newsweek*
reporter.

Other writers have approached the subject of working landscapes more in the tradition of nature writers or landscape painters, discussing what it is that they personally feel connected to
when they visit some special place in the working countryside—
some "great good place," in the Jamesian phrase. In a working
landscape, according to John Stilgoe, a Harvard landscape historian, "terrain and vegetation are molded, not dominated." As
a consequence, he maintains, when you enter such an area you're
always in the presence of a "fragile equilibrium between natural

and human force.'' The biologist René Dubos wrote in *The Wooing of Earth* about the ''charm and elegance'' and ''soft luminosity'' of one of his favorite places in the world—the farming country of the Île-de-France, around Paris, the landscape of his childhood—and addressed the question of how a life or a job or a vacation in the working countryside might affect someone's behavior or perceptions. When partial clearing of the wildwood changed the Île-de-France from a natural landscape into a working landscape, Dubos wrote, it gave rise to ''an environmental diversity that provides nourishment for the senses and for the psyche . . . from the mosaics of cultivated fields, pastures, and woodlands, as well as from the alternation of sunlit surfaces and shaded areas.'' For him, the ''profound origin'' of that nourishment was an ''increased awareness of the interdependence between human beings and their total environment.''

There's a darker shading to John Stilgoe's discussion of working landscapes than you find in Dubos's writing: Stilgoe's ''fragile equilibrium'' between people and the environment in farming areas sounds like an achievement that might slip away from humankind as easily as a handful of liquid. Dubos, with his robust celebration of nourishment, stability, and long periods of intimate association and interactions between human beings and the environment, made working landscapes sound like a subject that humanity had long since mastered and could now count on, like the use of language. Of course, the American working landscapes have only a short, problematical history compared with their European counterparts: The most seasoned and patriarchal working landscapes in New England—Stilgoe's part of the country—are now only ten or eleven generations old, while the Île-de-France and parts of the English working countryside are a hundred fifty generations old, at the very least.

And in New England, from long before the Second World War until very recent years, just as many old working landscapes vanished through reversion to old uses as through conversion to new ones. During this period, a great number of New England farmers going through hard times sold out to anyone who would buy and drifted westward to states where there weren't as many boulders in the fields. Although some of the land they left was put to new urban or suburban uses—covered with highways or tract-home subdivisions or long commercial strips—a lot of the New England landscape was merely left alone after seven or eight generations of being farmed, and, the partnership dissolved, it went back to being woodland, though these newer, second-growth woods are still dotted with old cellar holes and crossed at regular intervals by tumbledown stone walls.

To many present-day European minds, a partnership landscape like that of the Île-de-France is as clearly a part of the continent's patrimony as a major cathedral or château, or the Alps. One result of this way of thinking is that even the largest contemporary European cities have deliberately retained some age-old links to the nearby countryside. Compliment the Parisians, for instance, on the clarity of the famous golden, glowing light that suffuses their city, and they are quite likely to tell you that it wouldn't exist without the two woods just west and just east of the center city—the Bois de Boulogne and the Bois de Vincennes—because the trees in these two forests block out clouds of dust that might otherwise veil and choke the city.

For almost the last two centuries, the Europeans have been developing another idea about partnership landscapes—that the sense of partnership created in such areas is a public value, even if it may have been developed by the actions of innumerable private individuals. More than fifty years before Thoreau proclaimed that natural landscapes have an innate public value ("In wildness is the preservation of the world"), William Wordsworth's 1810 travel book, *Select Views in Cumberland, Westmoreland, and Lancashire,* put forward a similar thought about working landscapes. Walking through the great open moors and fells of his beloved Lake District, with its valley

bottoms occupied by small green fields and old stone farmhouses, Wordsworth reflected one day that the area, which had
by then inspired a whole generation of poets and painters, was
so precious for developing an understanding of life that in some
way it constituted "a sort of national property, in which every
man has a right and interest who has an eye to perceive and a
heart to enjoy."

The subsequent working out of this thought has led to several
further ideas, and also, in England and Wales, to a national
system of protected working landscapes, created "for the nation's benefit" after the Second World War. One of these ideas
has to do with "the right to roam," as it is sometimes called—
something of a modern form of the premedieval idea of the
common: a jointly owned, intricately used landscape. The old
idea was that the ownership of property was never all of a piece
but had to do with distributing a bundle of land-use rights—the
right to farm, for instance, and the right to graze animals, and
the right to gather firewood, and a right of way—among the
various members of a local community. And any one use had
to respect the other commonly established uses and not diminish
or trespass on any of them. In modern "common" thinking, the
right to roam—a right of access to the country's landscapes—is
distributed among the citizens of a whole country and remains
theirs even when different pieces of property change hands, but
it must itself be carefully exercised under some kind of partnership agreement, so that it doesn't interrupt or threaten a landowner's guaranteed right to privacy.

A second new idea also has to do with public value; simply
put, it warns that the sense of partnership available in a landscape can be undermined, or cropped, by changes that come to
an area. "Cropping public value" might mean, for instance,
building in a countryside region a house that gives its new owners a spectacular view but destroys the views previously enjoyed
by the other houses in the area. In this case, part of a public

value would have been stripped from a landscape and converted into cash value for private gain.

———————

Rural Flushing's sense of partnership began to ebb in the 1930s. In 1930, Robert Moses, the most powerful park and highway builder of the twentieth century, proposed a parkway program for the New York metropolitan region, including a Brooklyn-Queens Belt Parkway, a system of interlinked highways around the perimeter of both boroughs, which would connect on one end to an existing bridge to Manhattan, the Brooklyn Bridge, and on the other end to the Whitestone Bridge, a new bridge from northern Flushing over to the Bronx. The Belt Parkway, which was largely completed over the next decade, encircled rural Flushing, previously a remote area well beyond the reach of the city's mass transportation system. And since many of the subway lines planned for in a post–World War I building program never materialized, because money for subways, if not for highways, ran out during the Depression, the Klein farm is still a long subway ride, a long bus ride, and a hike away from Manhattan. In fact, the farm is in some ways less accessible by public transportation than it used to be, because fifty years ago there was a countryside trolley car line about a mile away, which extended from the town center of Flushing to the town center of Jamaica.

In 1930, Henry Keil founded Keil Brothers, a major garden center and plant nursery, and because he set up shop in Bayside, on the eastern border of Flushing, he was in a position to watch the unraveling of rural Flushing during the Moses years. His business is still in the same spot, although the street outside has been enlarged and renamed the Long Island Expressway. The first changes, as he remembers them, were invisible, or nearly so. Speculators bought up farm properties near the land where

the new highways would run. This was an invisible change, because in many cases the new owners didn't build on the land for
years. Instead, they installed tenant farmers on a temporary basis, and here changes began to show, if you looked carefully,
because the short-term tenant farmers took less care of the fields
they worked and, as weeds sprouted and were not cut down, the
open areas began to take on a raggedy, uncared-for appearance.
These final farmers of rural Flushing also neglected the old
farmhouses they occupied, instead of repainting and repairing
them, and so shutters sagged and porches drooped.

Twenty-two years ago, in a book called *The Last Landscape,*
William H. Whyte conducted the first precise survey of this phenomenon—"an inexorable sequence of events," he called it,
which brought about "the defilement" of a beautiful partnership
landscape. In the 1950s, Whyte had seen the same processes
consume his own favorite landscape in his home county: Ches-
ter County, Pennsylvania, twenty miles west of Philadelphia—
"an unusually beautiful expanse of rolling countryside," which
was, he wrote, "to some eyes, and not just my own, the most
beautiful in all the country." Speculators, Whyte discovered,
were always part of the chain of events:

> Much of the open space that remained . . . was being stockpiled
> by speculators for resale at a later date. They may have leased it in
> the interim to a farmer, but often they simply left the land idle. Soon
> it would revert to a dense growth of saplings and weeds and poison
> ivy. Some inhabitants would be reassured by this resurgence of nature
> but to the practiced eye it would be a sure tip-off the area was doomed.
> Thus does the speculator leave his tracks.

Whyte also identified a partnership-withering force whose approach any practiced eye could monitor. This was a laterally
moving change of heart he called a "greed line": "All this time
the main body of developers and new people moving out from

the city was getting closer. Somewhat in advance of them, moving at the rate of about half a mile or a mile a year, was a sort of greed line, and once touched by it an owner's fealty to the land was put to sore trial. The majority of landowners did resist it; some turned down extraordinary offers. Unfortunately, however, only a handful have to fall from grace to spoil things for others. One landowner, for example, might decide to sell a piece of meadowland for a drive-in theatre. This would be intolerable to the abutting landowner, and his property would go on the market. Then the next one.''

The Kleins fought a rearguard action against speculators and developers and highway planners for years. John Klein remembers his father telling him about actual pitched battles—"but only fisticuffs," he says—between his grandfather's farmworkers and gangs of laborers who had been hired by the New Deal's Works Progress Administration in the late thirties to widen Union Turnpike, at the south end of the old farm. The road gang would steal vegetables from the fields when they thought no one was looking, but John's father would send one of his men up to the attic of the farmhouse to spy out what they were up to and then would organize a countercharge. By the late thirties, Adam Klein thought that he could see the end coming: His taxes were rising, he told an interviewer in 1937, and Union Turnpike had become a stream of automobiles as soon as the WPA road crews finished their job and moved on. And around that time Robert Moses dispatched another WPA group, with steam shovels, to start laying out baseball diamonds and tennis courts in Cunningham Park. In the woods, where dogwoods and wild cherry trees had been, you now found abandoned cars and tree stumps chucked aside by the Moses men.

It was only a couple of years later that Adam Klein gave up the fight for the old farm. Henry Keil remembers going out to the Klein's big barn with a lot of other people on the day they auctioned off the farm equipment. Adam Klein was now living with his family in the new red-brick farmhouse he had built in 1930, on the smaller farm he now owned, over on the north side of Black Stump Road, and he began selling off chunks of his property in Flushing to real estate agents, starting with the old fields south of Black Stump Road. As the farms of rural Flushing disappeared, it looked at first as if at least some of the expansive, wide-open-spaces feeling of the area would survive, because so much land had been converted into golf courses, like the Fresh Meadows Country Club, next to the Kleins'. But after the war almost all the golf courses—including, of course, Fresh Meadows—were themselves developed, and when the Long Island Expressway was pushed through Flushing, in the mid-1950s, most of the still-surviving century-old specimen trees that Samuel Parsons had planted throughout the region were cut down.

There is now one old farmland tree still standing in Flushing—a knobby, ungainly, and, it appears, naturally seeded two-hundred-year-old black cherry tree a couple of miles from the Klein place. This tree grows near one edge of a small, overgrown sort of triangular lot that so far has proved to have too awkward a shape to build on. As improbable as the survival of the gawky old Flushing black cherry may be, I find the continuing existence of the two-acre Klein farm itself—and, through its existence, the continuing presence of old rural Flushing—an even more unlikely kind of event. Both the little farm and the large surrounding region could never have just happened to endure; they have had to be kept alive deliberately by four generations of Kleins (one of John Klein's sons, John, has recently decided to enter the family profession), a farming family whose loyalty to their land would not let them dissolve their partnership with their surroundings. Not that the Kleins find themselves remarkable. When I asked Mrs. Pfaff why her father had never sold out completely, she paused for a moment and then said, "Well, it still feels like country, and he didn't want to part with it."

Unlike the ancient black cherry, which lived on unnoticed by many Flushing residents, the Klein farm has long had a number of favorable reputations among its neighbors, most of whom know the place only from beyond its perimeter—from walking past the farm stand or peering through the chain-link fences around the sides and the back of the place. Local newspapers write stories about the Klein farm every few years, even though it is now so small, because it fits into three "last" and "only" categories: It is the only land in New York City still zoned for agricultural use; it has been used only for farming ever since the oak and chestnut woods on the land were chopped down more than two hundred years ago; and it is the last working family farm inside the city limits. (Twenty-seven percent of the city's land is covered by streets, and almost seventeen percent is parks. Almost forty-nine percent of the land has been zoned for three principal purposes: It is divided into industrial districts, commercial districts, and residential districts. Four percent of the city land is zoned for schools, hospitals, and other institutions, three percent is zoned for airports, and a little less than one thousandth of one percent of the land in the city has been set aside for working farms.) The farm grows mainly carrots, beets, turnips, cucumbers, scallions, dill, basil, and parsley, and everything that is grown on the property is sold fresh-picked in the farm stand on Seventy-third Avenue.

Still, most of the items sold at the stand are grown on Klein farmland farther east on Long Island and trucked in fresh early each morning by John Klein, who now has to commute to his Queens farmland. At this point, the Kleins have made about as many eastward moves as is possible on Long Island. First, in the forties, they bought land in Westbury and Hicksville, in Nassau County, about eleven miles east of the Queens farm. In the fifties, when those towns started to get built up as suburbs, they relocated seven miles or so to the east, in Melville, in western Suffolk county. But Melville has changed even more dramatically than Westbury and Hicksville—Route 110, which runs past their old Melville land, turned first into a manufacturing strip and then, in the 1980s, into a booming office center and research-and-development corridor, with several million square feet of office space occupied by major companies like Chemical Bank, National Westminster Bank, and Estée Lauder. Land along Route 110 now goes for a million dollars an acre. So in 1972 the Kleins moved forty miles farther east and bought a farm in Riverhead, at the west end of the North Fork.

The Kleins' Flushing neighbors have always recognized the value of having a farm stand within easy reach. And it is possible that even though most of them have never walked through the farm, they may also be responding to something present in the air: According, at least, to a new health discipline called aroma therapy, the scent of basil has a relaxing impact that releases tensions. And it looks as though something else could be at work in the area around the farm. Almost all the children attending P.S. 26 have written essays in language-arts, social-studies, or science class about how much they admire the farm, and this admiration, you find when you talk to them, reaches back behind the farm stand. Certain aspects of the farm's partnership sense catch their attention, if not that of their parents. "We thought it was a mansion on a hill, set on a gorgeous carpet of lawn, with a magical greenhouse behind it—magical because none of us had ever been inside," a P.S. 26 graduate now in her thirties told me recently. "There seemed to be an unwritten understanding among all the kids in the neighborhood—hands off the farm. Even the toughest kids would never think of defacing anything either on the farm or at one other place—a little old overgrown Dutch cemetery, farther down Seventy-third Avenue, that to us was 'the Indian cemetery.' For me, the farm and the old oak grove within Fresh Meadows were the two refuges I had in my thoughts—the two places nearby that I could summon up inside whenever life got too complicated."

6 After the Highways

According to some land-use experts I've been talking to recently
in this country and in France, Germany, and England—people
who are working out the details of what is sometimes called the
landscape approach or the regional approach to metropolitan development—all the produce on display at the Klein farm, the
partnership sense, and even the back-field evocation of a vast
rural region, may over the next few decades become thoroughly
commonplace parts of urban and suburban areas big enough to
cover parts of four or more states. The regional approach is
being created by an informal and loosely knit new public-private
partnership of local government agencies, college research programs, nonprofit environmental groups, and private individuals
with time to spare, who have discovered a common interest in
tackling an area's economic, environmental, and social problems simultaneously. One of the basic working assumptions
emerging from the new partnership, which is widely scattered
and is still fairly small in total numbers, is that the city-and-
working-country reality that in New York has been kept alive
only on the two acres of the Klein farm can be successfully
extended to landscape regions far larger than rural Flushing ever
was. Extended, and also compounded: The land-use experts are
convinced that three different forms of connectedness—the sense
of kinship with all life; the sense of partnership with working

landscapes; and the sense of community and companionability that is traditionally fostered by villages and urban neighborhoods—can be maintained in or, if necessary, brought back to even the most densely settled districts, old and new.

The regionalists say that much of their inspiration comes from the attention now being focused on both working landscapes and natural landscapes. In a quiet way, they are predicting that if some of the relatively small-scale landscape projects they're currently engaged in—such as a state landscape inventory; a series of town- and regional-character plans; a design manual for a forty-three-mile-long river corridor; and plans for both narrow, largely publicly owned linear greenway parks and broader, largely privately owned working-landscape parks—begin to multiply during the 1990s, it could mean that places like the Klein farm may have survived long enough to be recognized as the harbingers of a new form of human settlement.

According to the Green Cure Trust, a British group that has worked with city farms—like Windmill Hill in the heart of Bristol, which raises crops and a small flock of domestic animals—it's already possible to rebuild city soil so that it becomes again "a living organic thing, a basic and complex element in the life-support system." A New York City regionalist, Albert F. Appleton, talks about "a third round of cityscaping for the area"—to complete a system of open spaces for the New York metropolitan region started by Frederick Law Olmsted in the 1860s and 1870s and added to over a forty-year period by Robert Moses, beginning in the 1920s. Appleton, who has a knack for putting together projects in which government agencies and local citizens' groups share responsibilities—as will happen, for instance, at Dubos Point, a new city park and wildlife refuge on the southern edge of Jamaica Bay, named in honor of René Dubos—is himself almost a one-man public-private partnership. He currently serves as New York City's Commissioner of Environmental Protection, but until recently Appleton was a noteworthy

example of the spare-time regionalist: During the 1980s, he devoted his evenings and weekends to the volunteer job of conservation chairman of the New York City Audubon Society, while
on weekdays he worked as a senior legal manager on the staff
of New York State's deputy attorney general in charge of rooting
out Medicaid fraud.

A balance of three forces seems to be giving the regionalists
a rare infusion of energy and confidence: a new sense of urgency; recognition of an unexpected opportunity; and the impact of recent evidence that human beings need a countryside
component in their everyday surroundings if they are to function
effectively when it comes to learning, say, and recovering from
an illness or an operation.

The development boom in this country—a "crescendo," according to Grady Clay, the dean of American planning writers,
that "has gained the attention of a huge sector of the public that
never noticed before"—began getting noticed and creating concern in part because it's been the first construction surge we've
had since the beginning of what might be called America's post-
interstate period. Since the early nineteenth century, the United
States has put itself through a series of expensive clear-the-decks,
we-want-the-whole-place-completely-done-over transportation
changes that have no equivalent in any other nation. As soon as
we had completed a network of canals, we abandoned most of
them and covered the country with railroad lines. About a decade after the Second World War, we got tired of the railroads,
by then an intricate and sophisticated array linking thousands of
population centers, large and small, and decided to replace them
with airports and a new national system of freeways. Now, thirty
years later, at a cost of several trillion dollars, this enormous
highway-building program is almost finished, and American road
maps of the interstates, which run through every state except
Alaska, show only a few short gaps: places where thin black or
red lines have yet to be overshadowed by broad bands of deep,
rich blue.

Each change in the country's transportation system has changed the nature of its construction booms, by changing people's ideas of where it was convenient to have their workplaces (which must be convenient to transportation), where they could live (two or three hours, at the most, from work), and where they could go to get away from it all (something like a five- or six-hour radius from home)—time constraints that have themselves stayed more or less constant. The 1980s post-interstate boom suddenly, and for the first time, brought heavy development pressure on all sorts of settings simultaneously—center-city business and residential districts, older suburbs, shore areas, farmlands, resort communities, faraway deep woods— because with the interstates in place, a resort town like Mount Pocono, in eastern Pennsylvania, 114 miles west of New York City, is only a two-hour drive, with any luck, from Manhattan, and so can become part of New York's "commuter shed."

Similarly, tiny towns up in the middle of Maine's north woods—Abbot Village, say, and Greeley Landing, and dozens more—have become part of the weekend, or "second home," belt around Boston, because they're about 250 miles, or maybe just under a five-hour drive, away. Easterners began to realize the current extent of their second-home territory in February of 1988, when a French holding company, Générale Occidentale, decided to reduce its debt and sell almost a million acres of land in the Adirondacks, the northeast kingdom of Vermont, the White Mountains of New Hampshire, and the mountain ranges of Maine—private forest land that had always been open to the public for hunting, fishing, and camping. Developers were eager to buy in all four areas.

At the same time, some of the largest developers in the country have increased the size of their own operations, so that they can now think of taking on ten-thousand-acre, twenty-five-year "megaprojects," as they're called, such as the new city of Weston, Florida—sixteen square miles of farmland and ranchland fifteen miles west of Fort Lauderdale which by 2013 could have forty-five thousand inhabitants, an airport, an eighteen-hole golf course, two thousand acres of lakes and waterways, and millions of square feet of offices and warehouses.

And there's a further complication. Because America's first post-interstate development boom is also a post-industrial development boom, many white-collar workplaces that aren't directly dependent on raw materials are leaping out from the center cities, either into the suburbs or right past them onto the fields of the old working landscapes, beyond the farthest suburbs. Everything gets spread farther and farther out, which results in both reverse commuting—people live in the city and work in the suburbs—and suburb-to-suburb commuting. This puts the working landscapes within metropolitan areas at triple risk, because now they may be seen as immediately suitable sites for three kinds of development that used to arrive in stages: weekend homes, residential neighborhoods, and office districts. In this latest development era, "urban and suburban sprawl" is no longer descriptive, because the sprawl has been transformed into urban and suburban gobbling up and tearing at the ground, and it resembles the work of the great beasts of the last interglacial period, whose browsing destroyed large areas of thick forest.

Philip Lewis, a landscape architect at the University of Wisconsin in Madison, who for years has been tracking American development patterns by looking at nighttime satellite photographs of the glow given off by "urban stars," as he says, meaning the electric lights of North America, has identified an emerging doughnut-shaped, four-hundred mile-wide, four-state metropolis in his own region—an entity, or constellation, he calls "Circle City" that is coming into being as the outlying reaches of eight existing cities begin to converge: Chicago; Milwaukee and Madison; Minneapolis and St. Paul; and Mason City, Cedar Rapids, and Davenport in Iowa. The hole in the Circle City doughnut is a beautiful, rolling, enormous working landscape of rich peaceful farmland that's mainly in Wisconsin—

but also partly in Minnesota and Iowa, and with a smidgen in Illinois—known as the Driftless Area. The Driftless Area gets its name from the fact that it's the only preglacial landscape in the upper Midwest: For some reason, the Wisconsin glacier split in two to the north of the area and so never scraped the Wisconsin hills or dumped glacial "drift" onto them—scrapings from other places, farther north. The Driftless Area is already crossed by two interstates, one a north-south road and the other running east and west, and in another few years two more interstates will run through the place, paralleling the first two— which would make the whole area accessible to Circle Citizens looking to build second homes. The way Lewis sees it, two events will have to occur quickly if the Driftless Area is to have some kind of future as a working landscape. First, the residents of the six existing cities that ring the area will have to acknowledge that in some way they already constitute the chrysalis of an emerging supercity and now have interests in common. And then they'll collectively have to start treating the Driftless Area with great care, because it can serve as Circle City's Central Park.

The type of fused and embracingly aware metropolitan identity Lewis is hoping to find usually begins with a more preliminary sort of realization, a kind of shared dismay and wariness that gets shouldered or elbowed into people whenever the post-interstate development process touches their area. Traditionally, most American development decisions have been made at the community level, and many of the places that most of us know best are a product of thousands of local choices made for hundreds of personal and local reasons—such as Let's buy a house and Let's start a business and Let's put up a new office center and Let's bring some more tax dollars into the area. What is new about conventional post-interstate development is that a national decision to switch transportation systems has spread these same makes-sense-to-me-personally and makes-sense-to-us-locally development decisions across huge regional expanses, on the optimistic assumption that, whatever happened next, they would inevitably continue to produce the things that all people need, such as stable communities, cherished surroundings, and opportunities for full and fulfilling lives.

Instead, of course, they didn't. The initial responses to post-interstate development have, however, included a completely new combination of countermeasures, some old, some unprecedented, some a blend of old and new: They include reaching out; moving in and standing fast; and taking stock and forming new partnerships. All these activities seem to have at least one common theme, whether it is put into words or remains implicit—namely, that something is in danger or is already missing, and something has to be done about it now. Many of the people involved, when they read about the national environmental disasters that made headlines during the summer of 1988 (record heat wave, prolonged drought, enormous forest fires, miles of East Coast beaches closed when medical waste washed ashore), had an odd feeling that they were only reading local or neighborhood news that had vaulted out of the back of the newspaper and onto page one.

Reaching out is a community's first attempt to visualize, or somehow get some sense of, the size and shape and consequences of the post-interstate regions-in-formation and to keep track of the pace of change in its own region. It's proving hard to do, because region-focusing, or region-tracking, devices are not an automatic component of American communities. New York City, for example, has traditionally boasted of the purity of its drinking water. New York now receives water from an area almost as big as Delaware, but what can you tell about the size or the shape or the condition of that area by drinking a glass of water in Manhattan? True, the taste in your mouth occasionally gives you one piece of information. Every so often, when there's a bad drought in the region—and bad droughts may occur a decade or more apart—New York City tap water tastes chlo-rinated, because then the city has to supplement the water it routinely gets from Westchester, from the Catskill Mountains, a hundred miles northwest of the city, and from the Delaware River, a hundred twenty-five miles northwest of the city, and start drawing water out of the Hudson River—water that needs more chemical treatment before it's safe to drink. And last year people with low salt tolerances were advised to reduce their consumption of New York water, because the rock salt being used by towns in the Catskills to keep their roads ice-free in the wintertime had been leaching into the city reservoirs in the area. You can't taste this salt yet, but it's predicted that within a few years New York City water will have taken on a permanent new flavoring unless the Catskill road crews make other arrange-ments for keeping their roads open.

Is there anything else in New Yorkers' daily lives that can help them form a sense of the size of the watershed that supplies the city? According to Ellen Airgood, a researcher who pulled together "mountains of factual material on New York City's wa-ter supply" for a nonprofit regionalist group called Scenic Hud-son, which is interested in applying a landscape approach to new metropolitan development in the Hudson River Valley, it's hard for almost anyone to get a firm two-dimensional fix on the wa-tershed, or even to be certain how far away the edge of the watershed is—especially since the edge shifts whenever water-use levels in the city rise or fall. But, she says, many New Yorkers can easily gain a good idea of their watershed's third dimension whenever they're within sight of the Empire State Building, because the world's third-tallest building (the Empire State's current ranking among skyscrapers) is a sort of standing depth gauge of the whole watershed—that is, the highest reser-voir that sends water on to New York is about on a line with the television transmission tower on top of the Empire State. Or to put it another way, if all the water flowing into the city had to stay in New York and couldn't sink away into the sea, the city would eventually lie at the bottom of a lake as deep as the Empire State is high, with only the tops of the World Trade Center towers showing above water.

Putting the third dimension at people's disposal has become a specialty of Peter Powers, of Eugene, Oregon, a geographer and former cartographer for the United States Forest Service who five years ago developed two new interests at about the same time: bicycle touring—meaning bike trips of more than one day—and computer graphics. Powers's first five-day cross-Oregon bike trip surprised him by demonstrating to him, through his legs and lungs, just how little you could find out in advance about what a bike trip was going to be like—or a run or a hike, for that matter—by looking at a conventional map, the kind he had been producing professionally for years. On an ordinary map, even a topographical one, the countryside looks every bit as flat as the piece of paper the map has been printed on, and the roads move across the page in all directions but never seem to push out from or sink into the page itself. A topographical map does display different levels of terrain with wavy gray lines, but the predictive impact—the kind of impact you'll feel—is limited because, under the established customs of map-making, you, the viewer, are always directly on top of every single place on the map, even the places you're not looking at at the moment, and looking straight down at anything inevitably has the effect of flattening it out.

Ordinary maps are useful enough to drivers, because their cars are doing the climbing and descending, and anyway riding around in a car makes a place seem more like a map, since cars, like maps, are flatteners. Driving across the Fifty-ninth Street Bridge between Manhattan and Queens, for instance, feels like driving down a straight line, but running across it, according to a man I know who ran in the New York City Marathon last year, is more like sprinting along the Appalachian Trail—you become

aware that there's actually a thirteen-story-high hill between the
entrance to the bridge in Queens and the flat center span high
above the middle of the East River. As Powers himself puts it,
in the introduction to *Touring the Islands*—a guidebook, with
maps, to the islands near Seattle that he wrote with his wife,
Renee Travis—"Hills can become mountains and grades can
seem to go on forever when you are under your own power.
What looks like a winding road on a typical map may actually
be a series of switchbacks that climb up and over yet another
ridge separating you from the next campsite!"

After his first five-day bike tour around Oregon, it took Powers three and a half years to work out on a computer a way of
displaying on a flat map the kind of "computer generated 3-D
landscape" information, as he calls it, that would be of interest
to his own legs. Powers showed his first map to some other
bikers in Eugene, and also to some bicycle shop owners in the
area, and they all told him to make some more. In 1987, he
printed a book of maps, his first, *Touring Eugene,* which shows
fifteen looping trails through that city, in both 2-D and 3-D, side
by side. The next year, *Touring the Islands* made it to number
two on a regional best-sellers list published in August by the
Portland *Oregonian.* And according to a 1988 article about Powers by Karen Irmsher, a Eugene journalist, his maps have already started to gain a national reputation: "Assistant Bicycle
Coordinator for North Carolina's Department of Transportation,
Mary Paul Meletiou, one of five or six experts in the design of
bike maps in the United States, . . . said, 'The maps caused a
mini-stir here. As far as I know it's a completely new concept
in bicycle mapping. . . . I'm looking at it, and I can get a feel
for the steepness.' "

"To our knowledge," Powers says, "this is the first time this
technology has been used for recreational purposes. It's something like half cartography and half art." A Powers map shows
you steepness by changing one of the conventions of ordinary

maps, the point of view, and then adding two new graphic features: shading and an overlay grid of bending checkerboard lines. Viewers of such a map are still up in the air, floating over the terrain displayed, but they've descended closer to the earth, and now they're off to one side, hovering in a single, fixed location. This is a true bird's-eye view, in contrast to the omnipresent and extraterrestrial God's-eye view presented by traditional maps, and it immediately allows Powers to show one aspect of steepness, because now he can include, in outline drawings, the silhouetted shape of any hills and valleys sitting in front of the horizon. He uses shading the way painters have always used a smudge of gray when making a sketch, to darken one side of a hill. It's the checkerboard, a computer imaging technique, that seems to lock the image of the third dimension into place on a Powers map. Every piece of territory shown carries on its back a set of crosshatched lines, like the squares printed on a checkered bedspread or a tattersall shirt. And when the land on the map changes shape, the crisscrossed lines reflect the same bulging, or stretching, or sudden plunging, just as the grid of lines on a shirt sleeve changes shape when you put your arm through it.

In a suggested tour in *Touring the Islands* along a stretch of Whidbey Island, near the mouth of Puget Sound, about thirty miles north of Seattle, the red line of Zylstra Road, in the middle of the trip—straight, with only an occasional right-angle turn and restraightening—looks, on the 2-D map, as though it might be the place to dawdle and coast along. The 3-D map to the left corrects this assumption: The same red line is no longer straight but pushes up, and up again, and then up once more. Zylstra Road now looks like the steepest climb on the tour—a fact confirmed by a small "route profile" printed below both maps. A route profile is a sort of fever chart of the route, a thin red line that rises and falls with the elevations and descents along the way. Zylstra Road, as the Whidbey Island route profile shows,

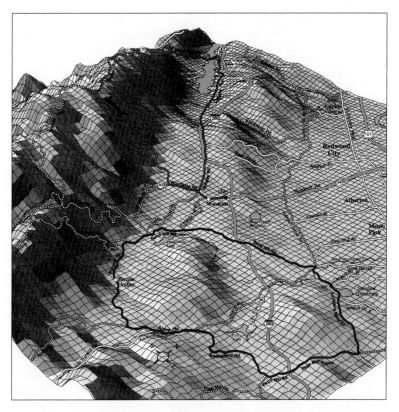

In Peter Powers' latest computer-generated bicycle maps—this one shows the Santa Cruz Mountains, south of San Francisco—the third dimension has taken on new vividness: The checkerboard grid has twice as many lines, and Powers can now show up to sixty shades of light and dark. *Map courtesy of Peter Powers*

climbs more than two hundred feet—the height of a twenty-story building—in just over four miles. The next mile and a half, on Fort Nugent Road and West Branch Road, is where you can take a breather as you slide back down to sea level. Earlier this year, Powers published two new books—*Touring the San Francisco Bay Area by Bicycle* and *Touring California's Wine Country by*

Bicycle—and he now plans, he says, to publish "similar guides for the most popular cycling cities and destination areas around the country." So far, though, no one has asked him for a 3-D landscape map of an entire watershed.

Perhaps, in the future, it will be possible to combine Powers's knowledge with some experimental techniques that the Environment Division of the Regional Planning Institute for the Île-de-France is developing in Paris. According to Raymond Delavigne, the director of the Environment Division, the generation of earth-observation satellites—including Landsat TM and SPOT—that was first put into orbit in the early 1980s may make it possible to keep track of regional changes by means of space-based "remote sensing," as it's now called. Pictures of the Paris area taken by a previous satellite, Landsat MSS, he says, were not as useful as had been hoped, because the MSS scanner wasn't sophisticated enough to pick up all the components of an "urban fabric . . . characterized by a mixture of heterogeneous objects of small size." But Landsat TM is equipped with devices that track a more extensive array of visible light and other electromagnetic radiation reflecting off the surface of the earth—and as a result, some images of the Île-de-France that were beamed to earth by Landsat TM on April 30, 1984, were later checked against eighty test sites on the ground and were found to reveal not only what was forest, what was farmland, and where there were buildings but also the relative age of the buildings, the shadows cast by high buildings, and whether the soil around them drained well.

In my office I have a couple of Delavigne's space-based pictures that he has had blown up to poster size—the 1984 Landsat TM shot of the whole Paris region and a 1986 SPOT picture of one section of the southwestern quadrant of the Île-de-France, which shows a number of the heterogeneous components of the area. Versailles, with its ornamental gardens and radiating paths, is near the middle of the picture, and you can clearly see the

intersecting arms of the mile-long artificial lake behind the
château; five miles southwest, and considerably bigger than
Versailles, is the "new city" of Saint-Quentin-en-Yvelines, a
planned community of office towers, shopping centers, apartment buildings, factories, and schools, which went up on open
fields in the 1960s as part of a project to relieve overcrowding
in Paris; south of Saint-Quentin stretches the still-farmed valley
of the Chevreuse River, an ancient and prosperous working landscape, where the playwright Racine went to school, along a
small tributary of the Seine; and at the bottom of the picture is
one edge of an enormous national forest, Rambouillet—it's almost as big as the more celebrated forest of Fontainebleau, over
in the southeastern part of the Île-de-France.

Delavigne's SPOT picture takes some getting used to; it has
been color-enhanced to emphasize the forested areas, and every
patch of woodland is a bright scarlet, whereas open water, like
the cross-shaped lake behind Versailles, shows up as a dark forest green. Fields are more fieldlike—they're either white or light
green—and the built-up areas are a pale dove gray. Most of the
colors in the Landsat TM picture are closer to reality: Paris is a
glowing gray, almost pewter-colored at its heart, the forests are
dark green, and the farmland strips are soft green and pale beige.
The only oddity in the Landsat view is the lakes—they're a vivid
emerald green. Unless you have a trained eye, you can't look at
these pictures and learn much about shadows or about how much
water the ground will be able to absorb, but when you put the
two pictures—taken two years and three months apart—side by
side, one feature emerges with amazing clarity. The satellites
allow you to see the shape of development as it flows across the
landscape: Beige fields to the east of Saint-Quentin in the earlier
picture have turned gray with buildings in the second.

Now four years have gone by since that second picture was
taken. What would a new picture of the same area show? Or
pictures taken every few months? Just how frequently do you

need to look at the spread of development in order to measure its pulse speed? Philip Lewis, Circle City's discoverer, would like every region, or every emerging urban constellation, to have at least one place within its borders fitted out with all the technologies that can bring into focus for its people both the resources in their area and the forces acting on them; Regional Discovery Centers is the name he proposes for the observatories. They could bring regionalists together and begin to answer the questions that pop up as soon as people start to see just how much information there now is about how to grow without sacrificing the connectedness of places.

Another new response in this country to post-interstate development processes—called moving in—is a phenomenon that has been unexpectedly turning up in the population statistics compiled by Calvin Beale, at the Economic Research Bureau of the United States Department of Agriculture. Beale, who is considered the top rural demographer in this country, says that in the 1980s, for the first time, large numbers of older Americans who have enough money to be able to choose whether they want to spend their retirement years in their own communities or move on to another place bought homes in countryside areas whose main attraction is an outstanding landscape—farmland, ranchland, mountains, forests, or some mix of natural terrain and managed land. He's found big population gains that include a high rate of incoming elderly residents in some five hundred or so beautiful rural counties around the country, including a couple in Montana, quite a few in New England, and one in northern Arizona, near Prescott. Most of these now burgeoning counties are quite remote, and some of them get extremely cold in the winter, and none of them has ever been thought of either as a resort region or as a likely retirement area—the way Florida and southern California are, and southern Arizona, around Tucson. And in the opinion of some rural analysts, a good number of the newcomers to the five hundred counties, and particularly the retirees, are people who have already made key decisions about the rest of their lives: For them, resettling in lovely surroundings is a sort of recruitment to a new career—the cause of the countryside—in which they enlist themselves as active guardians of the landscapes around them.

A recent issue of *Successful Communities,* a newsletter published by the Conservation Foundation, thinks that in addition, a more youthful group of movers-in is in formation: There's been a detectable population surge, according to a University of Idaho study, in counties adjacent to federally designated wilderness areas, and in these areas most of the new residents are "young and well educated"—"and forty percent say they are willing to sacrifice income to live in high quality environments." Now that American income levels, for the first time since the Second World War, are no longer rising steadily in all professions—a major change in the workings of the national economy that Barry Bluestone and Bennett Harrison, two American economists, are calling "the great U-turn"—some younger people may be discovering, as a few rural analysts have already suggested, that landscape connectedness is something they can still hold on to. For these people, working to protect connectedness may be part of a new process of coming up with alternatives to what other American economists call a love of material goods that has always shaped the Amercian consciousness.

Other types of responses to development pressures are emerging among people who want to stay where they are. There's the "slow-growth movement," for instance—a coalition of environmentalists and home owners that sprang up a few years ago in some of the well-to-do southern California suburbs that retired couples have recently started avoiding. This coalition (it includes a group named Not Yet New York) is already winning local elections and attracting national press coverage with a simple message: that there is a demonstrable link between private property values and public health—and equally strong links between

these two factors and the ease of physical mobility within a region, the region's economic security, and the resilience and well-
being of its natural environment.

The California Association of Realtors reports that more than
a hundred slow-growth plans have been put before California
voters in local elections in the last few years alone, and most of
them have been adopted, including the 1986 proposal that placed
height and bulk limits on earthquake-proof new commercial developments in San Francisco. Other West Coast cities outside
California—including Seattle, Portland, and Vancouver, British
Columbia—have approved similar downtown-growth-control
measures. "We were people who had worked hard to put together enough money to buy a home, only to find that it was
sitting atop poison," says Ruth Galanter, the first slow-growther
elected to the Los Angeles City Council. Also, slow-growthers
point out that the amount of money you can hope to sell a home
for can decline by as much as 27 percent if the trees around
the house have been cut down. And according to H. H. Hum-
phrey, Jr., of Short Hills, New Jersey, who is in the business of
recruiting senior executives to jobs in the New York area, "if
we make it so difficult for people to live in the suburbs and
commute to New York, there is only one thing that can happen:
The real-estate value of our homes and our largest investment
will go down."

In the elections of November 1988, a nonbinding ballot question asked Cape Cod voters what they thought about the idea of
taking development-approval power away from the fifteen town
governments on the Cape and giving it to a new, Cape-wide
regional-land-use commission, which would be authorized to
turn down any new construction project that might damage the
area's natural environment, water supplies, or coastline. A freeway now runs along two thirds of the Cape Cod peninsula—
from the shoulder to the elbow of this sixty-mile-long arm of
Massachusetts land. And although large stretches of the Cape's

beaches and duneland have been protected from development for some years, as the Cape Cod National Seashore, which is a unit of the National Park System, the Cape's population increased by 18 percent during the first six years of the 1980s— nine times the growth rate in the rest of the state. The suggestion of a Cape Cod commission had been put forward only a few months before the Cape elections, by former Senator Paul E. Tsongas, and, in what a Barnstable town selectman called "the Tsonganista revolution," it was enthusiastically endorsed, by a three-to-one vote—along with another nonbinding resolution asking for a moratorium on all Cape development until the commission could come into being. Paul Tsongas made his suggestion after serving as chairman of a Massachusetts advisory commission that had been asked to look at the condition of the state's environmental protection efforts and discovering that in Massachusetts, at least, there is a direct link between environmental protection and economic development. "If you look at why we have this prosperity in Massachusetts," he explained to a local reporter, Richard Stradling, in June 1988, "you really come down to the educational base. Thirty percent of the MIT graduates stay in Massachusetts. Twenty-five percent of all the Harvard graduates have stayed. That is an incredible balance of trade in brainpower."

But the advisory commission's investigations, Tsongas said, had also made clear that the Commonwealth of Massachusetts could no longer take its brainpower advantage for granted: "What we've come to understand is that if you destroy the quality of life, they're not going to stay. If you get people who refuse to live here anymore, then the Massachusetts Miracle of the future will not be." It was time to warn the Commonwealth, Tsongas said, because "by the time we wake up and realize we are Long Island, it will be too late." Tsongas's moratorium proposal—he calls it "the first shot of what will be the dominant issue in the next decade"—was approved by a two-to-one vote.

7 An Approach to the Next Generation

This past spring, Cape Cod residents voted to set up a new Cape Cod Commission. Even before that, a number of states, including Oregon, Florida, Georgia, Maine, Vermont, and New Jersey, have established statewide regional-growth-management plans, in response to a new realization about development patterns resulting from the interstate highway boom—one that is of special interest to governors and state legislators. The idea being expressed in state capitals—it's almost a "Just Say No" campaign directed at infrastructure—is that the interstate program, which started out as a single round of public spending on infrastructure and didn't even cost very much at the state level because the federal government put up ninety percent of the money, is now requiring a second round of public spending that will be far more expensive to both states and localities, because once the interstates have pulled people and businesses out into the countryside, they need more local roads and sewage lines and waste-treatment plants, most of which have to be completely paid for with state and local money. What regional-growth management does is to limit new state spending for infrastructure except in those areas that are already densely populated, to keep current costs at manageable levels, and to avoid bringing on in a decade or two a third round of infrastructure spending, which states might find themselves unable to afford.

Oregon, which adopted a statewide growth-management plan in 1973 to channel new development to existing cities, contains sprawl by defining outer limits for each built-up area—urban growth boundaries, these city edges are called. And at least one state is now talking about setting up a new system of countryside zoning, known as existing-use zoning, which would protect working landscapes from speculators by making them areas where traditional businesses like farming and forestry would be designated as the only appropriate uses for such land.

Yet another way of standing fast in response to development pressures has been showing up in Rhode Island: In the spring of 1987, the legislature of this smallest of all the states approved a $65 million bond act chiefly for buying land to protect it as open space, and in the summer it went back into session to pass a bill that would permit the thirty-nine cities and towns in the state to approve open-space bond acts of their own. Thirty-four of the Rhode Island towns, including the poorest ones and the richest ones, voted yes on these local initiatives, which added $61 million to the $65 million made available statewide for buying undeveloped land.

In November 1986, at a town meeting in Jamestown, population 4,500, there was a unanimous vote (575 to 0) to spend two million one thousand dollars to buy a local golf course that developers were preparing to build on. And a year later, at a special election, Jamestown voted to spend another five million dollars to buy farms and woods and ponds all over town. This happened only a year after the legislature's 1986 approval of a sixteen-million-dollar open-spaces bond act, and only two years after the legislature voted for the first time in twenty years to spend any money on open-space acquisition: In 1985, when open-space protection was still considered an untested idea in the state, and a politically risky one, the legislators adopted a nine-million-dollar bond act. That's $151 million altogether, in just over two years—and not much less than the $250 million worth of open-space financing that New York State voters agreed to in a 1986 election, though New York State has more than seventeen times as many people as Rhode Island (there aren't even a million Rhode Islanders) and is more than forty times as big.

Robert Bendick, who for eight years was director of Rhode Island's Department of Environmental Management (he's now New York's Deputy Commissioner of Environmental Conservation), is still astonished by the outpouring of feeling on this subject. He thinks that it could have happened only because post-interstate development forces have run up against a newly mobilized group of landscape guardians—people who have chosen to stay behind. Before the current development boom, Rhode Island had been losing great numbers of local families: Between 1960 and 1980, thousands of people pulled up stakes and drove off on the new roads to the Sunbelt and other regions in search of better jobs and better conditions. "When this tremendous out-migration began to slow down and people began to look around, it turned out that the people who were still there were the people who loved Rhode Island," Bendick says. "They had at least as much interest in finding the best place for a good life as the people who had gone elsewhere—but why should they move when they had already found it? These people had a deep attachment to the towns and the land of Rhode Island, and to the heritage of that land, and in many cases they came from families who had cherished these same places, often for generations."

Then, when development did come, and the economy of Rhode Island, after fifty years of stagnation, began to share in the boom being enjoyed by the two states next door, Massachusetts and Connecticut, the stay-behinds found themselves facing two different kinds of disruption of their connectedness to the land that meant so much to them.

"In Rhode Island, as in most eastern states, most of the land has always been privately owned, but in that state no one ever

The Pioneer Valley, Massachusetts: The 350-year-old working landscape of the Connecticut River Valley has been officially recognized as a distinctive landscape region by the *Massachusetts Landscape Inventory,* America's first statewide scenic survey. *Photograph courtesy of Mark S. Finnen*

felt the lack of the national parks they didn't have, or the national forests and other large public holdings that had never been established there,'' Bendick explains. ''Why? Because according to their own code of the countryside, an informal, unwritten tradition that was nevertheless widely acknowledged and accepted around the state, the owners of the farms and forests and shorelines of Rhode Island gave their neighbors the use of these places, so that private property functioned—very discreetly—as public open space. This tradition was perhaps a holdover from ancient land-use customs of common ownership and public access that the first European settlers in Rhode Island brought with them. But it began to be eroded, and then truncated, by the current wave of development, because now there were not only new buildings on a town's fields or near its beaches but also new owners, who didn't take kindly to trespassing. And people get much more excited about things they have enjoyed and are about to lose than they do about things they don't have—like national parks—but could have had if they had exercised some foresight. Loss of access made Rhode Islanders willing to throw their bodies in front of bulldozers—and helped persuade them to spend a great deal of money to do something about the situation.''

What Bendick doesn't say is that he himself helped crystallize the open-space forces in Rhode Island, with one well-timed remark. Normally a self-effacing man, who does a good job of presenting facts to political leaders while keeping his own name out of the newspapers, Bendick in April 1987 called a press conference in the statehouse rotunda and told Providence newspaper and broadcast reporters that ''the suburbanization of South County'' was now a fact—South County being the formerly rural southern section of the state, where all the beaches are. This statement—a year before Paul Tsongas told the citizens of Massachusetts that Cape Cod was being suburbanized—was the first public acknowledgment by a responsible Rhode Island official of the changes that development was bringing to the state. Bendick also permitted himself one further remark: ''We have five years to save all the lands in Rhode Island that are important to save.''

Bendick's statement, like Tsongas's, proved to be a critical factor, for once these statements were presented on TV and in the papers, the whole subject turned into something that people could talk about and do something about, and was no longer a silent and frightening nibbling away at the state that had to be mutely endured. Providence TV stations sent helicopters around the state and broadcast pictures of fields covered with tract houses and of barrier beaches cluttered with new condos on stilts. Within two years, Rhode Islanders were able to put to-

A loss and a gain: The recent subdivision of Silver Nail Farm, West Stockbridge, Massachusetts, identified as a distinctive site by the *Massachusetts Landscape Inventory,* has helped push the town toward adopting a new program to protect its remaining "areas of high visual quality." *Photograph courtesy of Mark S. Finnen*

gether an unusual working coalition—bipartisan and apolitical—of environmental groups and government officials who agreed on the need to protect open space in the state and backed up their plan by launching the largest per capita open-space-financing program in the country.

Bendick later joined an environmentalist and government group that two years ago took on an even bigger task: The six-state New England Governors' Conference (Rhode Island's governor was the 1988 chairman) agreed to put together a list of all the unprotected open spaces and working landscapes within the region that New Englanders, by consensus, consider special places that help create the distinctiveness of their particular corner of the country—some of the peaks in New Hampshire's White

Mountains, for instance, or farmland on Block Island, ten miles off the Rhode Island coast. Now that the list is complete, it will be used as a guide to regional identity and can serve as part of a framework for future development throughout New England. The six governors have all endorsed the preservation of every place on the list. So far, no other region in the country has even taken on the job of identifying the places it has that function as region makers, and Bendick hopes that the two-part regional-identity strategy that New Englanders have now devised—a commitment both to catalogue their own assets completely and, in the future, always to build around these characteristic places instead of on them—will, as it is put into effect over the next few years, disclose itself as a simple-to-follow procedure that other regions can adopt now, in the 1990s.

In addition to the newcomers to the countryside and old neighbors of the countryside who have been doing such stocktaking and reappreciating of open spaces and working landscapes, some of the original inhabitants of working landscapes in metropolitan areas—the farmers themselves—have been responding to post-interstate development pressures by standing firm and renewing their vows to the earth: celebrating the land they work with, recruiting new partners for these old partnership landscapes, and diversifying into an array of crops, such as prize-winning table wines, that convert the treasures of a landscape into a currency more familiar to city dwellers. For farmers anywhere close to New York City, this is almost a last-ditch stand, a final attempt to hold together a pattern stretched nearly to the breaking point. The future of the Klein farm in Queens, for instance, is more immediately threatened by events out on the East End of Long Island than it is by any changes within the city, because if the Kleins have to sell off their North Fork fields to developers, they

Eight percent of the landscapes of Rhode Island—including this farm on Betty Pucky Pond Road, Block Island, 7.5 miles offshore—have been catalogued as distinctive in the new *Rhode Island Landscape Inventory,* America's second statewide scenic assessment program. *Photograph courtesy of Elena Pascarella*

won't have a good-size cropland that's anywhere within trucking distance of their Fresh Meadows farm stand.

So far, thanks at least in part to the partnership action of some of the North Fork's farmers, and despite two new economic booms there and a recent environmental collapse, the North Fork—a narrow, tapered, eastward-pointing twenty-five-mile-long triangle of land—is still holding fast, and its farms are still the most productive farms in New York State, raising crops worth tens of millions of dollars annually. ("Despite" and "still" are two words that come up repeatedly in North Fork conversations nowadays.) A mid-eighties second-home boom—of waterfront-lot start-ups next to newly dredged marinas, and of four-hundred-thousand-dollar "custom homes" stuck out in the middle of big, flat fields—has been spilling up from Westhampton, Hampton Bays, Southampton, and East Hampton, the now crowded vacation villages down by the Atlantic Ocean, a few miles to the south, that had previously annexed such a great part of the South Fork's farmlands and woodlands and wetlands and dunes and beaches. Minimalls and commercial strips of franchise stores and used-car lots—the second boom—are proliferating on freshly bulldozed and asphalted sites on the outskirts of diminutive seventeenth- and eighteenth-century North Fork towns, obscuring old-time Main Street views of newly whitewashed picket fences and modest white clapboard or weathered shingle cottages flying outsize American flags.

Until only a few years ago, the North Fork was mostly two working landscapes side by side—one on the land and one in the water on either side of the land—and these two managed areas were jointly maintained by farming families and fishing families and a few families who did a bit of both. And there are natural landscapes on the North Fork, as well: saltwater creeks, beaches, sand flats, freshwater ponds, woods, marshes—a startling variety of terrains and habitats, considering how intensively used the expanses of open land and salt water have been down the years.

As recently as 1981, marine biologists marveled at the pristine state of the tidal waters that form the East End's Peconic system: Flanders Bay, Great Peconic Bay, Little Peconic Bay, Noyack Bay, and Gardiner's Bay—a linked sequence of shallow estuaries that separates the North Fork and the South Fork. The Peconic system produced large quantities of bay scallops, oysters, clams, mussels, weakfish, striped bass, and bluefish until the summer of 1985. Then, for the first time, a brown tide of algae covered the bay, killing off all the scallops, most of the oysters, and many of the fish, and ruining a number of multimillion-dollar shell-fishing and finfishing businesses. In the summers that followed, the brown tide returned, and although the bay has been clear

again for the last two summers, there are still no bay scallops in
Peconic Bay, and East End fish stocks are now probably about
a third of what they were just over five years ago. The number
of full-time baymen working the East End waters has declined
by at least fifty percent, and many of the remaining baymen "are
barely hanging on," according to Arnold Leo, the secretary of
a baymen's association on the South Fork.

These days, there is also heavier through traffic rumbling along
Route 25, the main east-west road of the North Fork and the
only direct paved connection between Orient Point and the Long
Island Expressway. Traffic has been increasing because New
York State now lets bigger ferryboats dock at Orient Point. For
over a century, there has been ferry service between the end of
the North Fork and New London, Connecticut, which is only
about fifteen miles northeast of Orient Point. In the past, the old
ferries brought manageable numbers of Connecticut day-trippers
and New England tourists down to the North Fork, but since the
end of the Second World War, when the new boats, with their
much higher car-carrying capacity, were put on the route, increasing numbers of long-distance New England drivers who
make frequent trips to New York City or places south of New
York—drivers who over the years have learned to loathe the almost constant congestion on Interstate 95, the Connecticut Turnpike—have started trying to save a few minutes on their overall
trip time by taking a left at New London across Long Island
Sound and using the alternate route south. And yet the land
component of the North Fork continues to function as a largely
intact working landscape, with a special and evolving partnership flavor all its own, and as a result, the North Fork has not
been suburbanized—which, I suppose, may simply mean that,
to use Paul Tsongas's phrase, it hasn't yet turned into Long
Island.

So there's still good news today on the North Fork, despite
everything, and one place you can hear about it is the front

porch of the Wickham farm, in Cutchogue, on Great Peconic Bay. Like the big house on the Klein farm in Fresh Meadows, the Wickhams' old farmhouse overlooks sloping land, and its front porch, like the front porch of the Klein house, has a small roof supported by two white columns, with two white wooden benches facing each other on either side of the front door. There is a more breathtaking view beyond the broad lawn in front of the Wickham house: a thick, low-growing orchard of semi-dwarf apple trees over on the right; a big, green-roofed barn straight ahead, with two little square cupolas perched on top; and, on the left, a glimpse of open water in the distance—Wickham's Creek, an inlet of the bay.

The Wickhams own 270 acres of land, and on 220 of these acres they raise twenty-two different crops—figures that don't begin to suggest the diversity and inventiveness of their undertakings. They grow at least seventy-five varieties of apples, and at least seventy-five types of peaches. When I met John Wickham, the eighty-two-year-old patriarch of the family, recently, and he invited me to sit down across from him on his front porch, I found myself thinking of old Adam Klein, a man who must have had the same kind of impressiveness John Wickham has. Wickham is a tall, strong, slow-speaking, white-haired, clear-eyed man who has remained trim. Except for Sunday mornings, when he goes to church, he wears high-topped working shoes and no socks, because that way, he says, his feet toughen up and then stay warmer in wintertime.

When you talk to John Wickham, you realize that on his farm every farming action furthers a number of interconnected partnership purposes at the same time. In the first place, Wickham says, working North Fork land is endlessly fascinating, and you feel privileged every day, because the rich soil and a protecting microclimate make it ideally suitable for agriculture, so that the land seems almost eager to be farmed. "The land is willing," Wickham says. "It's an irreplaceable situation. The soil is very,

very productive, and particularly here in Southold''—Cutchogue is one of the old villages within Southold, the main North Fork town—"where no place is more than a mile and a half from salt water, you can have two or three harvests a year and pick Brussels sprouts well into December. And, at least on our place, where we're fortunate enough to have a saltwater creek on either side of our fields, in the days when we used to grow cauliflowers, two years out of every three we could still take them out of the field for the Christmas market, and in one year out of every three they would keep growing for another week, and we could harvest them for the New Year's market.''

Wickham thinks of himself as only the most recent of fifteen or more generations of North Fork farmers—because Cutchogue was the site of extensive Indian squash, bean, and corn fields for perhaps hundreds of years before English families from the colony of New Haven began farming the same fields, in the 1640s. Plows turning over the soil out in the Wickhams' melon fields still occasionally bring up fragments of unglazed Indian pottery. Inside his house, Wickham gestured to an apple-size stone with scallop-shell markings that was sitting on a bookshelf—a stone of the sort that Cutchogue Indians had used to break open oyster shells. "Look what came up one day with a load of potatoes!" he said.

The Wickham family, down the years, has several times had to find new ways of remaining a part of the North Fork. The first Wickhams got to Cutchogue from the South Fork in 1698—John Wickham has a deed with that date on it hanging in the hall behind the front porch—and soon prospered. By the time of the American Revolution, they owned over two thousand acres of North Fork land, but all of it was taken away from them after the war, because the head of the family at the time, Parker Wickham, who was also supervisor of the town of Southold, was a loyalist sympathizer. "Just two families east of Brooklyn were tainted," Wickham says. "Both had large holdings, which were

entirely confiscated and auctioned off. The other family, like
most of the loyalists who were punished for their beliefs, reset-
tled in Nova Scotia, and their descendants live there today, but
the Wickhams chose another course. Parker Wickham himself
was banished to Connecticut by the New York State authorities,
but the rest of our family stayed on, partly because they always
felt that the confiscation had been engineered by local enemies
of Parker Wickham, who didn't care about his beliefs but used
them as an excuse to settle old scores. The family also stayed in
place because they had loyalties to the land and to the area that
went beyond their faithfulness to a lost political cause. The next
several generations worked on getting the land back.''

Their work was successful—the fields the Wickhams now farm
are only a few hundred yards east of the fields they had to sur-
render in 1783. Anne Wickham, John's wife, not too long ago
tried to explain to Steve Wick, a *Newsday* staff writer, how a
family's reasoning rearranges itself once it has established a
commitment to the land: ''John says a farm has to pay for itself
every generation if it is going to survive,'' she said. ''You have
to be able to buy the farm, essentially, if the next generation is
to continue.''

For North Fork farmers of John Wickham's generation, development pressures have added a special urgency to the job of
making a farm pay for itself, and third-generation Polish-
American and Irish-American farming families, as well as
longer-established farmers, like the Wickhams and the Lathams
and the Tuthills, have had to look hard to find new ways to keep
going, so that, as a number of them have said, they won't be
remembered as ''the generation that sold the land.'' For many
established North Fork farming families, this has meant getting
out of the potato business and the cauliflower business—the old
mainstays of the area—and starting to raise plants that can be
sold for higher prices. Some North Fork farmers now grow sod,
or ornamental shrubs such as rhododendron; some are growing

specialty crops, such as sorrel, baby carrots, and yellow cherry tomatoes, that they can sell directly to the public at their own farm stands; some have built greenhouses, so that they can grow year-round crops, such as potted geraniums, or springtime crops, such as early tomatoes. "You've got to keep broadening your base," John Wickham told me one fall. The Wickhams first put up a greenhouse when John Wickham was almost sixty, and they now grow thirty thousand pounds of hothouse tomatoes every year in two greenhouses before their field tomatoes get ripe, in July. And John Wickham told me he has found indoor tomatoes "fascinating plants—much more demanding than chrysanthemums or roses ever could be."

Other North Fork farmers have had a harder time adapting to new ways. "It's an emotional type of thing that means spring without spring plowing," William Talmage, a Riverhead farmer, told a *New York Times* Long Island reporter in 1988. Talmage's family went into the greenhouse-geranium business after raising potatoes for almost a hundred summers. "I try not to think it's a personal failure because other generations were able to grow potatoes and make money at it. But you have to know when to quit, and that day came for me when I saw that a five-pound bag of ice was selling for more than a five-pound bag of potatoes. That meant the water I was using to irrigate my fields was worth more than my crop." At the same time, Talmage thinks of himself as a success—or at least as an interim success. "I'm proud of what I've been able to bring about," Talmage said at one point in his interview. "Those three acres of greenhouse have paid my bills and preserved the rest of the farm." At another point, he said, "Our family has an unwritten moral. To use the land to make a living, and then pass it on. Maybe I'm not smart enough to grow food and make money at it, but maybe my son will be. What I can do is pay the taxes and support the family and buy time until the times change again." Talmage's idea is that each generation needs to make its own decisions and its own discoveries—which means that one of this generation's responsibilities is to see to it that the next generation will still have something left to discover.

Sometimes the changes that a North Fork farmer helps bring about buy time for people who are not blood relatives. John Wickham, for instance, served for years as chairman of the Southold Town Planning Board, and in the 1970s the board helped set up an innovative $21 million Suffolk County farmland-preservation program, the first of its kind in the country, which over the last decade has kept 6,500 acres of farmland—about a seventh of the remaining county farmland—in production by buying up what are called the development rights to the land. Essentially, the county strikes a bargain with farmers and pays them the difference between the price of the land as farmland and what a developer would be willing to pay for it. In return, the farmers agree never to develop their land, and anyone they sell to is bound by the same pledge. The county also agrees to continue taxing the farms as farmland. John Wickham enrolled in the county program early, putting more than half his land under development restrictions at a time when some of his neighbors were still wondering whether the program's only real purpose was to confiscate part of the value of their property. In more recent years, the town of Southold inaugurated a $2 million farmland-preservation program of its own. None too soon, it turns out: some land prices in Southold went up fifty percent during 1988 and 1989.

Twenty-five years ago, when John Wickham was already broadening his base, he planted a few table-grape vines because he had a hunch they might do well on the North Fork. The hunch was right: The grapes flourished immediately, and although table grapes have never become one of the largest Wickham crops, the Wickhams have kept on planting vines here and there ever since, and now have about seventy-five varieties of grapes growing on their land. Seventeen years ago, a young couple, Alex and Louisa Hargrave, who had an idea that they might like to start a business together as winemakers, happened to pay John Wickham a visit, heard him talk about the North Fork soil, the North Fork microclimate, and the North Fork growing season, and took a look at some of his grapevines. Alex Hargrave had been working in publishing, and he had a master's degree from Harvard in Chinese studies, but a back operation kept him off his feet for a number of months, and during his recuperation he and Louisa thought it would be enjoyable to find work that would keep them in the same place all day.

Soon after their call on the Wickhams, the Hargraves in 1973 bought a sixty-four-acre potato farm only a quarter of a mile from the Wickham farm. There they started planting vinifera grapes, the best European wine grapes, on a gently sloping forty-five-acre field, and opened the first commercial winery ever established on Long Island. The Hargraves released their first wines—a small bottling of Pinot Noir and Cabernet Sauvignon—in 1977. The early Hargrave wines were a quick success, winning medals at various New York fairs and tastings, and getting such a warm welcome from wine writers that other farmers—and even a few investors—started taking an interest in Long Island winemaking. Some international wine experts are already calling the area "one of the most promising viticultural areas in the United States," and others suspect that, after seven hundred years under cultivation, the North Fork may now have found its true identity as a working landscape—as a world-class wine-growing region that has a striking resemblance both to the Napa Valley in California and to the Bordeaux vineyards in France. This year, there are twelve wineries and twenty-five vineyards and more than a thousand acres of grapes on the East End of Long Island, almost all of them on the North Fork but only some of them on land already protected by Suffolk County's farmland-preservation program.

So the future of the area as a winemaking region is not yet

secure. Michael Zweig, an economist who teaches at the State University of New York at Stony Brook and has studied Long Island's wine industry, thinks that existing North Fork farmland-preservation programs, if they are "expanded and combined with large-lot zoning" of twenty-five acres or more, can protect agriculture in the area. "Wine grapes are a prime example of a new and economically viable direction for East End farming, although potatoes and other traditional crops will continue to be important as well," Zweig wrote in a recent report for the Southold town board and the Suffolk County Industrial Development Agency. Potatoes, he says, are actually making a comeback; three years ago, thanks to higher prices in the market, there was "a slight increase in potato acreage" on Long Island. But it is the wine industry that Zweig finds the "most promising." And he is willing to make an unusual claim. "The process which has so totally transformed the rest of Long Island in recent decades need not be repeated" on the East End, now that an alternative process is available, he declares. "Usually, the term 'developer' has connoted suburban residential, industrial, or commercial development, as though those economic activities were the only forms of progress," Zweig says. "On the East End, development can be driven by agriculture instead."

Several things will have to happen before Zweig's prediction can be realized. David Mudd, who is a North Fork vineyard manager, thinks the Long Island wine industry will gain a sound economic footing only after five or six thousand acres have been planted with grapes—three or four times as many as are planted with them at the moment. And with that many more grapevines to look after and to harvest, the area will have to attract a larger number of professionally trained farmers to serve as vineyard managers and winemakers. A number of the winemakers now working on the North Fork have degrees in enology from the University of California's campus at Davis, where winemaking is studied as an exact chemical science. Davis is only about forty miles east of the Napa Valley. The only academic program in enology offered in New York State at the moment is upstate, at Cornell. Zweig has suggested that the North Fork base its economy solely on three working-landscape-related industries: agriculture, fishing, and tourism. Conventional commercial and residential development will only endanger the health of the three primary businesses, he says. He wants to see Southold establish a nine-thousand-acre "agricultural district," from which any other business would be rigorously excluded. "The rural character of the area is slipping away," Zweig has said. "Yet it is exactly a rural character that will attract, and then be sustained by, grape growing for premium wineries."

Ronnie Wacker, the president of the North Fork Environmental Council, warns that there is still no agreement on the North Fork about a number of key issues. Scientists are still debating whether the brown tide in Peconic Bay is a natural phenomenon or a result of pollution. There is also disagreement about the carrying capacity of the North Fork's aquifer, its sole source of fresh water. Although the municipal water-supply system of the North Fork is dangerously tainted with fertilizer runoffs, relies on old pumps, and draws from a source whose size no one really knows, Suffolk County four years ago ordered the village of Greenport to hook up new housing developments to the old system. "On the North Fork, we have just a single lens of fresh water," according to a trustee of the Greenport village board, David Kapell. "It's not like up west, where they can drill to a lower aquifer. If we go any lower, we hit salt. What I'm thinking about is that one hot July day when everybody is out here and they all turn on the water at once—and a pump breaks down."

Meanwhile, as Ronnie Wacker points out, the town board of Riverhead has approved three new construction projects along Saw Mill Creek, a two-and-a-half-mile-long freshwater wetlands system, emptying into Flanders Bay: Bridgewater Estates, to consist of 162 condominium units and two office towers; Mill

Pond Commons, to consist of 100 condominium units; and the
Cross River Project, to consist of at least 380 condominium
units; and has yet to vote on two more developments proposed
for Saw Mill Creek, among them Peconic Park, a six-story hotel
and convention center, and East End Commons, a shopping
complex with three department stores. And there are well over
a hundred subdivision proposals pending in Southold. The North
Fork Environmental Council, through its Legal Defense Fund,
is now suing the Southold town board for having adopted new
zoning ordinances that fail to protect the town's most sensitive
waterfront areas and that, according to the council, will inevitably kill farming, fishing, and tourism in the town.

And the entire North Fork community, Wacker would argue,
has one paramount job to take on: protecting the public value—
the "rural character," as Zweig calls the partnership sense of
the place—that generations of villagers, baymen, and farmers
have added, and are still adding, to the landscape that now sup-
ports and enfolds all the people of the area. Creating public
value, Wacker says, is the only uninterrupted business venture
the North Fork has ever known, and now the North Fork needs
to devise a strategy for managing the future growth of its public
value.

———

Even while the first post-interstate boom is still accelerating,
many regionalists have gained an almost Wickham-like buoyancy after discovering that the coexistence of city and countryside—meaning both working countryside and natural
countryside—in a single area is easier to bring about than we
used to assume. If we're having to learn, that is, that no place
is automatically immune from development pressures these days,
we're also finding out that no place need ever be inevitably overwhelmed by development. Part of the learning process has to do

with getting a better understanding of the nature of development by looking at it carefully over a period of time. What you find when you do this is that because development does cluster around the transportation and energy systems in a place—and, more specifically, around those parts of the infrastructure that are considered modern in any particular period—development pressures tend to have an uneven impact, producing overwhelming changes in one spot and none at all in a spot a mile or two away. For instance, there's the countryside opportunity presented by the Blackstone River Valley, between Worcester, Massachusetts, and Providence, Rhode Island—an area that happens to be one of Robert Bendick's favorite places in the world. (Bendick was the planning director of Woonsocket, an old Rhode Island industrial city on the Blackstone, north of Providence, before moving on to the state's Department of Environmental Management.)

The Blackstone River Valley, which is forty-three miles long and only a couple of miles wide—the river runs between two parallel ridges of hills on its way from Worcester to Narragansett Bay—was the first area in North America to be industrialized. Beginning in the 1790s, several decades before steam engines came into general use in this country, a succession of cotton mills was set up along the Blackstone—huge mills that used the waterfalls on the river to keep giant waterwheels turning with enough force to power their looms. The northern stretch of the river, the Massachusetts part, which is bordered by large and spectacular wetlands, stayed mostly undeveloped, but in Rhode Island, mill villages dotted the hillsides. A canal was dug in the valley floor, on a course that ran parallel to the river, so that finished goods could be shipped downstream. Every town on the river was supported by a mill, and every waterfall on the river had a mill next to it, but even within this heavily industrialized corridor, development had only local effects on the landscape; any area that was beyond walking distance or out of range of a canal barge stayed as it had been.

Almost two hundred years later, the textile industry has abandoned the mills, but the hillside mill towns are still vital and serve as bedroom communities for both Providence and Boston as well as Worcester and Woonsocket. Mid-twentieth-century industrial pollution in the cities along the Blackstone fouled the river's waters, but since the early seventies the states have spent $150 million to make the river clean again. An expressway from Providence to Woonsocket, which runs about two miles west of the Blackstone, is bringing a lot of new residential development to the ridge of hills just west of the river valley, but much of the valley itself is almost remote these days, almost a wilderness: Between the villages and cities there are heavily wooded pockets, with a few old bottomland and hillside farms; the air smells sweet and stays cool all summer long, even when temperatures are soaring in Providence and Woonsocket; visitors find that they can't see any of the new development beyond the hilltops; and it's so quiet in these wild parts of the valley that the loudest noises are made by the waterfalls. Down there, Bendick says, you can't help realizing that human changes are often not as durable as we intend them to be and that natural forces, left to themselves, prove to have a resilience and a regenerative power we often don't suspect.

A freight railroad, the Providence & Worcester, has tracks running through the Blackstone River Valley, and several two-lane roads run into the valley—each comes down one of the hills on one side, crosses a narrow bridge, passes an old mill, and goes up the other side—but no continuous road has ever been built down the length of it, and if you don't have friends who work for the P. & W., the only way to get from one end of the Blackstone River Valley to the other is by canoe. And the valley, though it is surrounded by an almost unparalleled development boom, of far greater intensity than the mill boom that began two hundred years ago, has become almost an invisible place and is now practically unknown to its neighbors in the once poor and now prosperous countryside next door. Development, then, can be self-focusing and can have an impact on people's mental maps of the landscapes near them even when it leaves the landscapes themselves untouched.

Bendick began to use his discovery about development impacts, along with two other new pieces of information about landscape use, to open up the Blackstone River Valley for local recreational use and, at the same time, to initiate a change in regional and national recreational habits. While he was working on the New England Governors' Conference's list of special places throughout the six New England states, it became obvious to Bendick that many of these places were already part of "use patterns" that had become truly regional in scope. "Nearly everyone in New England, if you ask him to name a favorite area for skiing, or for hiking, or for looking at autumn leaves, will mention Vermont's Green Mountains, either right away or after a minute or two," he says. "And other, equally well-known scenic areas, such as Acadia National Park, in Maine, or the Presidential Range of the White Mountains, are now getting such overwhelming use, and the volume of people using them compared with the number of acres available is so staggering, that you just can't conceive of how to deal with it all. Except, perhaps, by siphoning a bit off here and there and rearranging things to make the East Coast a bit more like the West Coast and the mountain states, so that adventures outdoors in this part of the country are not so far away anymore from our own front doors.

"Rhode Island has already started to build a fourteen-mile bicycle path along the Blackstone River, which will bring people into the area, and they're also working with Massachusetts parks people and with the National Park Service on projects they're thinking about. The Park Service is involved because four years ago Congress designated the entire Blackstone River Valley a National Heritage Corridor, which doesn't make the area a national park or a federal property but does mean that the national government is willing to try to coordinate the thinking of the two states and the twenty local communities involved. But what I've had in the back of my mind is bringing east a successful Colorado white-water experiment known as rapids enhancement, which had to do with increasing the rate of flow in a river near Denver by moving some of the rocks around, to make the river more exhilarating for canoers and kayakers."

Bendick goes on: "People get itchy to get out of the house and into an encounter with the countryside, and if nothing has been provided for them nearby, they'll go travel some distance. But when they're given the choice, they'll usually stay in their own area. If we could provide mini-adventures in and near the major New England cities, we could take some of the pressure off the Green Mountains and the White Mountains, and also off the special places outside New England that draw a national or an international crowd, such as the Grand Canyon or, closer to home, New York State's great wilderness park, the Adirondack Park—the largest American park in the first forty-eight states. The Grand Canyon had three and a half million visitors in 1987 and nearly four million visitors in 1988—a ten percent increase in just one year, although it seems to have leveled off in 1989. There's a five-year waiting list for private rafting trips through the Grand Canyon, and when you do get a chance to ride the rapids out there, you find chartered airplanes and helicopters roaring overhead almost all day long.

"If New Englanders can spend their weekends outdoors in their own home towns, they can save the Green Mountains for a longer trip and the Adirondacks for a special occasion. And if families from New England and New York and Pennsylvania and Quebec and Ontario who cherish the wilderness qualities of the Adirondacks found themselves making just two fewer visits there every year, because now they had wilderness connections in their own landscapes, we would be in a position to preserve that huge wilderness from the development booms that will begin after the present boom has exhausted itself.''

Twenty-two years ago, William H. Whyte noticed a facet, or quirk, of people's ordinary perceptions about development in the countryside—a seemingly built-in tendency closely related to Bendick's discovery about the cloak of invisibility that development sometimes casts over adjacent landscapes. Whyte's name for this phenomenon was "tremendous trifles." He thought that it opened up great opportunities for protecting natural landscapes and working landscapes, because simply by changing the focus of people's attention you could make it clear to them, even during a development boom, that there is considerably more countryside at hand than they thought. Where Bendick saw development pulling people's attention away from any piece of countryside out of the reach of the transportation infrastructure, Whyte saw that people also start to discount a landscape, and lose their sense of connectedness to it, as soon as even a few blemishes crop up. In other words, you can make people look away either by not calling attention to yourself at all or by having a spot on your sweater.

Albert F. Appleton, New York City's Environmental Protection Commissioner, has even come up with a rough mathematical formula to measure landscape degradation: "The first five percent of development in a countryside region generally does fifty percent of the damage, in terms of altering people's mental geography of an area," he says. "And the second five percent of development enlarges this damage by another fifty percent. The environmental damage caused by the first development in a region varies tremendously from place to place, depending on the nature of the terrain and the kind of development involved, but the disproportionate initial-impact formula seems to apply across the board."

The precise numbers might change from one boom to the next, but there was also welcome news here, Whyte thought.

"In these disproportions lie great opportunities," he wrote. "If relatively small elements of the scene have such a leverage effect, relatively small actions can, too. A scenic clearing to open up a meadow, a row of sycamores planted along a river bank, a screen of signs removed at the crest of a hill: individually, such projects seem trivial." But taken together, "these tremendous trifles can have a major impact on the environment."

It's all a matter of dovetailing uses so that they're brought closer together in an area without diminishing its public value. For instance, as Whyte explains, "open space . . . and the effect of open space are not quite the same, and . . . effect is more important." The public value of a place gets maintained by treating cause and effect as separate variables—so that "the more crowded landscape of tomorrow can be made more pleasing, more expansive, more green, than the relatively more open one of today. No technological breakthrough is necessary—the spade and the saw have been invented. What is necessary is a systematic effort by communities to look at their landscapes—as most people see them most of the time." What every community needs, in other words, is a systematic assessment of its own landscape character, an inventory of the connectedness it has—and of any broken connections that need mending. Working with the "tremendous trifles—the brook by the side of the road you do not see for the second growth, the wall that hides the skyline," Whyte warned, might not seem like "the grand-sweep approach to regional design," but it's the job that awaits us, because "in the aggregate, it is the host of small pictures and the perception of them that is, for people, the true regional design."

What might a greener and more pleasing but more crowded natural landscape or working landscape look like? The easiest way to find out, according to Richard R. Gardner, a land-use expert with the National Oceanic and Atmospheric Administration, in Washington, who has an intimate knowledge of many

of the backcountry roads in the mid-Atlantic states, is to go see
one that already exists; and Gardner, after some systematic wan-
dering, has found a Pennsylvania landscape of tomorrow—or, at
least, a fraction of one—in southern Lancaster County: a stretch
of working landscape where, more than eighty years ago, a hulking new piece of transportation infrastructure was installed in a
way that respects small pictures and ordinary perceptions. The
place is a pretty little valley of farms—most of the farmers are
Old Order Amish—about ten miles long, running east to west,
and about a mile wide, and most outsiders don't know it, because it's about ten miles south of the principal Amish settlements in the region. And many of the visitors it does get don't
notice its secret, so cleverly have the small pictures been constructed. Gardner himself came across the place only because
he invented a hobby several years ago, which was to get in his
car on a weekend or a few days off and head for New York City
but try to make the entire 237-mile trip over a route pieced
together solely out of two-lane rural roads. The goal was never
to get onto a major highway. So far, he has been able to track
down half a dozen rural routes through the Northeast Corridor
that have only a few gaps in them, and recently he offered to
drive me out to the unknown valley so I could see it for myself.

The valley, whose official name seems to be Valley—the
stream that runs through it is called Valley Run, and the road
that parallels the stream is called Valley Road—has the small
town of Quarryville at its west end and the smaller town of
Christiana at its east end. Most of its land is sloping meadows
and cornfields and pastures, framed by two gentle waves rolling
across a calm, green sea of landscape—that is, there are rounded
hills to the north, then a smooth dip down to the valley floor,
and then an equally effortless bobbing up toward the same kind
of rounded hills to the south. There are a few groves of trees,
some long hedgerows, and several big white barns. When Gardner pulled his car over to the side of the road, we were both

struck by the quiet of the place and by the timelessness it evoked. Since most of the Old Order Amish have never started using cars or tractors, there was almost no machinery to listen to; and since most of them also don't use electricity, there were no electric poles or telephone poles along many of the two-lane roads that cross the valley. The roads are paved, but otherwise the valley still looks much the way it has since German farmers first settled here, in the first part of the eighteenth century. Occasionally, an Amish horse and buggy passes by.

Gardner, who has something of a magician's flair, drove on and then stopped again, without saying anything, a few feet from one of the long hedgerows. We were close to a small bridge, which, I assumed, crossed the Valley Run. We still hadn't seen anything that hinted at the presence of any major public works projects. Gardner stretched, strolled out onto the bridge, and leaned his arms on a steel guardrail at one side. When I joined him and looked down, I was jarred to find myself staring at a wide, well-maintained two-track freight-railroad right-of-way running along a deep, straight cut in the ground eighteen feet below the bridge. What I had thought was a hedgerow was in fact a line of trees that had been planted to conceal the lip of the cut and two rows of tall utility towers flanking the tracks. These trees made such an effective screen that as soon as I stepped off the bridge and walked a few feet down the road, I was no longer aware of being anywhere near a railroad.

Back on the bridge, Gardner began telling me about this concealed railroad—the Low Grade Line, as it's called, one of the most ambitious construction projects ever undertaken by the old Pennsylvania Railroad. "The Low Grade Line was part of the master plan for the railroad mapped out in its glory days at the turn of the century by its greatest president, A. J. Cassatt, whose younger sister was Mary Cassatt, the painter," Gardner said. "It was A. J. Cassatt who built the original Penn Station in Manhattan, which gave greatness to the Pennsy as a passenger railroad. And the Low Grade Line, as he conceived it, would have transformed the freight end of the business as well, taking freight trains off the steep grades of the heavily used and circuitous main-line tracks.''

In Cassatt's grand design for the Low Grade Line, no curve between New York and Chicago would ever be sharper than two degrees and no slope steeper than one degree, and the entire line would be completely grade-separated. The Pennsylvania leg of the line was built, and so was a second section, in Ohio, both of them running over fairly level ground, but Cassatt died before the next part of the project, which would have involved tunneling through the Alleghenies, could get started, and in later years the whole enterprise was postponed and finally shelved.

As Gardner told the story to me, "The great achievement of the Low Grade Line is a railroad that is practically a straight line and almost a flat plane, and never comes into direct contact with other types of vehicles, because all the roads and highways that meet it pass either over it or under it, on bridges or through tunnels. The existing Pennsylvania segment of the Low Grade Line is now owned by Conrail, and the first consequence of that change in management was to make the Low Grade Line not quite as good a neighbor to the Amish as it once was, because Conrail, to save on operating costs, deelectrified the line and began running diesels through the valley. You still never saw a train in the valley, but for the first time you could hear it roaring toward you and past you—a sound that, once it has passed, only gradually dies away in the distance. Of course, for Conrail managers the landscape has never been a full partner in their business plans, and Conrail has recently stopped running any trains across the Low Grade Line, and has now filed plans to abandon it altogether. It may continue to have a place in the valley, however, because Lancaster County officials who have a strong interest in landscape management are working to see whether the county can acquire thirty-five miles of the line as a greenway—

a hiking and biking trail that could also be used for horseback riding and cross-country skiing.''

———————

Shortly after my trip to the forgotten valley, Jim Riggle, director of operations for the American Farmland Trust, a national non-profit organization devoted to preserving working landscapes around the country, told me he may have to start taking Pennsylvanians on field trips to the Low Grade Line—so that today's road builders will know what an invisible incision in a working landscape actually looks like. In 1988, the AFT was part of a fierce battle about how to change the transportation infrastructure of central Lancaster County, only five miles north of the Low Grade Line. Thanks to the Amish and the careful farming practices of the other Pennsylvania Dutch farming families in the area, the agricultural industry is Lancaster County's biggest business, which every year produces farm goods worth almost three quarters of a billion dollars—and tourism is almost as big an industry, because so many people want to come see the landscape the German farmers have created. ''In two hundred and fifty years,'' Riggle says, ''these farmers have built up an absolutely incredible tilth, as we call it, in this area—meaning that the land there is now far more productive than it was before cultivation began.'' But Lancaster County is also a developing urban area that's only an hour's drive west of Philadelphia. There are now endless traffic problems on the main road through the area—the old two-lane Lincoln Highway, U.S. Route 30, which, back before the Second World War, was the first coast-to-coast federal highway built in this country. According to Riggle, this road, the main link between the city of Lancaster and the farmland around it, has also served as an Amish distribution network for more than half a century: Satellite Amish farming communities that have been set up in Ohio, Iowa, and Illinois are all within striking distance of the alignment of Route 30.

"Everyone in Pennsylvania," Riggle says, "thinks that a new road is necessary, and a while ago the engineers at PennDOT, the Pennsylvania Department of Transportation—this kind of planning is done at the state level—prepared a map that displayed twelve alternate routes for the new road: They stretched across the county almost like guitar strings. The trouble came when they made their final choice—a four-lane controlled-access expressway that would have cut right through the heart of the best farmland, severing the Amish community, paving over the tilth, and pushing up land prices from about four thousand dollars an acre, which is an agricultural value, to perhaps twenty or thirty thousand dollars an acre, which is a residential and commercial price. The changing economics would probably have been the death knell of the Amish community, because even the best husbandmen can't produce enough to buy land at those prices."

Riggle says that the PennDOT engineers, when they made their disastrous choice, were actually trying to be responsive to environmental concerns. As he explains it: "Section 4-F of the United States Transportation Code, drawn up in 1966, soon after the first national alarms had been sounded about the country's deteriorating environment, virtually bars any new highway construction on parkland, on wetlands, and on wildlife habitats. What nobody thought about at the time was that by adopting only these restrictions, Section 4-F in effect literally directed transportation engineers to build all future highways on the best farmland—which is predominantly flat, and so cheap to build on anyway, and isn't wet, because it drains well, and doesn't have too much wildlife, because farming activities have chased many animals away. Fortunately, existing laws also direct PennDOT to hold a series of 'scoping meetings' in an area where a highway is projected, to address any local concerns about the impacts that a new road will bring. The Amish, traditionally, do not participate in the public process; but in 1988, on the night of the Lancaster County scoping meeting, more than a thousand

Old Order Amish drove their buggies to the meeting hall and expressed their concern by simply sitting quietly in the audience in their black homespun suits while testimony was taken. The silent eloquence of their unprecedented turnout produced a dramatic impact of its own—a short time later, Pennsylvania's governor, Robert Casey, announced that he had ordered the Pennsylvania Department of Transportation to abandon work on the proposed alignment for the new road and to find a more suitable alternative. So now there's an opportunity to build a road in partnership with the existing landscape.

"Today's highway engineers have not yet been trained to look at, or even to recognize, whole landscapes, but there are several encouraging new developments: PennDOT's environmental impact study of the new highway has now been expanded to include a $713,430 cultural impact assessment of how the road will affect the Amish community. For almost a generation now, highway engineers have paid attention to monuments left behind by vanished cultures—Interstate 55, for example, was rerouted around Collinsville, Illinois, to avoid cutting through Cahokia Mounds, the site of a major American Indian metropolis that may date back eight thousand years. But PennDOT's new study is the first time a state transportation department has ever looked into the question of how a work of engineering will alter a way of life with the idea of actually protecting an ongoing, living culture. At the same time, Lancaster County officials are working to see if they can get the new road designated as the country's first National Agricultural Scenic Highway, which would make federal funds available for preserving some of the best Lancaster County farmland."

If Carole Neidich-Ryder can make her passion a reality, recognizing landscapes could become an easier task in a few years.

Neidich-Ryder, who is a biologist on the staff of the Nassau
County Recreation and Parks Department, on Long Island, and
lives in a Levitt-built house in Hicksville, thinks that an opportunity now exists—by combining the established habits of her
suburban neighbors, the landscape suggestions coming from a
new school of American landscape designers known as the naturalizers, and some pioneering golf course designs created by
Karl Grohs, a West German landscape architect—to reconstitute
the outlines of a lost landscape: the sixty-thousand-acre built-
over Long Island prairie that used to be called the Hempstead
Plains. "I have some very radical ideas," she says, "but I think
it makes sense for everyone to pick one thing to fight over, and
I've been living on the Plains since I was three, so I already
know what they can do for people."

Officially, the Hempstead Plains are not quite a lost landscape, because there is now a sixty-acre Hempstead Plains preserve adjacent to the Nassau Coliseum, and in addition, there is
a nineteen-acre tract on the grounds of Nassau Community College that, biologically, has been determined to be a remnant of
the Plains—though if you're not a grasslands expert it looks like
just one more weedy, shrubby, overgrown Long Island lot.
Neidich-Ryder wants to see both preserves fully restored. That
means bringing back all the wildflowers that have disappeared
and removing all the invasive shrubbery. But that's only the preliminary part of her plan. "There has always been a tremendous
amount of open land in the Long Island suburbs—golf courses,
campuses, and, in Levittown, a front yard and a back yard for
every house," she says. "That's one part of it. Of course, all
this land has traditionally had to have a distinctive look. Golf
courses, for instance, with their sand traps and ornamental lakes,
are fictionalized re-creations of the seacoast of Scotland, the
region where the game was first played. And there are laws in
most communities about how high the grass can grow in people's yards—usually four inches, or eight inches at the most. It

used to be thought that an unkempt lawn meant that a property was being neglected, which made it a threat to real estate values in the area.

"But the naturalizers, who are interested in saving the botanical heritage of different regions of the country, have recently demonstrated, first, that it costs a lot more to grow an imported species of ornamental grass than it does to raise the grasses that are natural to an area—grasses that are looked down on as ordinary old things but are part of the plant community that originally evolved successfully in that place. And the naturalizers have also shown that people get a lot more enjoyment out of looking after a taller lawn filled with wildflowers that change with the season. Karl Grohs, in Essen, West Germany, has been making the same discovery about golf courses—the game itself is played on only about thirty percent of the land set aside for it, so there's plenty of room for the designer to make changes without obstructing the golfers. The tees and the greens are sacrosanct, of course, but when the rest of a *Golfplatz* is 'renatured,' as he says—that is, planted to be continuous with the existing landscape of an area—the game gets more exciting, because you're never in the same place twice when you play among surroundings that change from day to day. At least, that's what people tell him after they've played one of his courses, such as the new championship course in Düsseldorf, where the German Open is now held every third year. The first question a golf course designer must ask, Grohs says, is not how many strokes to make a hole but what kinds of birds it should have, and what kinds of amphibians."

Neidich-Ryder thinks that Nassau County people could easily enough be brought around to the idea of welcoming home the Plains. "Now, I haven't yet talked to many Long Island golfers," she says. "But I know my neighbors, and that makes me think that out here we're ready to give a great number of our open acres back to the Plains. That's because in the suburbs, front lawns are not for use. Using your front lawn is something you might do in the city, where you don't have enough space, and have to use every inch that's yours. In Nassau County, the back yard is where you live—it's where the kids play, it's where the barbecue is, it's where you hang the laundry out to dry—and the front yard's only purpose is to look beautiful and show off the house. We live the same way indoors: We keep the living room clean and watch TV in the den. To me, this means that almost half the land in Levittown is available to the Plains—as long as the grasses and the wildflowers don't grow too tall and hide the houses that we want you to see.

"And there's a reason for all this that goes beyond beauty and delight and not having to spend as much money or take care of the lawn as often. And that is that we now know that the Plains have an ecological function we didn't know about before: They are the grass roof over and the principal component of the underground aquifer that supplies drinking water to all the towns in the county. We're all one family when we turn on the faucet, and I think that having the Plains outside again will start making it easier for me and my neighbors in Hicksville to realize that the people to the east of us, in Bethpage, are drinking what we drink, and we're drinking what the people up north in Jericho are drinking, and anything I pour into the water here will reappear in the houses down in Bellmore, six or seven miles south. This is something all my neighbors have always really wanted to know more about—after all, we came out here to have clean air and clean water. And it's ours. It just turns out that as rooftop dwellers, we have to do our chores. And the chores turn out to include *not* mowing the lawn, and learning to live more lightly on the Plains."

8 Creating Public Value

Landscapes, in the view of some land-use experts, interested in a regional approach to development, are now showing themselves to be a cake that you can eat and have too. People can build on a landscape, that is, without eating away at it. All this seems to take, as the new regionalists have pointed out, is a simple, slight shift in the way people look at a place; then, almost abruptly, they can notice areas nearby that still present a countryside sense of kinship, or partnership, or community and companionability.

In fact, people are finding such a variety of opportunities for landscape connectedness that some regionalists have started to ask themselves why it is that a "both/and" sense about landscapes—the idea that places can change within an overall context of continuity—is only now becoming widespread. These regionalists are beginning to think that the opposite point of view—an "either/or" approach to landscapes—was an early by-product of the environmental and social dislocations created during the first years of the industrial revolution, two hundred years ago, and that ever since, often without realizing it, Western Europeans and Americans have been carrying around with them as part of their mental baggage a deeply felt and despairing assumption that progress demands degraded surroundings. You put up with such surroundings as long as you have to, and you run away from them as soon as you can afford to; but, this belief has it, deteriorated landscapes and debased communities and bad smells and hideous noises are simply a given—something we all have to live with.

In a book called *Placeways: A Theory of the Human Environment*, published in 1988, Eugene Victor Walter, a retired professor of sociology who taught at the Harvard Medical School and Boston University, looks at the interactions of people and places, and demonstrates that slums are a late-eighteenth-century phenomenon, brought on by the change of thinking that accompanied the industrial revolution. A new idea about places took over (a "new topistic ideal," he calls it), and it became acceptable "to segregate good and bad experience, locating wealth and illth in separate spaces." ("Illth" is his word for poverty and ill health.)

Walter's work confirms earlier social-geography studies by the architect and planner Clarence S. Stein, who served as chairman of the New York State Commission of Housing and Regional Planning in the 1920s. In a 1925 article in *Survey Graphic* titled "Dinosaur Cities," Stein noted that New York City's first housing shortage and slum areas appeared in downtown Manhattan during the 1830s, when the city was in the middle of its first great development boom and population explosion, brought on by the opening of the Erie Canal, in 1825. Manhattan had 124,000 residents in 1820 and nearly triple that number in 1840, and the only response of the city's prosperous families to the new industries and the new immigrants was to move away, in a series of hops, one every generation, "proceeding up the length of Manhattan Island," an associate of Stein's wrote, "and submerging in time the quaint little colonial villages of Greenwich, Chelsea, and Harlem."

Imposing New York City residential neighborhoods were thrown together—almost overnight, it seemed—on top of old fields and pastures. And only a few doors down from the rows of new houses, you could expect to find elegant new stone churches: Their serene, lofty spires created a new skyline, which looked as though it might last for centuries. Across the street from the houses and the churches you might find yourself stepping into a meticulously maintained new private park, such as St. John's Park (close to where the entrance to the Holland Tunnel is now)—"a spot of Eden loveliness and exclusiveness," as it was called in the 1840s. That park was enclosed by a cast-iron fence, laid out with gravel paths, and planted with flower beds and specimen trees, which, according to Charles Lockwood, a New York architectural historian, included catalpas, cottonwoods, horse chestnuts, and silver birches. But such neighborhoods proved ephemeral, no more than elaborate tent camps along an inexorable and restless flight to the north. In 1866, Cornelius Vanderbilt bought St. John's Park for a railroad freight depot, and today all traces of that building, too, have disappeared. But, as Clarence Stein pointed out, one of the consequences of running away from the problem rather than solving it was that New York "never caught up with its original shortage" of housing and settled instead for a permanent state of crisis—a state that eventually began to seem a natural condition.

By now, people in this country have been subjected to so many landscape upheavals that the both / and idea about landscapes—that new uses can always find a way of working together with longtime partnership uses—may sound at first like wishful thinking or, at best, a dubious oddity of some sort, as if the Klein farm's linking together of modern New York City and old rural Flushing were just a gimmick or a happenstance or a tourist attraction.

Recent work in a number of research fields, such as education and health care, has been advancing the regionalist approach by making it clear that certain essential human activities, including both learning and healing, can be enhanced when they take place in a setting that offers people countryside connections in addition to the support systems already in place. In the next few years, it will be possible to see what some familiar small-scale institutional settings will look like once they've been recountrified, so to speak. In some ways, oddly, they will resemble certain very early photographs of New York City, taken in the mid-1850s. In England, a three-year-old national research program—the Learning Through Landscapes Project—is under way to investigate how schools can restructure a number of paved and windswept schoolyards to give them a country look and so provide "a complete environment for learning." The idea is that "the landscape in which the school stands . . . can provide a rich and stimulating resource and setting . . . for learning and teaching."

The study is based on a number of modern research findings, such as a UNESCO survey of children's needs, which was written about by the late urban planner Kevin Lynch. In the UNESCO study, summarized in the book *Growing Up in Cities,* Lynch compiled interviews with children from Argentina, Australia, Mexico, and Poland about their reactions to their surroundings and found that no matter where they came from—it might be an inner-city neighborhood, a provincial capital, or a rural village—"the hunger for trees is outspoken and seemingly universal."

Another modern researcher, Colin Ward, the education officer for the Town and Country Planning Association, in London, has written that "the rural needs of the urban child are not just the sights of the farm or the pleasures of running untrammelled through the woods or exploring the country park. They include vital personal experiences and discoveries like silence, solitude, and the sensation of utter darkness." Neglecting children's rural needs, according to Roger Hart, director of the Children's Environment Research Group at the City University of New York, can impair their healthy development as adults. "Part of being a responsible adult is having a sense of responsibility for the environment," he says. "And you can only care for something you've grown to feel a part of."

The Learning Through Landscapes Project also represents, according to some observers, part of a belated attempt to put into practice a previously ignored countryside component of the educational teachings of the nineteenth-century German educator Friedrich Froebel, who is best remembered in this country as the inventor of the kindergarten—"an environment in which children grew freely, like plants in a garden," he said. Although in Prussia in the 1850s kindergartens were banished for nine years as subversive institutions, they have since flourished throughout the world—without, for the most part, a countryside setting. But according to Froebel, children need more than toys, games, music, dedicated teachers, and a pleasant classroom in which to develop their intellects and their feelings.

In Froebel's formulation, which was based in part on the many days he spent outdoors as a child—his stepmother had no time for him—people are created both as wholes and as parts—that is, they have to learn how to function both as separate individuals and as participants in larger patterns that include harmonious relationships with other people and with all of life. And, Froebel asserted, it was only outdoors that a person could learn empathy with the rest of creation: "On the first spring day [when] the shining sun beckons through the window and the clear blue sky is seen through it, the doors open as if of themselves," he wrote, and kindergarten children, once they are out on a nature walk, not only are immediately open to the "new observations and perceptions for which God's free world offers occasions" but also notice within themselves "increased feelings of life"—sensations that serve as powerful positive reinforcement for closely observing nature and opening up to it. Froebel also thought that nature study, and all the other pleasurable activities of kindergarten life as well, should form part of the curriculum of higher schools: "Possibly our sons may thereby finish school life a year or two later; but is it not better that they should thereby attain a worthy aim than . . . an illusory one?''

Writing a few years after Froebel, Frederick Law Olmsted, according to his biographer Albert Fein, suggested that college campuses also needed to be thought of as a ''total environment'' and proposed that if campus buildings were set around a common open space, like the town green in a New England village, this would foster a social connectedness that would exert ''an incalculable effect on future attitudes.'' By the time Olmsted began working on college designs—including fragrant and visually complex plantings in the grounds of Gallaudet University, in Washington, a college for deaf students—New York City had turned away from such notions, and Columbia College had been squeezed into a cluster of institutional buildings in midtown, on Madison Avenue. An old photograph I have seen shows the original, late-eighteenth- and early-nineteenth-century campus of Columbia College when it was way downtown in Manhattan, a couple of blocks southwest of City Hall. In the picture, taken by a former president of the college in 1854, the trees are not in leaf, but still you can barely see the main building, because the elms on the green in front of the old structure are so thickly crowded together.

The ideas in a celebrated 1984 study by Roger S. Ulrich, a University of Delaware geography professor, ''View Through a Window May Influence Recovery from Surgery,'' published in *Science,* have been incorporated into the design of a hospital in Newport, on the Isle of Wight, in southern England. Professor Ulrich, who is now at Texas A & M's College of Architecture, found that over a nine-year period, gallbladder patients who could see a cluster of trees instead of a brick wall outside their hospital window ''had shorter post-operative stays'' and ''took fewer moderate or strong'' painkillers. Richard Burton, who is one of the architects of St. Mary's, the new hospital on the Isle of Wight, had been asked by British health authorities to design a structure that had space for more artwork and at the same time used less energy than conventional hospitals. One of his design solutions was to place the hospital in the middle of a thirty-acre public park whose centerpiece is a duck pond fringed with willows. You can stand on a solarium balcony at the end of one of the wards and look down two stories and out at a lawn and the pond, with a few willows, a reed bed, and a couple of old oaks and pine trees nearby. Raising your eyes, you can see beyond the houses and warehouses of a Newport suburb in a small valley to hilltop fields, woods, and pastures on the horizon, two miles away.

An old photograph of the original site of New York Hospital in Manhattan, in what is now a warehouse and office district northwest of City Hall, shows a building set far back from the street, behind a large lawn and two stately rows of elm trees. Lying in bed, you can't see many trees from the high-rise windows of the current New York Hospital, on the Upper East Side of Manhattan, but the hospital does operate a separate psychiatric hospital, in White Plains, which is in a 230-acre park with landscaping designed by Olmsted. The future of the Olmsted landscape is now in doubt, though: The hospital has announced that it wants to develop most of the property in order to have more money for health care.

The city of Boston has approached the Isle of Wight model of health care, but there's still something missing: In the 1970s, under a program called Urban Wilds, Boston began protecting undeveloped city lots that had long been untouched and had remained often spectacular natural areas—woods, wetlands, meadows, rock outcroppings. More than nine hundred acres have since been permanently set aside as public open space—a figure that may soon be expanded to include a lush hilltop meadow in Mission Hill, where, behind a profusion of wildflowers, you can just make out the distant, shimmering tops of Boston's downtown skyscrapers. This meadow is close to, but not next to, New England Baptist Hospital, which is on the same hilltop but has no such view, because what was once half of a much larger meadow—the half closer to the hospital buildings—has been paved over and surrounded by a chain-link fence, and now serves as the hospital's staff parking lot.

New work in the field of social medicine is beginning to discover further possible public health connections of trees and meadows with human settlements—for instance, there is the idea of "the enabling environment," which Susan Toch, an environmental planner, defines as the unbreakable connection between the condition of the environment in an area and the well-being of the people who live there. As a graduate student at the University of Waterloo, in Ontario, Toch, who was one of the first researchers to look into this relationship, discovered during fieldwork in the Île-de-France that health authorities should be able to set up a new generation of "integrated epidemiological studies." These studies, once completed, would show direct spatial correlations between ecological damage, such as that to lichens in the Île-de-France (lichens are sensitive to air pollution); heavy concentrations of man-made pollutants (automobile emissions, for instance); and the specific illnesses people get, such as respiratory disease or cardiac distress.

Susan Toch says that while "the inherent links between medical and ecological information are rarely acknowledged," volunteer work she did in France with a local emergency medical squad showed her where integrated epidemiological studies of the area could begin to collect evidence: She found that local pharmacists often learned about new environmental problems long before the regional public health officials did. Talking with small-town druggists, she discovered a new kind of early warning system: When something gets into a town's water supply that can give people stomachaches, not every household will know right away that people are getting sick, or why, but within a single day the local drugstores will often be selling more than twice the usual number of stomach-settling pills and syrups, and the druggists will have started putting together a picture of the problem. Toch says that, just as canaries used to be taken down into coal mines to act as "indicators" for coal gas, because the birds would be affected by it long before the miners could tell that anything was wrong, these days we have to be our own canaries, and the people in the French towns have become "indicators" for a problem with the water supply. In other words, a major part of the business of taking care of the environment has to do with learning how to keep at least one eye on ourselves.

———————

Some of today's regionalists—among them Robert D. Yaro, senior vice president for plan development at the Regional Plan Association, a private, nonprofit planning agency in New York City—think that there's a fourth reason (beyond the urgency of the moment, the opportunities at hand, and the evidence from related fields) that regionalist projects can find a welcome in this country in the middle of the largest national development boom in American history. That is that such projects are not doing anything innovative, after all; they're only resuming work, on some jobs and some principles that were fully spelled out in *The New Exploration: A Philosophy of Regional Planning*, a recently rediscovered and now much pored-over book by an American forester and planner named Benton MacKaye, which was first published sixty years ago. In the 1930s, MacKaye was a cofounder, with Aldo Leopold and several other conservationists—many of whom had served in the United States Forest Service—of the Wilderness Society, a nonprofit group set up in Washington to promote wilderness preservation of federally owned forest and other land. And a dozen years earlier, in New

York, he had joined with Lewis Mumford and Clarence Stein and a few other planners and architects who had taken an early interest in land-use reform to set up the Regional Planning Association of America, their own informal clearinghouse for new thinking, a group that operated separately from the larger and more New York–oriented Regional Plan Association. The tiny RPAA incubated many of the land reclamation and social development policies later put into effect by the New Deal, such as flood control, rural electrification, and the reforestation of logged-over mountain tracts by the Civilian Conservation Corps.

Until only a few years ago, when some of the new regionalists in this country began prowling the stacks of local libraries in search of old copies of *The New Exploration*, MacKaye (the name rhymes with "high") was remembered primarily as the father of the Appalachian Trail, which in 1937 became the first two-thousand-mile-long hiking path in the United States and the first interstate ridgeline greenway park: a linear inland strip of wilderness that parallels the Atlantic Ocean and runs from mountaintop to mountaintop down the East Coast. The trail begins on the top of Mount Katahdin, in Maine, and eventually climbs to the top of Springer Mountain, in Georgia, after crossing through fourteen states.

Other long-distance interstate trails are now being blazed through wilderness lands, two of them in the western United States. The Pacific Crest Trail, 2,560 miles long, is almost a mirror image of the Appalachian Trail; it's a ridgeline path along the Cascades and the Sierra Nevada that parallels the Pacific Ocean and extends from Canada to Mexico. And the Continental Divide Trail, through the peaks of the Rockies, will eventually provide a hiking path of more than three thousand miles between Canada and Mexico, once the Forest Service and other groups select and mark a route for the Colorado–New Mexico–Mexico segment of the trail. Along with the Appalachian Trail, the two newer trails are now National Scenic Trails and thus part of the national park system. Another National Scenic Trail in the making, the North Country Trail, a 3,200-mile-long trail now almost one-third complete, will provide a continuous forest and farmland path through seven states between Lake Champlain in New York and Lake Sakakawea in North Dakota. There it will link up with the Lewis and Clark Trail, a National Historic Trail now under construction, which retraces the steps of the two explorers and will eventually extend west all the way to the Oregon coast, where the Columbia River meets the Pacific Ocean.

Three years ago, the President's Commission on Americans Outdoors, a bipartisan panel established by the Reagan administration to think about the country's recreational needs in the first decades of the twenty-first century, proposed creating a national "green mosaic" of hiking trails, jogging trails, bicycle paths, bridle paths, and scenic highways and byways—a "network of greenways across the country" that would link every community to all the state parks, state forests, national parks, and national forests in the country and "tie this country together with threads of green that everywhere grant us access to the natural world." The commission also proposed setting up a new national outdoor trust fund authorized to spend up to a billion dollars a year to help bring the green mosaic and other recreation projects into being. The commission's chairman, Governor Lamar Alexander of Tennessee, wrote to President Reagan that he foresaw, as he tried to look ahead, "a prairie fire of concern and investment" to preserve and create outdoor opportunities for the next generation of Americans.

Since MacKaye's proposal for an Appalachian footpath is still less than seventy years old—he first mentioned the idea in an essay published in 1921—the recent national embracing of his plan might make him seem a worthy minor prophet whose mission has come to fulfillment in an unusually short time. But from the first, in every paper and book he wrote, MacKaye was really talking about something larger, about landscape connectedness and the role it can play in a special kind of enabling environment. For him, making wilderness hiking a regular part of American urban life was simply one element in a new national undertaking that could diminish some of the impact of the automobile; halt the headlong, panicked flight from blight; and, at the same time, reinvolve all modern Americans in the patterns of kinship and partnership and neighborly and intellectual connections that can operate in what he called "three basic 'elemental environments' ": natural landscapes, working landscapes, and cities—or, to use his terminology, "The Primeval," "The Rural," and "The Urban."

And there was more than this. In *The New Exploration* MacKaye talked again and again, in almost quantifiable terms, about the effect that making or breaking daily landscape connections inevitably has on the lives of large populations. To paraphrase MacKaye's underlying formula slightly, what he saw happening could be expressed as "three minus one equals zero" but "one plus one plus one equals four": that is, people's lives are immediately diminished whenever their connections with any one "elemental environment" are blurred or broken—because, he said, the "personality" of a place evaporates whenever "unthinking" development covers an area with "structures whose individual hideousness and collective haphazardness present that unmistakable environment which we call the 'slum.' " He went on to explain: "Not the slum of poverty, but the slum of commerce. . . . These souls live all in a single environment: not city, not country, but wilderness—the wilderness not of an integrated, ordered nature, but of a standardized, unordered civilization." MacKaye's prose is always pungent: "A rootless, aimless, profoundly disharmonized environment" is his description of standardized development.

This is the immense threat—that when we lose one set of connections we end up severed from all connectedness. "Together," MacKaye says, the three elemental environments "seem to form, when normally developed, a complete and rounded external world adapted to man's psychologic needs." But "depletion in any one of them means a corresponding depletion in man's life." MacKaye also points out an unsuspected quality inherent in all properly connected places. When all three of the elemental environments are readily available to people, he says, they form the terrestrial basis of "a fundamental world of man's needs as a cultured being"—a basis that makes possible a kind of collective forethought, or anticipation of the future, which is otherwise not ordinarily available. "A higher estate in human development," MacKaye calls this, and he also refers to it as "a gradually awakening common mind."

The promise here is that people properly grounded in a complete and rounded environment could begin to get a better feeling for the day-to-day aspect of the many multigenerational decisions in modern life—those actions we initiate that pile up assets or debts for our children and grandchildren. If our own landscapes could help us live more lightly, it would be easier for us to feel the weight we were piling on the backs of people who will be arriving here in a few years. Human consciousness, with its multiplicity of awarenesses, evolved in surroundings that provided several kinds of connectedness to the "common mind." We're only now learning that there's yet another, concealed danger in indiscriminately altering the environment: By inadvertently severing connectedness and thus dulling some of our own awareness, we can begin systematically ignoring our surroundings without quite realizing that our alertness has faltered; we can damage natural systems; we can put our own safety and health in peril, by cutting ourselves off from settings that— undefaced, as MacKaye said—could let us live as one "unit of humanity" with the next two or three generations after our own time.

For MacKaye, thinking about connectedness evoked regional thinking, because he thought you would need to have a piece of land at least thirty miles by forty in order to set up an urban area, a rural area, and a wilderness area big enough to function on a sound economic and environmental footing; he called such an area a "regional city." And a transregional project such as the Appalachian Trail was more than just a delivery system that would bring countryside connections to your front door and link small regions together. It would be an underpinning for all the landscapes of—in this case—the eastern United States: a framework that would give stability to local wilderness areas and partnership landscapes, and would also nourish and replenish them, by serving as a source of supply. Lewis Mumford wrote in 1962 that it was instantly apparent to the regional planners of the early 1920s that the original Appalachian Trail proposal was a "decisive departure" from previous plans for paths and trails. "I well remember the shock of astonishment and pleasure that came over me when I first read this proposal," Mumford wrote. MacKaye had "conceived this new trail as the backbone of a whole system of wild reservations and parks, linking together by feeder trails into a grand system, to constitute a reservoir for maintaining the primeval and the rural environment at their highest levels."

MacKaye realized early in his life that landscape connections are often unwittingly severed by major technological innovations and that transportation systems in this country always serve two functions: They move goods from place to place, and they are put to use by America's internal immigrants—the people fleeing the approach of industry and slums by moving to new neighborhoods. Long before the first interstates were built, he could see that automobiles would have a decisive effect on the dynamics of urban flight, because, unlike canal boats and railroad trains, they could head in almost any direction. In one of his most memorable phrases, MacKaye declared that in the twentieth century, "Pygmies have become centaurs," with the result that "the weakling man, seated in his motor car with hand on wheel and foot on lever, becomes a locomotive.'' But the Appalachian Trail, together with similar transregional dikes and ramparts of countryside that might be created in the future, could be thrown across the path of the motor cars. ''Here is the barrier of barriers,'' MacKaye wrote about the Appalachian Trail, within a ''world-empire of industrial and metropolitan upheaval.'' It was, he said, ''the backbone levee of the whole Atlantic border from Canada to Georgia.''

The countryside, in other words, could rescue the cities, because a reshaped countryside would now be an urban design too—a means, Mumford wrote in his 1962 essay, ''of designing a better urban pattern for the flow of population that was already making the whole coastal area from Boston to Washington into a formless 'conurbation,' as Patrick Geddes had long ago called it, before Jean Gottmann, in a recent study, gave it the less accurate name of 'megalopolis.' '' As MacKaye saw it, you changed people's mental maps by first altering their physical maps. The partly completed Appalachian Trail of the 1920s had ''already laid, both on the ground and in the public mind, the thread on which to weave . . . the main open way across the metropolitan deluge issuing from the ports of the Atlantic seaboard,'' he wrote, and ''this open way, when once it really opens, would form the base throughout eastern populous America for controlling the metropolitan invasion.''

For some of today's regionalists, to read MacKaye and then find on a road map of the eastern United States the dotted red line of the Appalachian Trail, connecting dozens of national forests, state forests, and state parks, and even two national parks—Great Smoky Mountains National Park, in Tennessee and North Carolina, and Shenandoah National Park, in Virginia—''makes it impossible for any of us to feel like a pioneer,'' one of them told me recently. He went on, ''But that is more than made up for by finding ourselves to be members of an established American profession. Sometimes I think the only way to describe

MacKaye's impact is to rewrite the Johnny Appleseed story, because I get a feeling that's almost like growing up in a country where no one has ever even heard of apples, and then, when news about apples finally makes its way to you, you look outside and see that there are apples hanging outside your window, ready to eat. And then you find out that two generations ago someone came through the area planting a few apple trees, which you had always assumed were just ornamental shrubs. And then you see that there's a package with your name on it, left behind by the apple planter, and inside are more seeds, a couple of shovels, and detailed instructions for setting up an orchard.''

9 Thinking Regionally

Benton MacKaye never thought of himself as an innovator. In *The New Exploration,* he wrote that the pattern of the regional city "is no invention of mine nor of any other single human brain" but "is merely an attempt at the restoration, and extension through modern instrumentalities, of the basic scheme of regional development, which arose naturally and spontaneously in the endeavor to adapt a given American setting to certain fundamental human desires." And quoting an early essay by Lewis Mumford, he reminded his readers that in the years before nineteenth- and twentieth-century transportation schemes set off wave after wave of urban flight, regional development had normally been of service to "man's evolution" by creating for people a connectedness that widened their "mental and spiritual horizon." The public value of regions had increased at the same rate as private property values. By 1850, according to Mumford, "the communities that were planted on the seaboard and up the river valleys during the seventeenth and eighteenth centuries . . . had achieved their maximum development; they had worked out a well-rounded industrial and agricultural life, based upon the fullest use of their regional resources through the water-wheel, mill, and farm, and they had created that fine provincial culture, humbly represented in the schools, universities, lyceums, and churches, which came to a full efflorescence in the scholarship of Motley, Prescott, Parkman, and Marsh, and in the literature of Emerson, Thoreau, Melville, Whitman, and Poe.''

Because MacKaye made it clear that regions can begin to work as enabling environments only when all three of the elemental environments that serve to define a region can offer a well-rounded range of public values, some regionalists in this country now see reason to pay special attention to America's working landscapes. First of all, to play catch-up—since working landscapes in the 1990s are often the environments that have the least protection and are disappearing the most rapidly. New York State, for example, has recently lost vast amounts of farmland; close to a million acres went out of production just between 1982 and 1987. Across the country, 372 of the most productive American farming counties—over half of all the High Market Value Farming Counties in the United States—are either already within or directly adjacent to metropolitan areas. At the same time, city people have been rediscovering natural areas inside their own borders. In a recent book called *Urban Wilderness: Nature in New York City,* by Jean Gardner, with photographs by Joel Greenberg, there's a picture of tall evergreens, crisp, fresh-fallen snow, and a roaring waterfall; the picture turns out to be a contemporary view of the Bronx River.

''New York City has one of the most diverse natural environments of any American city,'' Gardner has said. On her master list of the ''natural complexity'' in the city are, among other features, a pine barren, a hemlock grove, estuaries, rivers, and even one of the highest elevations along the Atlantic coast (Todt Hill, on Staten Island). New York City now has more than 19,000 acres of parkland that are being officially preserved as wild countryside; in the 1970s, the 9,100-acre Jamaica Bay Wildlife Refuge, in southern Brooklyn and Queens, was turned over to the National Park Service and became part of the Gateway National Recreation Area; and then, in 1984, the city's Parks Department got into the wilderness business itself, setting up a

new Natural Resources Group to develop management plans for
7,000 acres of undisturbed woods, wetlands, meadows, and
meandering streams inside dozens of city parks in the five
boroughs.

Wilderness areas are actually increasing in New York City.
Gardeners from the Green Guerrillas, a local environmental
group, have spent the last five summers creating Brooklyn Bridge
Meadow by planting native wildflowers—many of them collected
from vacant lots in Brooklyn—on a small triangle of once dusty
land between City Hall and the entrance ramps to the Brooklyn
Bridge. A New York State environmental-conservation program
is now financing the efforts of a volunteer group devoted to
restoring the most densely built-up section of the Bronx River's
banks—several miles south of the waterfall. In a still more ambitious project, a Buffer the Bay program, launched in 1984 by
the New York City Audubon Society, later joined by a national
nonprofit land conservation group named the Trust for Public
Land, has targeted several broad, quiet tidal creeks and other
natural areas around Jamaica Bay as new city parkland. These
creeks were left out of Gateway for a variety of reasons, and if
they could be added to the parkland in the city, says the city's
Environmental Protection Commissioner, Albert F. Appleton,
"these natural-habitat areas would become greenways that would
bring Jamaica Bay across the Belt Parkway and into the neighborhoods of South Brooklyn and South Queens."

Hiking trails and bicycle paths—greenways of a more conventional sort—are also under construction in New York. The
grandest of these is the Brooklyn/Queens Greenway, a forty-
mile-long bicycle path and pedestrian path from the Atlantic
Ocean to Long Island Sound. This is a project of the Neighborhood Open Space Coalition, an alliance of 125 community-
gardening and environmental groups in New York, and it has
been designed as a ribbon of open space that will unite thirteen
city parks, two botanical gardens, and several eminent New York

City cultural institutions, including the New York Aquarium, the Brooklyn Museum, and Shea Stadium. The plan is getting a warm reception in New York, where an editorial in the *Daily News* called it "an urban version of the Appalachian Trail." Tom Fox, the executive director of the Neighborhood Open Space Coalition, says that the Brooklyn/Queens Greenway, which he would like to see completed by 1995, can increase the reach of existing open spaces in a way that will help millions of city people feel closer to the out-of-doors: Half the population of New York City lives in Brooklyn and Queens, but only nine percent of Brooklyn, and only ten percent of Queens, are parkland.

A third greenway system now being planned for New York—a project by the city's Parks Department to restore bicycle paths along the Shore Parkway in Brooklyn and Queens—will eventually link the first two greenway projects by creating, at its eastern end, a fourth greenway, the Brooklyn/Queens South Shore Greenway, or Blue-and-Greenway, as Parks Department planners have nicknamed it. As currently proposed, the Blue-and-Greenway would be a bicycle path, running east and west, that would cross all the Buffer the Bay wilderness greenways extending north from Jamaica Bay. And several miles to the west, the Shore Bikeway, which has been planned as the western extension of the Blue-and-Greenway, will meet up with the southern end of the Brooklyn/Queens Greenway on the boardwalk at Coney Island.

And even this isn't the end of it: Hooper Brooks, who directs the Regional Plan Association's Regional Open Space Program, is drawing up a "greenway framework" for the whole New York metropolitan area; it would take in, among other large-scale projects, the one-hundred-fifty-mile-long Hudson River Valley Greenway, which now has the sponsorship of Governor Mario Cuomo. One element of RPA's Regional Open Space Program, a Palisades Conservation Plan, would be visible from New York

City. It's a plan for a fifteen-mile-long greenway that will protect the cliffs along the Hudson River which cut through ten New Jersey towns just west of Manhattan. To make the Palisades Conservation Plan work, RPA is suggesting that all ten towns agree to two kinds of growth controls. First, no future structures built on the flats below the Palisades could ever obstruct any of the panoramic views you can get at the top of the cliffs: the Hudson River down below; the Manhattan skyline straight ahead; the open sky above it all. And second, any new building put on the flats would have to preserve one of the feelings still available on the land down at the foot of the Palisades—the sense that your nearest neighbors include towering dark-red basalt cliffs almost two hundred million years old.

But what about the working landscapes of the New York metropolitan region? In Benton MacKaye's definition, regional connectedness needs such landscapes as much as it needs greenways, because delivery systems can bring you only those qualities which pour into them from reservoirs. It's possible to hook up a local wilderness reservoir, like Jamaica Bay's twelve thousand acres of marshland, upland, and open water, to a city greenway, like the forty-mile-long Brooklyn/Queens Greenway, and it's also possible, by adding only the smallest of detours, for the Brooklyn/Queens Greenway to start giving New Yorkers a taste of working countryside: The Queens section of the path, as it is now planned, will cut through Cunningham Park on a route that is only a few hundred yards east of the Klein farm. In MacKaye terms, though, the two-acre Klein farm is nothing like a working-landscape reservoir, only a clear-running spring.

Robert Yaro, who until this year was director of the Center for Rural Massachusetts, a research institute at the University of Massachusetts—Amherst, was once a Boston city planner, who later went on to become chief planner, and then deputy commissioner, of the Massachusetts Department of Environmental Management. In his various capacities, Yaro spent much of the

1980s on two aspects of the working-landscape-supply problem: first, finding the regional reservoirs before they were all drained by approaching development; and second, setting up local management plans for all identified working landscapes—plans that treat working landscapes as regional assets. When you act locally while thinking regionally, Yaro says, you welcome growth and new development in working-landscape areas, but you also arrange any changes around two unchanging principles: you keep at least fifty percent of the land in production—a big enough block so that the farmers in an area can make a decent living—and you conserve the rural character of the place, the existing sense of connectedness, by seeing to it that new buildings capture the spirit of the place. Doing that, Yaro explains, is mostly a matter of thinking about creating two kinds of views at once— the views *of* a new building and the views *from* it—and involves finding sites for buildings that let them fit in with the contours of the land and at the same time offer what Randall Arendt, a planner and associate director of the Center for Rural Massachusetts, has called "uninterrupted views across long, open fields or pastures, permanently protected from future development."

Benton MacKaye, in the 1920s, thought that the population of a "regional city" could increase by more than forty percent without any loss of connectedness, provided that the newcomers settled only in new villages within the working landscapes of the area, so that the old central city of the region stayed at its original size and nearby wilderness land was left completely unoccupied. MacKaye's vision was a challenge to traditional either/or planning methods and also called into question the conventional real estate practice of calculating equity values by looking only at the rise and fall of private property values in an area. In such an expanded definition of equity, the public value of a landscape or a neighborhood formed a permanent surplus, which could always be enriched during a development period that made private equity values rise. And when public value went up, private value would go up along with it—for example, people would be willing to pay more for a new house in a beautiful setting that had a beautiful view. But at the same time, public value had to be treated as a separate equity account, with an established minimum balance that was never available for conversion into private value by speculators or through old-fashioned landscape-skimming techniques, such as building a new house that gives its owner a stunning view but spoils the views from all the other houses within, say, a five-mile radius.

MacKaye never actually built a regional city, but he did keep suggesting strategies for getting started; he thought, for instance, that "modern inventions" like electric power and commuter buses would make the job easier. And in *The New Exploration* he found several ways of expressing a central idea, which was that designating and caring for a regional city would always mean working directly with connectedness—with "the vital forces, rhythms, and aspects of definite desirable environments," as he put it at one point. "The job is not to 'plan' but to *reveal*," MacKaye said, by which he meant that what gets added to a place is less important than what you can stay close to. MacKaye also said that you remodeled a place through living in it and reminded his readers that the point of developing a region is "not so much an affecting of the countryside as of *ourselves* who are to live in it." Almost at the end of his book, MacKaye confessed to a certain doubt about the task ahead: "The forces set loose in the jungle of our present civilization may prove more fierce than any beasts found in the jungle of the continents—far more terrible than any storms encountered within uncharted seas. . . . Can we control their flow before it controls us? Can we do it *soon enough?* This is a crucial question of our day. What instructions can we issue to our modern-day explorer (whether technician or amateur) to guide him in coping with this modern-day invasion?" But then optimism returned, and he

wrote: "Our last instruction to our new explorer and frontiers-
man is to hold ever in sight his final goal—to reveal within our
innate country . . . *a land in which to live,* a symphonious
environment of melody and mystery."

Yaro says that regionalists can now show that MacKaye's innate optimism was well founded and that several of his predictions about regional growth were highly accurate, among them
the one about the ability of rural areas to take on large numbers
of new nonfarming residents while preserving a partnership sense
created by generations of farming families. MacKaye had specifically estimated in *The New Exploration* that the rural population of a regional city could grow without any difficulty from
a low of around 4,000 to a high of about 23,000—an increase
of almost 500 percent in the number of working-landscape
residents.

In *Dealing with Change in the Connecticut River Valley: A
Design Manual for Conservation and Development,* a recent
book by Yaro and three associates (Randall Arendt, Harry L.
Dodson, and Elizabeth A. Brabec), the Center for Rural Massachusetts presents a full-length analysis—complete with photographs, site plans, model bylaws, and vivid full-color drawings
of future construction—of how a large, three-hundred-year-old
working landscape can absorb high suburban densities of development over a forty-mile stretch of river terrain without jeop-
ardizing future private property values or sacrificing its ancient
partnership sense. All the new housing would be detached single-
family homes, as in most existing suburbs (research by the Center for Rural Massachusetts has shown that the average New
England family still dreams of having a house and a lawn that
are all its own), but the net gain in density would actually be
higher than what is permitted in most suburbs and closer to what
you'd expect to find in a residential neighborhood of a small
city, because the *Design Manual* makes room for the same number of people that could ordinarily be accommodated only by

blocks of attached row houses. Yet in the *Design Manual* stud-ies, none of this growth would bring about the look of even a low-density suburb; the whole region, all forty miles of it, would still look like a working landscape and function as a working landscape.

The basic design ideas in the *Design Manual* are that most new houses, shops, and offices should be gathered together in clumps, usually at the far edges of open fields, and that wherever it is possible, existing villages and woods should be used as closets for higher density—places where new construction can be neatly stowed away without diverting attention from partner-ship values. The proposed bylaws give meticulous consideration to the question of just how visible new projects can get, stipu-lating, say, the kind of "softly illuminated" nighttime signs that would be appropriate in front of roadside stores, so that you'd still have a sense of driving through moonlight and starlight.

The landscape under examination in the *Design Manual* is the Pioneer Valley—a local name for the Massachusetts portion of the Connecticut River Valley and, more specifically, for the small towns and broad expanses of richly productive riverfront farm-land between Holyoke and the Vermont–New Hampshire bor-der, which have remained essentially unchanged since the seventeenth and eighteenth centuries. The long view north along the river, particularly from a vantage point such as the summit of Mount Holyoke, at the southern end of the rural portion of the valley, became a famous tourist attraction in the early nine-teenth century, so the Pioneer Valley, like the Hudson River Valley, is a place where even the partnership sense has been carefully documented over the years, by landscape painters and by writers. For instance, there's *The Oxbow,* Thomas Cole's gigantic, panoramic, thundercloud-laden canvas of the gliding sailboats and golden haystacks and grazing sheep, the plumes of smoke from farmhouse chimneys, and the soaring, wheeling birds he saw from the peak of Mount Holyoke in 1836—a painting that hangs in the Metropolitan Museum of Art. Standing on that peak several years earlier, Timothy Dwight, the president of Yale University who became America's first epic poet, called the scene before him "the richest prospect in New England, and not improbably, the United States," and "a collection of beauties to which I know no parallel." And in his book *Travels in New York and New England,* Dwight wrote: "When the eye traces this majestic stream, meandering with a singular course through these delightful fields, forcing its way between these mountains, exhibiting itself like a vast canal . . . it will be difficult not to say that with these exquisite varieties of beauty and grandeur the relish for landscape is filled."

Pioneer Valley farmland is now more vulnerable to development than it used to be—the major farming business in the area, the Consolidated Cigar Company, which used to grow the kind of large-leaf tobacco used for wrapping cigars in the fields next to the Connecticut River, picked up stakes in the mid-1980s and moved its operations to Latin America. But the valley by now has a long history of making room for change while maintaining its sense of roominess, and has already absorbed some conspicuous nonfarming uses without compromising its integrity. It contains five major colleges—Smith, Amherst, Mount Holyoke, Hampshire, and the University of Massachusetts. And since the late 1960s, the valley has attracted so many craft workers—more than a thousand of them, including potters, weavers, woodcarvers, calligraphers, jewelers, glassblowers, blacksmiths, silversmiths, printers, bookbinders, and people who make musical instruments—that it has acquired a new reputation, as an East Coast Santa Fe.

Now the natural countryside in the Pioneer Valley is coming under the guardianship of several new Connecticut River regional environmental programs. In Connecticut, Massachusetts, Vermont, and New Hampshire—the four states along the river's 407-mile course from the Canadian border to Long Island

Sound—over $900 million in federal, state, and local funds have been spent since 1970 to improve water quality in the river, and in 1987 the Nature Conservancy, which operates the largest privately owned nature-preserve system anywhere in the world, set up a Connecticut River Protection Program to save 7,000 acres of wild areas near the river, such as floodplain forests and riverside grasslands—"the best of the river's remaining natural communities," according to a recent issue of *The Nature Conservancy Magazine,* including all "those that still possess enough biological integrity to maintain themselves as functioning systems well into the future." Dennis Wolkoff, who is the Nature Conservancy vice president in charge of the Eastern Regional Office, says, "The Connecticut River is the ecological thread that ties New England together."

There is so much at stake in the Pioneer Valley that the *Design Manual,* with its proposals for concealing density, has been causing something of a sensation in planning circles: A development company known for carving up whole mountains into small lots bought 110 copies of the book for the use of its acquisitions and planning staff; the American Society of Landscape Architects gave the book a design award in 1988 as one of the best landscape books of the year; and both the water commissioner of Texas and the director of a national rural-planning institute in West Germany have asked for copies. But Bob Yaro, who considers himself a close student of Benton Mac-Kaye, has a slightly different, and more complicated, explanation for the instant success of the *Design Manual.*

Yaro thinks that the conclusions in the *Design Manual* are workable only because two more MacKaye hunches about development have turned out to be true: Areas can conceal density only by working directly with connectedness; and the process of working with connectedness is politically acceptable, because it's basically a democratic procedure rather than something outsiders can control or impose—all they can do is tap into local people's hidden expertise about connectedness ("The job is not to 'plan' but to *reveal.*") What MacKaye couldn't guess was that in a post-interstate boom, there would be a couple of additional, equally compelling reasons for building a region around connectedness: It's cheap; and you can get it done quickly, while there's still a landscape around you to work with. And there was a gap in MacKaye's thinking—the gap that led him to have doubts. He didn't see the full force of the discouragement built into people after two hundred years of development decisions that ignored connectedness. Yaro discovered early in his career that to attract people's interest to regionalist projects he needed to take the psychology of regional planning one step beyond MacKaye's work: Often, he found, before you could hope to make the public value of a place part of the local process of thinking about land-use decisions you had to take a preliminary step, which involved reconnecting people to their own sense of connectedness. Ever since, the first part of any Yaro project, urban or rural, has involved revalidating connectedness and helping it to find a voice.

————

Part of Yaro's approach has to do with learning how to avoid any oncoming development storm. "When I was growing up, in the 1950s, my grandparents had a farm outside Hartford, in a place called Andrews Corners, where their farm was actually one of the four corners of a crossroads," Yaro told me one afternoon last year at the University of Massachusetts faculty club. "The farm was surrounded by orchards, and there was a skating pond for the winter and blueberry bushes for July and August picking. By the time I was a teenager, the three other corners were being filled in, and there were supermarkets and gas stations standing on old farmland. By the time I got out of college, my grandparents' farm had become a regional shopping mall. Almost all the regionalists I know have had this kind of experience, growing up—it's what gets them started. Part of the appeal of a movie like the first *Back to the Future* is that it lets you see instantly what going back thirty years can do—the suburban mall vanishes, and old fields and barns reappear. One of the few human rights that aren't officially guaranteed in this country is an agreement that the places you grow up caring about will be there for you when you're ready to start a family of your own.''

Yaro paused, and then said, ''Until very recently, it seemed as though we had two land ethics in the United States—five percent of the nation was set aside as national parks, and treated as special places where we talked about things like 'America the Beautiful' and 'We, the People.' This was neutral territory, but it seemed that different rules had to be obeyed through most of the rest of the land: either 'Take the Money and Run' or 'Private Property: Keep Out.' But all the time, the first land ethic was in place inside vast numbers of people, who would have told you if you asked them—and I have—that they never thought about the land and didn't have an opinion on the subject. But given the right setting, the right evocation, the right stimulus, many of those people who put themselves in the 'Don't Know' column turn out to be very articulate and outspoken concerning the special qualities they care about in their own communities. People can become vehicles for places. These are the feelings and this is the understanding now bubbling up from real people who live in real places—and as a result, there's a ferment in the country about land values that hasn't been seen since MacKaye was writing, in the 1920s. Even the environmental movement, when it emerged in the 1970s, didn't tap all these concerns; at first, we were paying so much attention only to clean air and clean water that I used to think that any visitors from outer space would immediately ask each other, 'Are these creatures really *terrestrial* beings?''

"Of course, where the environmental movement did get involved with land-use issues, as in the case of wetlands, hardened
attitudes began to melt in short order, and we now have a tremendous amount of official machinery to protect swamplands,
which a generation ago were thought to be disease-ridden places
that generated only poisonous, putrid miasmas. In the meantime, the legal system has caught up with the biology. I think
we're now maturing as a nation in our thinking about land-use
issues. Until very recently, much of the rationale behind American economic development plans boiled down to something
close to 'Put up a shopping center, hope that it will eventually
create some jobs nearby, and then call it a success.' And now—
it's fascinating—here we are, living in an era in which New
Jersey doesn't want to be New Jersey anymore: It helped build
a consensus for land protection on Cape Cod last summer when
people who had given up all hope heard the governor of New
Jersey declare that he was going to save the Jersey coast by
limiting development. After that, discussion began anew. 'You
can't buy back the Cape,' some people said. And other people
started to say, 'They shouldn't be allowed to treat Cape Cod as
if it were any old place.'

"A new approach to community development is in the making—one that asks people to think about the long-term needs of
a place and of all its residents. We're in the process of building
local institutions that take over the job of looking after public
value on a volunteer basis, and we're learning how to reinvest
in areas so that they'll be more valuable to the next generation
than they are to ours. After all, the postwar era has been this
country's great age of wealth, and during such periods you're
supposed to embellish your civilization and your country with
something that can endure—like the Roman aqueducts. Most of
what we've been doing is throwaway stuff—it can't be sustained.
Sometimes part of the problem is learning how to bypass the
gatekeepers—the entrenched local interests who can think only

about increasing real estate values. I think we can now show that stewardship springs from connectedness—it gives people back a sense of thinking responsibly on behalf of the whole community, and it sends a shiver up the spines of the gatekeepers, by reminding them that someone can take away their keys.''

Yaro smiled, and went on: "It's not development that causes problems—only *patterns* of development. And since the country now needs at least a couple of million new units of housing every year just to keep even with population growth, if we start constructing houses now that build public value for the future we can create a new national pattern of development within thirty years. I began working on this problem more than fifteen years ago, when I had a job as a neighborhood planner in Dorchester, an old blue-collar section of Boston. It was bleeding to death, because the people there thought there was nothing left in the community they could hang on to. The housing stock in the area was in fact sensational—Victorian mansions and big old triple-decker, three-family frame houses. These houses have now been rediscovered and sell for as much as a quarter of a million dollars, but at the time Dorchester folks were just walking away from them, and you could get one for eight thousand or less. My colleagues at City Hall and I devised a strategy—we started with the easy stuff. We got a couple of neighborhood houses listed on the National Register of Historic Places, and we conjured up a new name for the area—Melville Park. Then we organized tours and got members of the Victorian Society in Cambridge and Wellesley—people who had ignored Dorchester for years—to visit the stately homes of Melville Park on Saturday afternoons. It worked. People stopped moving away—because if people from the suburbs would stop by, people who could choose to live anywhere, it had to be a decent place to live.

"When I moved over to the Department of Environmental Management, I found I could apply the same kind of thinking to whole cities, and it was still just as important to start with the easy stuff, because DEM was an absolute bargain-basement type of operation, with a consistently low budget. The Massachusetts Miracle was under way—an economic development boom in a state that had been a backwater for decades. But because this was a boom of the modern era, most of the development headed straight for the prosperous suburbs, and federal statistics officially classified twenty-nine of the thirty-five cities in the state as economically distressed. It was already a policy of the Dukakis administration to do something about this—'We don't throw away cities,' Mike Dukakis had told all his state agencies—and there was a hazy notion abroad that it might be possible to give cities a lift by setting up urban state parks that had some kind of education-and-preservation component. My Melville Park days had taught me how to find the special qualities of a place that supposedly didn't have any left. A few of us began to think that a park, bringing a visible physical improvement into the heart of a city that hadn't had a nickel of private money invested in it for fifty years, might turn out to be a new way of attracting developers' attention. In Lowell, we looked at the magnificent old mill buildings downtown, and we later went down to Fall River, a riverside city of a hundred thousand people, more than half of them Portuguese families who used to fish for a living. In Fall River, we walked along the waterfront and found only rubble-strewn lots, chemical tanks, and gas tanks—and not one single foot of public access.

"We set up what we called Urban Heritage State Parks on these two sites, and they were followed by new state parks in a dozen other Massachusetts cities, as part of an ongoing project that has now cost the state a hundred million dollars. And so far that public investment has generated half a billion dollars of spending by private developers. The property right next to the new parks has shot up in value, but most of the private money— I'd say up to eighty percent of it—gets spent on projects in other parts of the Urban Heritage State Parks cities. Now each one of these cities is considered a good place to live and do business in—a place that has been officially recognized as special enough to deserve a state park of its own. Most important, these places are back on their feet and are pulling their own weight, thanks to what the easy stuff helped bring about.''

———

Once the urban parks had become a repeatable success, Yaro turned his attention to another problem—the countryside. Bringing the cities back into the economic mainstream meant that something like a fifth of the private money for new economic development could be redirected from the suburbs to the downtown. But four fifths was moving outward from the suburbs and grabbing at the working landscapes just beyond the last streets of houses. Was there any way for the state not to throw away the countryside? Yaro and his associates, still operating on a shoestring, worked out a two-step approach to the question. The first step involved giving specialness official recognition, as embodied in the Department of Environmental Management's *Massachusetts Landscape Inventory,* a 268-page book published in 1982. The follow-up step, which had to do with hooking into local connectedness, was launched in 1988, when the Center for Rural Massachusetts brought out the *Design Manual,* with its local strategies for protecting one of the distinctive landscapes previously identified in the *Inventory.*

The *Massachusetts Landscape Inventory,* which surveys five million acres of land, was put together mainly by three and a half people—Neil Jorgensen, a geologist; Mark S. Finnen and Harry L. Dodson, two landscape architects; and Bob Yaro, as a part-timer, shuttling between projects. The group was able to avoid making invidious comparisons—deciding, say, whether the Berkshires are more beautiful than Cape Cod—by a simple device. They divided the state up into six "physiographic regions,"

large areas with broadly similar landscapes and cultural char-
acteristics, and then looked for the best landscapes in each of
them. The regions were the Coastal Plain, the Seaboard Low-
land, the Central Uplands, the Connecticut Valley, the Berkshire
Hills, and the Taconic Section. Massachusetts had a history of
inventorying its scenic features—an earlier survey had been made
in 1929. But the 1929 report, which led to protection for Mount
Holyoke and other outstanding natural features of the state,
largely ignored its working landscapes, though the state was then
still forty percent farmland. Farmland seemed an endless resource in the 1920s, and besides, it was considered to be just
"ordinary" scenery.

By the early 1980s, the situation had changed: Three quarters
of the farmland in the state had disappeared between 1950 and
1980. The new inventory-takers therefore knew they had to work
fast. But they found that they had two obstacles to overcome.
They could turn to knowledgeable local people for hints about
where to get started, but even the most concerned local people
tended to be hazy about sites a few miles away from their own
villages. So the surveyors had to weave together a series of local
suggestions in order to get a complete picture of the distinctive
qualities of a region. Also, it turned out that existing American
scenic-assessment techniques concentrated exclusively on natural features, such as mountain ranges and waterfalls; farmland,
even though it was vanishing, was still officially an "ordinary"
commodity. So Jorgensen, Finnen, Dodson, and Yaro adopted
a scenic-assessment method used by the Countryside Commission of Scotland—a technique developed to give "a central position" to landscapes that have "undergone centuries of human
influence," according to the *Inventory*. The Scottish work could
be welcomed in New England, according to the completed *Massachusetts Landscape Inventory*, because "while the primeval
forests of Massachusetts were undoubtedly beautiful environments, today's second-growth forest provides only limited inter-

nal views in most areas"—that is, as the *Inventory* went on to explain, "in a region of generally subdued topography, second-growth forests tend to limit visual quality. If cultural, agricultural, and historic landscapes did not exist in Massachusetts, scenic areas would generally be limited to the seashore, lakes, rivers, wetlands, and the few areas of sharp relief."

Working with the tips provided by local landscape authorities, the survey team pored over topographic maps published by the United States Geological Survey, looking for basic information they could spot-check in the field, such as changes in elevation, whether the land was open or wooded, and the likelihood of coming across vistas. The maps also helped them rule out areas with very little potential. Then they drove around the state looking at everything they had heard about or found on a map and, back in the office, prepared new maps, on which they ranked as "distinctive," "noteworthy," or "common" the landscape features in each of the physiographic regions. When they totaled their finds, four percent of the land in the state, about two hundred thousand acres, seemed to deserve a "distinctive" rating, and five percent, or a quarter of a million acres, could be considered "noteworthy."

The rankings didn't change the legal status of any Massachusetts landscapes, although the Department of Environmental Management at once adopted the *Massachusetts Landscape Inventory* as a guide for future purchases of state parkland. But three years later, in 1985, the *Inventory* listings gave farmers in the towns of Ashfield and Hawley, in the Berkshire Hills, a way of successfully resisting the United States Air Force, which had announced plans to build a "telecommunications facility" on a six-hundred-acre hilltop potato field straddling the Ashfield-Hawley town line. The main components of the facility were to be thirty-one freestanding antennas, ranging in height from 240 to 300 feet. The antennas would have been lighted at night, and they would have been clearly visible from the summit of Mount

Greylock, the highest point in the state, twenty miles to the west.

Farmers at first pointed out that potatoes were already a dwindling crop in Massachusetts, and that the field the Air Force was looking at represented ten percent of the potato-growing land left in the state. The Air Force, in its reply, said that the field was suitable for antennas in part because farming had already made the ground clear and level. And an Air Force spokesman also said that the site had been selected "because of its remoteness, so it isn't in someone's back yard." The site was, however, in the middle of one of the "distinctive" landscapes mapped by the *Massachusetts Landscape Inventory,* and as a result, James Gutensohn, the commissioner of the Massachusetts Department of Environmental Management, toured the site with the state's agriculture commissioner, Gus Schumacher, and both officials later announced their opposition to the project. They were joined by Silvio Conte, the area's congressman (who sits on the House Appropriations Committee and threatened to cut off the airplane allowance), and by the Boston *Globe,* which declared in an editorial that "the antenna farm is wrong-headed and ill-advised," and urged the Air Force to start looking elsewhere. Several months later, the Air Force agreed to do so. In 1988, the *Inventory* won a second major victory when the New England Power Company withdrew plans for a new coal-fired generating plant on a "distinctive" landscape at the north end of the Connecticut River Valley.

Harry Dodson, who is also one of the coauthors of the *Design Manual,* suggests that the *Inventory* serves another statewide, or regionwide, function, beyond helping to protect landscapes from such encroachments: By assembling a comprehensive and panoramic picture, it enables different groups of people to detect the distortions lodged in their own thinking about landscapes. "What we're often finding is that people in any area have at least two levels of feelings about their region," Dodson told me.

"And these feelings don't always quite mesh—some of them are clear-eyed visions and others are based on squinting, and very few people have ever sorted them out. There's usually a broad consensus among local people on the special places in their own neighborhoods—though they may not be aware of how widely shared their own attachments are until someone brings them together and starts a conversation on the subject. At the same time, they may hold very odd views about areas beyond their daily reach. Many state officials who work in Boston, for instance, think of Massachusetts as the United States in miniature, and for some of them the Connecticut River Valley is in the boonies, a place as far away as the Great Plains. 'How's your view of the Rockies?' is a typical statehouse joke. This is all because of the Snowbelt, as it's called. There's heavy snow every winter in the hills west of Boston, so Bostonians have decided that the valley is unreachable. One result is that most of the tourists we get in the valley come from New York State and not from eastern Massachusetts."

According to Bob Yaro, there is one more piece of landscape thinking that often needs rearranging before the countryside of America can be considered safe. Land-use decisions in New England are made by local towns, and there are more than a thousand towns in the six New England states. The trouble is that many of these towns think they have already protected their open spaces by adopting one-acre or two-acre zoning—a guideline that guarantees the preservation of at least a full acre of unbuilt land between new houses. What the towns don't seem to be able to see in advance is that those zoning laws actually require them to suburbanize, because a town that has one house on each acre is a town that has open space but no openness. As Yaro says, the only land left over is in "pieces that are too big to mow and too small to plow."

Greenbelt Alliance, a nonprofit regionalist group in the San Francisco Bay Area, has developed a new technique for showing an area which of its towns are most immediately threatened by suburbanization. The nine-county Bay Area includes almost four million acres of ranches, farms, vineyards, parks, open space, and watershed lands, and the Alliance used to publish a gray-and-green "Greenbelt" map of the region—gray identified urbanized areas, most of them contained within a strip of land bordering San Francisco Bay. Around the gray was what looked like almost an ocean of dark-green open space. "A beautiful map," says Larry Orman, executive director of Greenbelt Alliance. "And that was the problem with it. Our entire huge greenbelt looked serene and stable. When in fact development pressures have been increasing wildly in some areas and almost not at all in others."

So Orman and Jim Sayer, a research associate, looked at existing zoning, freeway locations, and other planning and growth factors at work in the Bay Area, and in 1988 published "Threats to the Greenbelt," a new map in five colors that vividly identifies the areas most at risk. The gray areas are unchanged from the old map. But now there are only patches of dark green nearby—representing parks and other securely safeguarded open spaces, such as private open space protected by conservation easements. A much larger area is now colored light green, indicating farms, ranches, and other properties that seem to be safe in the short run. Running through the light-green lands are bands of pink—"Medium Risk" areas, where land-use controls are sketchy or only partly effective. Finally, there are splotches of angry red: the "High Risk" lands along highway corridors and around the edges of the gray urbanized zones. It's a map that seems to be almost violently in motion, and when you look at it intently you can almost begin to see the pink areas intensifying into red and the red lands fading to gray.

The Connecticut River Valley *Design Manual* uses its four-color drawings, grouped into what Randall Arendt calls a series of triptychs, to show rural towns the inevitable consequences of suburban development, whenever it comes. You are shown three views of the same spot: a contemporary view, followed by two different tomorrows—first, the tomorrow that has been ordered up by one- and two-acre zoning, and then an alternative tomorrow, based on connectedness. The two future views, as the text explains, contain the same number of new buildings. The first picture, of the existing landscape, is always printed on a right-hand page, so you have to turn the page to look into the two futures—a conventional suburban build-out on the left, and the regionalist alternative on the right. This is a deliberately arranged shock to the senses, because it is at first almost impossible to see any difference between today's landscape and the regionalist vision of tomorrow; there are big fields and small villages in both pictures.

People who are looking through the *Design Manual* for the first time often find themselves flipping pages back and forth so that they can stare at these two views. It's almost like a puzzle-page game of "What's Hidden in This Picture?" Only after careful comparison can you notice that, yes, in the third picture a new little street has been tucked inside the village, just south of the church, and it has on it the same five new houses that in the second view are sitting on four fifths of the big open field between the village and the Connecticut River.

Since the *Design Manual* restricts not development but only the pattern of development, Yaro sees it as a mechanism for building private equity and public value simultaneously. And he points out, too, how much money can be saved by learning to think regionally. In the last decade, the Commonwealth of

OPPOSITE AND OVERLEAF: This landscape triptych was left out of the Connecticut River Valley "Design Manual," partly for lack of space and partly because, even three years ago, it seemed almost too shocking: The intense level of development it shows as possible and typical was then still practically unheard of in the area's hill towns. *Drawings courtesy of Kevin Wilson, based on plans by Dodson Associates*

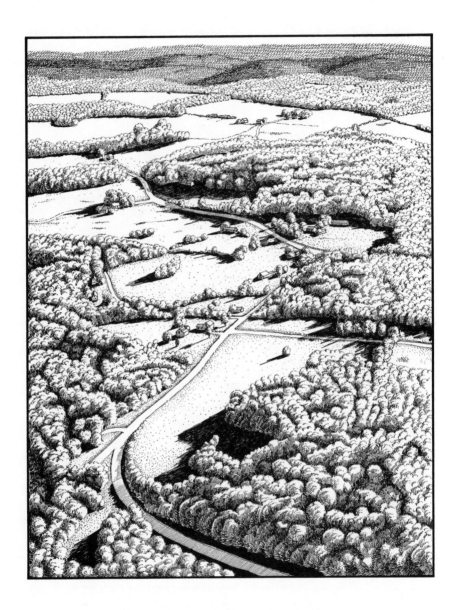

A TYPICAL NEW ENGLAND LANDSCAPE

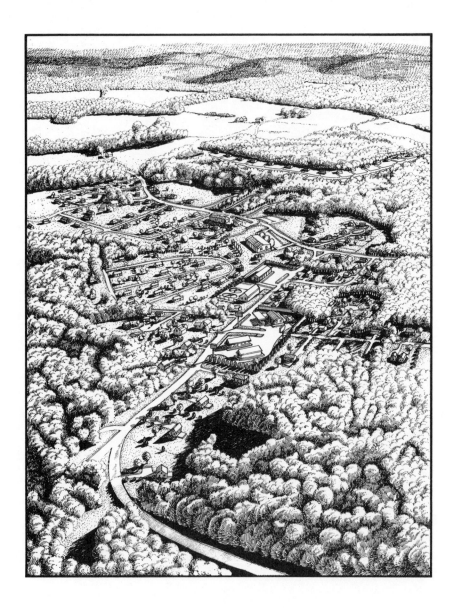

DEVELOPED CONVENTIONALLY

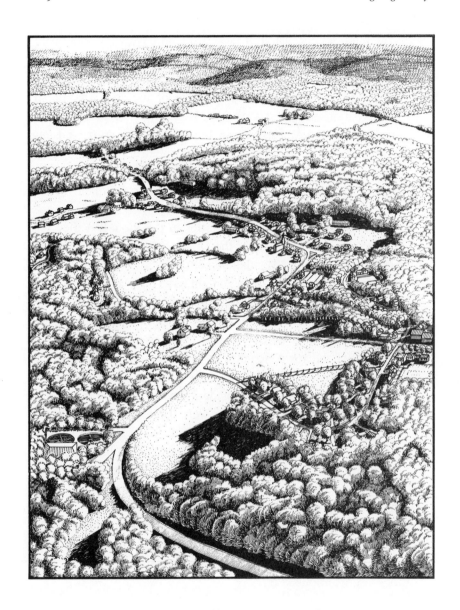

A REGIONALIST SOLUTION FOR THE SAME DENSITY

Massachusetts has acted to save farmland by buying up farmers' development rights, but land in Massachusetts is now so valuable that the huge new purchasing funds were able to acquire the rights to only a small percentage of the state's farmland. "Acquisition alone can't work," Yaro says. "If states have to buy the land, the best we can hope for is preserving postage stamps of green surrounded by seas of metropolitan and resort development." The *Design Manual* plan, by contrast, immediately reserves for farming purposes half the farmland in any working landscape, at no cost to anyone.

The voters of the towns and cities in the Pioneer Valley will have to agree to the ideas of the *Design Manual* before they can become reality, and Randall Arendt has been touring the valley—and the many towns in the United States and Canada that have asked him to come—with a slide show of triptychs and photographs. Sometimes he comes home at night feeling encouraged. "I have to tell you that I had an almost mystical experience at the town meeting in Belchertown, just east of the Pioneer Valley," he told me recently. "The meeting was to vote on two zoning proposals. I made a seven-minute presentation, and I couldn't even tell if people were listening to me. Only one voter in ten turns out for a town meeting, so you never know who it is you're talking to—and this is a town that has voted down cluster zoning three years in a row. Then the voting began: Article One, which permitted cluster zoning for all new buildings hooking into town water supplies and sewage lines, passed by one hundred and ninety-six to eight, and Article Two, which allowed cluster zoning for any new buildings that would use well water and septic tanks, passed by two hundred and four to nothing—a unanimous vote."

A Beginning

Over the next hundred years or so, America will essentially complete itself. At least, the Census Bureau sees it that way: The current United States population of 250 million is about five-sixths of the population predicted for fifty years from now—an all-time high of 301 million people. After 2040, the numbers are expected to start gradually declining, and ninety years from now, in 2080, there will be 292 million Americans. Most of that future population will live in urbanized surroundings within a hundred miles of a major shoreline—the Atlantic, the Pacific, or one of the Great Lakes. The lasting shape of those late-twenty-first-century surroundings will to a large extent be determined by thousands of short-term decisions we will be making during the next thirty years. This is partly because most of the remaining surge of American population growth will take place before 2020. Another part is that patterns of settlement, once launched, tend to have great staying power: The sites of most of the cities in this very young country were all chosen long ago, some of them back in the seventeenth century. How can any of us see to it that the fully grown America we're already preparing for—or the America after that—will continue to make available to people the kind of richly varied and nurturing experiences people have always needed? Will the next American cities work to help people fulfill themselves? Will the city dwellers of that time have full access to wilderness experiences, or to expanses of partnership landscapes?

We need to get started now—for our own sake, as well as theirs—and this means seeking out some experiential goals that we can use to guide the development process. For instance, there's the idea of "No Net Loss," which has recently been adopted by the state of Maryland as its official environmental policy for wetlands. From now on, any wetlands filled by developers or highway engineers must be replaced elsewhere in the state. President Bush has also declared it his intention to make No Net Loss a national wetlands goal. And we could just as easily extend this idea and adopt a new national No Net Loss policy for the place experiences that are important to people in this country. The first step here is easy enough—compiling a list of the existing experiences that are treasured.

There's also the idea of dovetailing, or reconciling, experiences—the idea that has already been put forward in a countryside context by the Center for Rural Massachusetts in its development plans for the Connecticut River Valley. Build farmland to suburban densities, if you have to, but don't interrupt the existing farming uses or the traditional countryside character. In cities, where retaining character is equally important, simulation laboratories can economically perform the same service, by helping us know in advance the consequences of any proposed development, so that we can rebuild cities without damaging their ability to help people come together.

And we can also develop habits of experiential watchfulness. For a start, here are several sample experiential checklists:

1. *America the Beautiful.* Other than parks, what landscapes do you know and care about that you would nominate to a list of Outstanding National Landscapes? How secure are these places at this point? Who's in charge of them? What kind of changes to what you see, hear, smell, or touch would damage your sense of connectedness to these landscapes?

2. *Sweet Spots.* What are your favorite nearby places—rural or urban, public or private—within walking or driving distance of where you live or work? What's the nature of the experience there, and is it different during the daytime, at night, on a weekday, a weekend, a holiday? Is anything missing, or neglected, or not regularly maintained? Have any recent changes to such places changed what you can experience? Do you go less often? How vulnerable are these places?

3. *Reaching Out to a Region.* How closely connected do you feel to the people in neighboring communities, to other living creatures around you, to the land nearby? How many towns, counties, or states are part of your region? What are the region makers in your area—rivers, mountains, valleys, forests, lakes, trails, railroad tracks? How far do you have to travel to get a feeling not available in your own neighborhood—for instance, if you live in a city, where's the nearest place that feels like countryside? Where's the nearest wilderness?

The experiences that places make available to people, as we're learning, are an inheritance that has been entrusted to our care. Guarding these experiences and championing them, as we're also learning, are skills that are natural to people—because each one of us has direct access to the experiences that pour into us at any moment. So getting good at replenishing the places around us will just need a small stretch in our understanding.

Bibliography

Alexander, Christopher, et al. *A Pattern Language: Towns, Buildings, Construction.* New York: Oxford University Press, 1977.

Appleton, Jay. *The Experience of Landscape.* London: John Wiley, 1975.

Balling, John D., and John H. Falk. "Development of Visual Preferences for Natural Environments." *Environment and Behavior.* Vol. 14, No. 1, January 1982.

Barth, Gunther. *City People: The Rise of Modern City Culture in Nineteenth-Century America.* New York: Oxford University Press, 1980.

Bluestone, Barry, and Bennett Harrison. *The Great U-Turn: Corporate Restructuring and the Polarizing of America.* New York: Basic Books, 1988.

Clay, Grady. *Close-up: How to Read the American City.* Chicago: University of Chicago Press, 1973.

Dubos, René. *The Wooing of Earth.* New York: Charles Scribner's Sons, 1980.

Ehrenzweig, Anton. *The Hidden Order of Art.* Berkeley: University of California Press, 1967.

Fein, Albert. *Landscape into Cityscape: Frederick Law Olmsted's Plans for a Greater New York City.* Ithaca: Cornell University Press, 1968.

Froebel, Friedrich. *The Education of Man.* New York: D. Appleton & Co., 1898.

——.*Pedagogics of the Kindergarten.* New York: D. Appleton & Co., 1898.

Gardner, Jean. *Urban Wilderness: Nature in New York City.* Photographs by Joel Greenberg. New York: Earth Environmental Group, 1988.

Gratz, Roberta Brandes. *The Living City.* New York: Simon & Schuster, 1989.

Hall, Edward T. *The Silent Language.* New York: Doubleday, 1959.

——. *Beyond Culture.* New York: Anchor Press/Doubleday, 1976.

Hart, Roger. *Children's Experience of Place.* New York: Irvington, 1979.

Jacobs, Jane. *The Death and Life of Great American Cities.* New York: Random House, 1961.

Kaplan, Stephen, and Rachel Kaplan. *Cognition and Environment: Functioning in an Uncertain World.* New York: Praeger Publishers, 1982.

King, Alexander, Martin Holdgate, Eugene Grebenik, Kenneth Mellanby, and George McRobie. *An Eye to the Future.* London: Institute for Cultural Research, 1975.

Lam, William M. C. *Perception and Light as Formgivers to Architecture.* New York: McGraw-Hill, 1977.

———. *Sunlighting as Formgiver for Architecture.* New York: Van Nostrand Reinhold, 1986.

Leopold, Aldo. *A Sand County Almanac.* New York: Oxford University Press, 1949.

Lewis, Philip H., Jr., Bruce Murray, and Ben Neiman. *Regional Design for Human Impact.* Kaukauna, Wisconsin: Thomas Publishing Company, 1968.

Lockwood, Charles. *Bricks and Brownstones: The New York Row House, 1783–1929.* New York: Abbeville Press, 1972.

Lynch, Kevin. *The Image of the City.* Cambridge: The M.I.T. Press, 1960.

———. *Growing Up in Cities.* Cambridge: The M.I.T. Press. 1977.

———. *A Theory of Good City Form.* Cambridge: The M.I.T. Press, 1981.

MacKaye, Benton. *The New Exploration: A Philosophy of Regional Planning.* Introduction by Lewis Mumford. Urbana: University of Illinois Press, 1962.

Maslow, Abraham H., and Norbett L. Mintz. "Effects of Esthetic Surroundings: I. Initial Short-Term Effects of Three Esthetic Conditions Upon Perceiving 'Energy' and 'Well-Being' in Faces." In *People and Buildings,* edited by Robert Gutman. New York: Basic Books, 1972.

Mintz, Norbett L. "Effects of Esthetic Surroundings: II. Prolonged and Repeated Experiences in a 'Beautiful' and an 'Ugly' Room." In *People and Buildings,* edited by Robert Gutman. New York: Basic Books, 1972.

Mumford, Lewis. *The City in History.* New York: Harcourt, Brace & World, 1961.

———. *The Myth of the Machine.* Vol. 1, *Technics and Human Development.* New York: Harcourt, Brace & World, 1966.

———. *The Myth of the Machine.* Vol. 2, *The Pentagon of Power.* New York: Harcourt Brace Jovanovich, 1970.

Orman, Larry, and Jim Sayer. *The Bay Area's Greenbelt At Risk.* San Francisco: Greenbelt Alliance, 1989.

———. *Reviving the Sustainable Metropolis: Guiding Bay Area Conservation and Development into the 21st Century.* San Francisco: Greenbelt Alliance, 1989.

Ornstein, Robert, and David Sobel. *The Healing Brain.* New York: Simon & Schuster, 1987.

Paddock, Joe, Nancy Paddock, and Carol Bly. *Soil and Survival.* San Francisco: Sierra Club Books, 1986.

Powers, Peter. *Touring Eugene.* Eugene, Ore.: Terragraphics, 1987.

———. *Touring the Islands.* Eugene, Ore.: Terragraphics, 1988.

Rackham, Oliver. *The History of the Countryside.* London: J. M. Dent & Sons, 1986.

Roper, Laura Wood. *FLO: A Biography of Frederick Law Olmsted.* Baltimore: The Johns Hopkins University Press, 1973.

Shoard, Marion. *This Land Is Our Land: The Struggle for Britain's Countryside.* London: Paladin/Grafton Books, 1987.

Simpson, Jeffrey. *Art of the Olmsted Landscape: His Works in New York City.* Edited by Mary Ellen W. Hern. New York: New York City Landmarks Preservation Committee/The Arts Publisher, 1981.

Stegner, Wallace. *The Sound of Mountain Water.* Garden City, N.Y.: Doubleday, 1969.

Stein, Clarence S. *Toward New Towns for America.* Cambridge: The M.I.T. Press, 1966.

Walter, Eugene Victor. *Placeways: A Theory of the Human Environment.* Chapel Hill: University of North Carolina Press, 1988.

Ward, Colin. *The Child in the City.* London: The Architectural Press Ltd., 1978.

Whyte, William H. *The Last Landscape.* New York: Doubleday, 1968.

———. *The Social Life of Small Urban Spaces.* Washington: The Conservation Foundation, 1980.

———. *City: Rediscovering the Center.* New York: Doubleday, 1988.

Wordsworth, Jonathan, Michael C. Jaye, and Robert Woof. *William Wordsworth and the Age of English Romanticism.* New Brunswick, N.J.: Rutgers University Press, 1987.

Wordsworth, William. *A Guide Through the District of the Lakes in the North of England.* London: 1835.

Yaro, Robert D., Randall Arendt, Harry L. Dodson, Elizabeth A. Brabec. *Dealing with Change in the Connecticut River Valley: A Design Manual for Conservation and Development.* Amherst, Mass.: University of Massachusetts, 1988.

Yaro, Robert D., Neil Jorgensen, Mark S. Finnen, and Harry L. Dodson. *Massachusetts Landscape Inventory.* Boston: Massachusetts Department of Environmental Management, 1982.

Index

Note: Numbers in italics denote illustrations.

A NOTE ON THE TYPE

The text of this book was set in a digitized version
of Times Roman, a typeface designed by Stanley
Morison for *The Times* (London), and first intro-
duced by that newspaper in 1932.

Among typographers and designers of the twentieth century, Stanley Morison was a strong forming
influence, as typographical adviser to the English
Monotype Corporation, as a director of two distin-
guished English publishing houses, and as a writer
of sensibility, erudition, and keen practical sense.

Composed by Creative Graphics, Inc.,
Allentown, Pennsylvania

Printed and bound by R.R. Donnelley & Sons,
Harrisonburg, Virginia

Designed by Dorothy Schmiderer Baker

DATE DUE

DEC 1 4 1998			
MAR 1 9 2002			
GAYLORD			PRINTED IN U.S.A.